W9-CUA-362

Astrology

Publisher and Creative Director: Nick Wells
Project Editor: Cat Emslie
Art Director: Mike Spender
Layout Design: Robert Walster / Big Blu
Digital Design and Production: Chris Herbert
Copy Editor: Sonya Newland
Proofreader: Dawn Laker
Indexer: Helen Snaith

Special thanks to Chelsea Edwards, Ray Barnett, Vicky Garrard,
Elizabeth Huddlestone, Julia Rolf and Polly Willis

This is a **STAR FIRE** Book
First published in 2002
This edition published in 2007

07 09 11 10 08

1 3 5 7 9 10 8 6 4 2

STAR FIRE
Crabtree Hall, Crabtree Lane, Fulham,
London, SW6 6TY, United Kingdom
www.flametreepublishing.com

Star Fire is part of
The Foundry Creative Media Company Limited

Copyright © 2007 The Foundry Creative Media Company Ltd

ISBN 978 184451 925 5

All rights reserved. No part of this publication may be reproduced, stored
in a retrieval system, or transmitted in any form or by any means, electronic,
mechanical, photocopying, recording or otherwise, without the prior
permission of the publisher.

A copy of the CIP data for this book is available from the British Library

Printed in Dubai

Astrology

AN ILLUSTRATED GUIDE

KIM FARNELL, CAT JAVOR, HELENE SCHNITZER

GENERAL EDITOR: KIM FARNELL

STAR FIRE

CONTENTS

Introduction	❖	6
History	❖	**8**
People	❖	10
Places	❖	22
Fields	❖	26
The Zodiac	❖	**34**
Signs of the Zodiac	❖	36
Divisions of the Zodiac	❖	54
Planets and Aspects	❖	**60**
The Planets	❖	62
Aspect Patterns	❖	70
Major Aspects	❖	72
Minor Aspects	❖	74
The Chart	❖	**78**
House Systems	❖	80
Houses	❖	84
Chart Points	❖	90
Interpretation	❖	94
Prediction Methods	❖	102

Measurement ❖ **106**
Astronomy Measurements ❖ 108
Astrology Measurements ❖ 114
Time Measurements ❖ 118

Terminology ❖ **122**
Astronomy Terms ❖ 124
Astrology Terms ❖ 138

Glyphs ❖ *166*
The Horoscope ❖ *168*
Ascendants and Cusps ❖ *170*
Time ❖ *172*
Planets ❖ *173*
Aspects ❖ *174*
Planetary Strength ❖ *176*
Relationships ❖ *178*
Predictions ❖ *180*
Fixed Stars ❖ *184*
Bibliography ❖ *186*
Credits ❖ *188*
Index ❖ *190*

Astrology. To most people that means reading a column in their daily newspaper that will tell them when they are going to meet a tall, dark, handsome stranger. Something to look at while drinking a morning coffee, a little light entertainment.

However, there is much more to astrology than that. It has a long and rich history, it is an integral part of our culture, and it is still used regularly by vast numbers of people. Serious astrology is very different to what we read in the popular press. It can be used as an adjunct to counselling, is associated strongly with psychotherapy, provides a guide to character and even predicts the weather. Its uses are innumerable.

The history of astrology goes back to ancient Babylon, where people first began to notice that cosmic phenomena were related to the seasons. The need to plan harvests and predict the weather led to more detailed observations being made. Over time more sophisticated observations enabled astrologers to offer predictions for states and rulers. By about 1700 BC the cast had been assembled: the seven planets, counting the Sun and Moon, the Sun's path around the Earth and the 12 sections of that path, the zodiac. What was essentially a farmer's calendar became an instrument for the foretelling of events.

By the third century BC astrology had reached classical Greece from Babylon. The mathematician Pythagoras placed his imprint on the concept of the movement of the heavens. The Earth was maintained as the centre of the Universe and was a sphere surrounded by other spheres fixed to a vast crystal sphere. As each moved at a different speed they were supposed to emit a note of a different pitch. This was the music of the spheres, in which notes blended into one pure, harmonious sound. Greek mythology and culture permeated the whole of astrology and still retains an influence today.

The Egyptian writer Claudius Ptolemy, writing in the second century AD, produced the *Tetrabiblos* – widely regarded as the greatest astrology book ever written, and still in common use. By this time astrology was well established. It continued to flourish until the Dark Ages. In medieval times texts from Arabic scholars became available and these provided the next advances in astrology.

In the seventeenth century the first work in English was published, *Christian Astrology*, by William Lilly. However, with the move towards rationalism and the division of areas of study, astrology began a decline that was not to be reversed until the late nineteenth century.

In the early twentieth century astrology began to regain popularity, and in 1930 the first sun-sign column appeared in the popular press. From this time onwards almost everyone would at least know the sign that their Sun was in when they were born.

Astrology is still fundamentally the same today as it was several thousand years ago. A chart is cast for a specific moment in time, at a specific place, and by

LEFT: The signs of the zodiac

applying time-honoured and tested rules the astrologer may describe the character of the subject and make predictions about what is likely to happen to them.

In casting a chart the astrologer calculates the position of the planets – including the Sun and Moon – and draws them on a circular chart at their zodiac degrees. The positions of the ascendant or rising sign and midheaven are then calculated. These vary by about one degree every four minutes of real time, and according to latitude. The ascendant is drawn on the left-hand side of the chart and the midheaven at the top. From these points tables are used to calculate the other house cusps until the chart is divided into 12 sectors. Finally, the angular relationships between the planets – aspects – are calculated and the chart is ready to be interpreted.

The process of analyzing a chart is very much like putting together a jigsaw. The planets represent defined energies. Their sign placements show how these energies are manifested and their house placements show in which areas of life they are apparent or most powerful. The aspects between the planets modify their meanings, allowing them to act in combination.

Depending on the astrologer's approach to their work, a number of refinements are often included at this stage to give more information. For example, note may be taken of the planet that rules or has a strong affinity with a house. The position of this planet relates then to matters of that house.

When making predictions a variety of different techniques are available to the astrologer. These range from looking at the relationship between the positions of the planets at a specific date and comparing them to the birth chart (transit), to using a symbolic method (directions) to move the planets forward and comparing those positions to the ones in the birth chart.

ABOVE: *Arabic astrologers observe the sky*

To those who are not used to astrological concepts, this may sound rather arcane. What use is it to know where the planets are and what their relationship is? The horoscope is basically a map of our lives. It describes the sort of person we are and who we can become. Few astrologers today would suggest that the planets cast down rays that affect our lives, as was believed in the past. But rather, most believe that the configurations and patterns made by celestial bodies are reflected down on Earth. Centuries of observation enable us to interpret and judge a horoscope in amazing detail.

Once you have taken a look at what astrology can offer there is no going back.

Kim Farnell

THE ORIGINS OF ASTROLOGY

At times regarded as a science, astrology has exerted an extensive or a peripheral influence in many civilizations, both ancient and modern. Its origins lie within the astral religion of ancient Mesopotamia of the third and second millennia BC. From Mesopotamia, astrology spread to the adjacent regions, changing its form as it went. Astrology is often defined as a pseudo-science and considered to be diametrically opposed to the findings of real science. Although there have been periods when astrology has fallen out of favour, it has never completely disappeared. Although scientists continue to rail against the discipline, it has gained in popularity since the late 1980s. Astrology is now part of popular culture and everyone has a smattering of knowledge of it, even if it only extends as far as knowing their Sun-sign.

HISTORY

PEOPLE

An astrologer is someone who studies celestial patterns and makes analysis of character and predictions based on them. For many centuries the terms 'astrologer' and 'astronomer' were synonymous – meaning one who studied the movements of the skies. In the earliest times astrologers were priests and scholars, and many ancient astrologers worked for the most important people in the land.

Aristotle

Aristotle was born in 384 BC at Stagirus in Thrace. He studied under Plato and later began to lecture. His divergence from Plato's teaching prevented him from being elected to leadership of the Academy. He was the tutor of Alexander (the Great) and set up his own school at the Lyceum. On the death of Alexander in 323 BC the Athens government was overthrown. A charge of impiety was trumped up against him and to escape prosecution he fled.

Aristotle and Plato are responsible for reinforcing astrological thought through attempts to define time. Aristotle wrote a summary of astrology accounting for planetary motion. His views were based on philosophical speculation rather than observation, although he did acknowledge the importance of 'scientific astronomy'. He also believed that celestial bodies were composed of ether – in addition to the four other elements of earth, air, fire and water. Aristotle was responsible for developing a mechanistic view of the Universe as opposed to the earlier models that focused on the divine. Through Thomas Aquinas and others' writings, Aristotle gained great popularity in the Middle Ages and was a common source for all astrologers. Numerous texts were falsely attributed to him. Aristotelian thought was reintroduced to Europe through Arabic writings.

❖❖ see THOMAS AQUINAS p13

Manilius, Marcus

Little is known of Marcus Manilius's life. He is likely to have been a Chaldean by birth and was a Roman poet, who followed the style of Lucretius, Virgil and Ovid in his work. He wrote the first Roman work on astrology, dedicated to the Emperor Augustus. This, the unfinished *Astronomica*, was written in about 45 BC, according to the book's dedication, although there is also evidence that this work was written around AD 14. In five books, this poem gives an outline

LEFT: *Aristotle studied under Plato and was the teacher of Alexander the Great; his work was popular in the Middle Ages*

LEFT: *Ptolemy's understanding of the planetary system*

against other astrologers who hid their lack of knowledge with difficult speaking and writing skills, he would also make his own writing difficult in order that the ignorant could not just pick up one of his books and understand his methods. When astrological predictions failed he believed it to be the fault of the astrologer. Astrology to Valens was a means of participating in the divine

of astrology, beginning with an account of celestial phenomena and including instructions for calculating the ascendant and details of decans, zodiacal geography and other technical matters. The work was rediscovered in the fifteenth century and published in various editions.

❖ see CLAUDIUS PTOLEMY p11

and attaining union with God. He made many mentions of keys hidden throughout, and weaving the general matters with the specifics. It is believed by many that he was the originator of the Porphyry house system. His *Anthologiae* is the longest extant astrological work from antiquity and contains more than 100 horoscopes.

❖ see HOROSCOPE p138

Valens, Vettius

Valens led an ascetic life, believing the pleasures of men would interfere with his knowledge and learning of astrology, and it is reported that he lost all his money searching for an astrological teacher. Valens ran an astrology school, where students swore oaths, and believed in a process of initiation. He worried that his astrology would fall into the wrong hands and had a disdain for people who only learned small bits of the discipline. While Valens made many remarks

Ptolemy, Claudius

Little is known for certain about Ptolemy. He was an Egyptian astronomer, mathematician and geographer who lived near Alexandria about AD 150. He is believed to have been head librarian at the famous library in Alexandria. He worked from the data of past astrologers to map over 1,000 stars. He compiled a list of 48 constellations and described the lines of latitude and longitude on the Earth. He believed Earth was the centre of the Universe and outlined his theories in his most famous work, the *Almagest*. These theories remained the basis for all astronomical thought for more than 1,400 years. *Tetrabiblos* also proved to be one of the foundations of modern astrology. The four books of this work became familiar to Europeans, as Latin translations were available from 1434.

❖ *see* EGYPTIAN ASTROLOGY p22

Augustine, Saint

Augustine (AD 354–430) was born at Tagaste (now Souk-Ahras) in Numidia. In his youth he consulted astrologers and shared the common belief in the efficacy of their art. According to his *Confessions*, this belief was undermined on the day that he discovered a very wealthy landowner had been born at the same moment as one of the slaves on his estate. His final condemnation of astrology came in *The City of God*, written after the Sack of Rome in AD 410.

He claimed that astrology was a fraud which usurped God's power over the Universe. If a planet could predict a future event, this limited the Creator's power to alter that event. Primarily because of Augustine's writings, astrology was dismissed as a fool's goal for more than four centuries. However, it was never formally proscribed by the Church and an underground movement kept the art alive in Europe.

❖ *see* THOMAS AQUINAS p13

Abumassar

Abu Ma'Shar (AD 787–886), known in the West as Abumassar, was born in Baghdad and died in Mesopotamia. He began his career as a student of the Hadith (a collection of traditions from the Prophet Muhammad) but he grew interested in astrology and eventually turned his complete attention to astrology, in which he became a leading authority. His book *Introductorium in Astronomiam* had an enormous influence on Renaissance astrologers. Abumassar displayed an interest in comets, and his account of their significance in each of the signs of the zodiac was often repeated by Latin authors. He also dealt with the problem of Free Will and the degree of control exercised by the planetary bodies. He made a distinction between the influence of the planets and fixed stars.

❖ *see* BYZANTIUM p24

Al-Biruni, Abu Rayhan

Abu Rayhan Al-Biruni (AD 973–1048) began his astrological studies at an early age under the astronomer and mathematician Abu Nasr Mansur. Al-Biruni wrote over 100 books and treatises on subjects such as mathematics and geography as well as astronomy and astrology. His *Book of Instructions in the Elements of the Art of Astrology* follows a logical progression from first principles and discusses mathematics, astronomy, geography and chronology before going on to discuss astrology. Al-Biruni occasionally criticizes

LEFT: *Saint Augustine, originally a believer in astrology but later disillusioned, is shown in his cell in this painting by Sandro Botticelli*

LEFT: *Abumassar studied the significance of comets in the various signs of the zodiac*

Aquinas wrote on natural science and alchemy and asserted that astrology played an important role in these disciplines. He believed that the divinatory arts were permissible as long as they had a natural base. Aquinas reflected in his works that if the Moon could influence the tides, there was no reason to deny that the planets could influence humanity. However, he did not believe that such knowledge should be used for predicting the future.

❖ see ARISTOTLE p10

Bonatus, Guido

Guido Bonatus (c. 1230–c. 1300) was born in Friaul. Professor of astrology at Bologna University, he wrote a book on astronomy and a theory of the planets, as well as books on astrology. He made his living by advising princes, and was for some time employed by Count Guido de Montefeltro. When that prince was involved in a dispute that led to military action, Bonatus would climb to the top of his castle, and at the auspicious moment strike the bell once for the Count and his men to don their armour, again for them to mount their horses, and a third time for them to ride forth to battle. Filippo Villani, a contemporary historian, claims that Montefeltro won many battles by following his astrologer's advice. Bonatus died around 1300 after being assaulted by robbers. He was the astrologer Dante described as one of the sufferers who had spent too much time trying to predict the future, and were now condemned to pace about with their heads on backwards.

❖ see NOSTRADAMUS p15

Copernicus, Nicolas

Born in Poland, Copernicus (1473–1543) studied mathematics at Cracow University and canon law at Bologna. He was appointed canon in the cathedral of Frauenburg, and it was from here that he carried out his astronomical observations from a turret situated on a wall

certain techniques, although in the main he presents astrology as a natural part of Islamic philosophy and science. During his lifetime Biruni's fortunes changed drastically and he was often forced to spend time in abject poverty. He spent many years in India and is credited with translating a large number of works to and from Arabic and Sanskrit.

❖ see ABUMASSAR p12

Aquinas, Thomas

Born at Rocca Secca in the Kingdom of Naples, Thomas Aquinas (c. 1225–74) began his study of astronomy at the age of 11. He became a Dominican monk in 1240 and was ordained a priest 10 years later. In 1257 he was made a doctor of theology. During the Middle Ages the teachings of Aristotle gained enormous popularity and Aquinas was one of the scholars of his time who subscribed to Aristotle's theory that the stars had an effect on human destiny; it was Aquinas's defence of Aristotle's works that ensured the former his place in astrological history.

around the cathedral. In 1530 Copernicus completed his great work *De Revolutionibus*, in which he asserted that the Earth rotated on its axis once a day and travelled around the Sun once a year. This heliocentric (Sun-centred) system overthrew the traditional geocentric (Earth-centred) view of the Universe. The work was clearly controversial and Copernicus was in no hurry to publish it, although it was circulated. His work was forbidden by the Church in 1616 and only removed from the Index of banned books in 1835.

❖ see FRANCIS MOORE p18

BELOW: *The Universe as understood by Copernicus*

Cardan, Jerome

Also known as Cardanus Hieronymous or Cardano Girolamo (1501–76), Cardan taught mathematics and wrote commentaries on Ptolemy. He completed his studies at Padua in 1526, earning a doctorate in medicine and setting up a practice locally. Marrying in 1531 he had two sons and a daughter. Beset by financial problems, Cardan turned to gambling in an attempt to make his fortune. In 1534 the family moved to Milan where he took up teaching. His reputation in medicine grew and he was appointed Chair of Medicine at Pavia. In 1560 his son was beheaded after being charged with poisoning his wife

while in childbirth. Cardan fled from Milan in disgrace and became professor of medicine at Bologna. In 1570 he was imprisoned by the Inquisition for casting the horoscope of Christ. In 1571 he went to Rome where he received a pension from the pope and resumed his profession. Cardan was the astrologer for Henry VII and Edward VI. After Henry's death, he came to England expressly to calculate the chart of Edward VI. Having cast his own horoscope predicting he would live to the age of 75, he committed suicide on 21 September 1576.

❖ see JOHN DEE p15

Nostradamus

Michel de Nostre-Dame (1503–66) was born in St Rémy de Provence. After studying law he went on to study medicine and developed an interest in astrology. He first made his mark by his successful treatment of plague victims. During his travels in Italy he discovered his faculty of seeing into the future. The most famous story about him tells of how he met a young monk and fell to his knees before him. This young man was later to become Pope Sixtus IV. By 1550 Nostradamus had produced a yearly almanac and after 1554 *The Prognostications*. On 4 May 1555 the first edition of his *Centuries* was published. He came under the protection of Catherine de Medici as physician, drawing up horoscopes for the famous Italian family. He ended his life drawing up horoscopes and completing his prophecies.

❖ see HOROSCOPE p138

Dee, John

Born in 1527, Dee studied mathematics and astronomy at Cambridge and took his MA in 1548. He had to leave England after accusations of being a conjurer. On his return he was already well known as an astrologer and was granted a pension by King Edward. On the accession of Mary he was imprisoned and charged with using enchantments against the queen's life. When Elizabeth I took the throne he elected a date for the coronation and

ABOVE: *Sixteenth-century Danish astrologer Tycho Brahe, at work in his observatory in Uranienborg, Sweden*

became a court astrologer. In 1581 he came into contact with Edward Kelly and their lives became completely entwined. Kelly was an Irishman who had lost his ears for forgery. He was reputed to be able to summon spirits. They involved themselves in alchemical research and necromancy. For eight years they travelled abroad together before quarrelling and separating. When Dee returned to England in 1594 he stopped dabbling in spiritualism and alchemy. James I ejected Dee from his sinecures and he retired to his small estate in Mortlake, Surrey, where he died at the age of 81.

❖ see NOSTRADAMUS p15

Brahe, Tycho

Tycho Brahe (1546–1601) was born in Skane, then in Denmark, now Sweden. In 1572 he observed a new star in the constellation Cassiopeia and published a brief tract about it the following year. In 1574 he gave lectures on astronomy at the University of Copenhagen. He was convinced that the improvement of astronomy hinged on accurate observations. Brahe accepted an offer from Frederick II to fund an observatory, which he built near Copenhagen. He designed and constructed new instruments, calibrated them, and instituted nightly observations. He also ran his own printing press. Brahe trained a generation of young astronomers in the art of observing. After falling out with Christian IV in 1597, he left Denmark; he settled in Prague in 1599 as the Imperial Mathematician at the court of Emperor Rudolph II, and died there in 1601.

❖ see JOHANNES KEPLER p16

Shakespeare, William

The works of William Shakespeare are full of imagery from many sources. Mythology, magic and science all find a place in his texts. One of the richest sources of imagery in his works is astrology. In Shakespeare's 37 plays there are

ABOVE: *Johannes Kepler, German mathematician, astrologer*

BELOW: *William Shakespeare, English playwright and poet, who used astrology as a rich source of imagery*

more than 100 allusions to astrology and many of his characters' actions are said to be favoured or hindered by the stars. The signs of the zodiac are mentioned in six plays and the planets are blamed for disasters. The references would have made sense to his audience and are no indicator of whether or not he personally believed in astrology. In Shakespeare's time the discipline was held in high regard. Both high-born and commoners employed astrologers and were familiar with astrological terms and concepts. *King Lear* in particular contains numerous references, most famously: 'This is the excellent foppery of the world, that, when we are sick in fortune (often the surfeit of our own behaviour) we make gaiety of our disasters the sun, the moon and the stars…'.

❖ see JOHN DEE p14

Kepler, Johannes

The German astrologer Johannes Kepler (1571–1630) was born in Wiel, in Wartemberg, and joined Tycho Brahe in Prague in his early adulthood. At Graz, in 1594, he took up a post as teacher of mathematics and astronomy. During this tenure he produced four almanacs. In the first of these he prophesied very cold weather and an invasion by the Turks. Both occurred and for the rest of his life he was to some extent considered a professional astrologer. In the introduction to *Tertius interveniens* he warned readers that while justly rejecting the stargazers' superstitions, they should not dismiss the true value of astrology. Kepler was convinced that mundane events could be predicted using this science. He discovered a harmonic, musical relationship between the planets and musical scale. Many of the minor aspects used by astrologers are also attributed to Kepler. Though appointed Imperial Astronomer, he could hardly keep his family from starvation and died from a fever worsened by disappointment and exhaustion.

❖ see TYCHO BRAHE p13

Lilly, William

Lilly was born on 16 May 1602 in Leicestershire. After his family ran into financial problems he left for London. Working as a servant, he married his master's widow on his death, and when she died some years later, he was left property that brought in an annual income of £1,000, making him a reasonably wealthy man. This gave him the freedom to study astrology from 1632 and he became a professional astrologer in 1641. A prolific writer, he produced almanacs with increasing frequency. In 1666 he was examined by a parliamentary committee investigating causes of the Great Fire of London, which he had predicted. This was to guarantee his name going down in history. In 1647 *Christian Astrology* was published – the first astrological text ever to be published in English. During his lifetime he judged thousands of charts. The problems he dealt with ranged from the everyday concerns of ordinary people to larger political issues. He was thought of as the leading English astrologer and played a prominent role in the Society of Astrologers. A recent revival in traditional and horary astrology has led to new adherents of his work.

❖ see HORARY ASTROLOGY p28

Culpeper, Nicholas

Nicholas Culpeper (1616–54) is a legendary figure in the field of herbal medicine and is popularly regarded as the figurehead of alternative medicine. A member of an old noble family, he was born fatherless in Surrey, squandered a fortune in Cambridge and tried to elope with a rich heiress who was killed by lightning. His study of astrology began at the age of 10, and he was taught astrology by William Lilly in 1635. Although it was intended that he should study theology, he began attending anatomy lectures. He trained as an apothecary in London, and by producing an unauthorized critical translation of the *London Dispensatory* he became the enemy of the

ABOVE: *Fourteenth-century manuscript depicting healing herbs*

physicians. Working as an astrologer and herbalist he saw up to 40 patients a day. During the Civil War he joined the Parliamentarian forces and was wounded. He fought a duel and was accused of witchcraft. In 1652 he wrote his famous herbal, *The English Physician*, and before that the first English textbook on midwifery and childcare.

❖❖ see WILLIAM LILLY p17

Moore, Francis

Dr Francis Moore was a physician at the court of Charles II, and his original broadsheet combined herbal recipes and remedies with favourable astrological times for taking

them. He died in 1715 and the title was bought by the London Liveried Stationers Company, who sold it to its present publisher, Foulshams, in the nineteenth century. His name was adopted by Henry Andrews in the late 1770s. During Andrews's time as compiler of the tables sales rose from 100,000 to 500,000 per year. He received the same remuneration throughout his 43 years' association with Old Moore's – £25 per annum. *Old Moore*'s became a more esoteric publication in the years following Andrews's death. It became an assortment of advertisements for the

BELOW: *William Herschel, who discovered Uranus in 1781*

sale of mystic objects, household hints and astrological forecasts concerned with national celebrities and the rise and fall of nations. Since Andrews's death innumerable astrologers have been 'Old Moore'.

❖ see JOHN DEE p15

Herschel, William

Born in Hanover, Herschel (1738–1822) was a successful musician. An amateur astronomer, on 13 March 1781 he observed an unusual object presenting an extended disc-like shape and thought he had discovered a comet. Continuing his observations, however, he discovered the orbit lay beyond that of Saturn and was fairly circular. This was no comet – it was a new planet. Different names were suggested, including his own. It was eventually named Uranus, after the mythological god of the skies. Herschel was granted a pension of £200 a year, knighted and made King's Astronomer. He made numerous discoveries. He observed sunspots and confirmed the gaseous nature of the Sun. He discovered not only the planet Uranus, but two of its moons, and two of Jupiter's. His principal works were on stars and he discovered nearly 1,000 double stars.

❖ see JOHANNES KEPLER p16

Zadkiel

Zadkiel means 'angel of genius of the planet Jupiter' and was the pseudonym of two astrologers – Richard James Morrison (1795–1874) and A.J. Pearce (1840–1923). Morrison worked in the Royal Navy until 1818; he became a professional astrologer in 1830. He launched *Zadkiel's Almanac* at this time. He studied astrometeorology and was a member of the London Meteorological Society. Morrison's speculative activities bordered on the fraudulent and in 1862 he brought a libel action against Sir Edward Belcher after an article published in the *Daily Telegraph* accused him of

taking money for using a crystal ball. He won the case but was refused costs. He is best known for his *Grammar of Astrology* and an abbreviated version of Lilly's *Christian Astrology*. He died in 1874 and the name of Zadkiel was handed down to a Mr Sparkes. Unfortunately, Sparkes also died soon afterwards, and Alfred Pearce became the new Zadkiel. Son of a notorious homeopath convicted of manslaughter, Pearce edited *Zadkiel's Almanac* until his death in 1923.

❖ see WILLIAM LILLY p17

Raphael

The name Raphael means 'God has healed' and it is associated with the planet Mercury, the traditional ruler of astrology. The first time Raphael was adopted as a pseudonym was by Robert Cross Smith (1795–1832). At the age of 25 he became the editor of *The Prophetic Messenger* which survives today in the form of Raphael's *Ephemeris*. There were few astrologers at this time and Smith led the revival of nineteenth-century astrology.

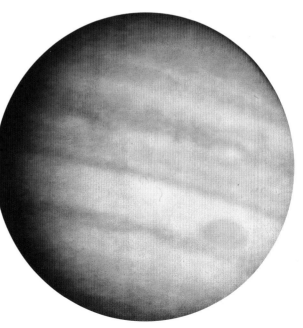

RIGHT: *Zadkiel, the pseudonym of two astrologers, means 'angel of genius of the planet Jupiter', shown here in a colour photograph from 1973*

He wrote innumerable works on astrology and other occult subjects and gained huge popularity. Smith's favouring of the Placidean house system led to the spread in popularity of this system. After his death in 1832, John Palmer took over editorship of the PM until his death in 1837. A man called Medhurst was the next Raphael until 1847, followed by Wakely until 1852 and Sparkes until 1875. Finally, the name was adopted by Robert Thomas Cross. Cross became as renowned as Smith, and was an equally prolific writer.

❖ see MERCURY p62

Leo, Alan

Born in 1860, Leo (born William Allen) is thought of as the father of modern astrology. Brought up by his mother, Leo was a member of the Plymouth Brethren and began life as a commercial traveller. Whilst managing a grocer's shop in Manchester, he began studying astrology. With Frederick Lacey he launched the *Astrologers Magazine* in 1889. This was later to become *Modern Astrology*, one of the longest running astrological journals ever published in English. From 1898 it was edited by his wife Bessie. Business was so good that he employed a staff of nine and developed a system of facsimile horoscopes, the forerunners of computerized horoscopes. A member of the Theosophical Society, he twice visited India. In 1914 he was prosecuted for fortune-telling but was acquitted. He wrote numerous textbooks and ran a correspondence course in astrology. His highly simplified books have remained in print and his approach was the forerunner of psychological astrology.

❖ see HOROSCOPE p138

Jung, Carl

Dr Carl Jung (1875–1961) was born in Kesswil, Switzerland. He studied medicine and became assistant professor at a psychiatric clinic in Zurich. He remained there for nine years, at the end of which he was created instructor of psychiatry. During this time he became increasingly interested in Freud's methods of psychoanalysis. After meeting Freud in 1907 the two became friends. Jung set up in private practice in 1909.

By 1911 the relationship between Freud and Jung was under strain because of Jung's interest in astrology. In a letter to Freud in 1911, he wrote: 'My evenings are taken up largely with astrology. I make horoscopic calculations in order to find a clue to the core of psychological truth. Some remarkable things have turned up which will certainly appear incredible to you… I dare say that we shall one day discover in astrology a good deal of knowledge that has been intuitively projected into the heavens.' The friendship was broken in 1913.

❖ see WILLIAM HERSCHEL p19

BELOW: *Raphael's* Manual of Astrology

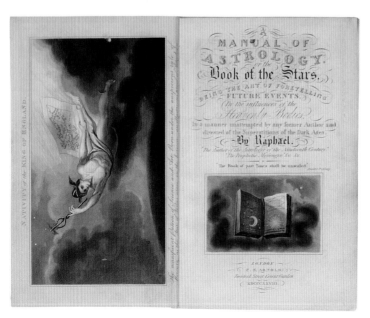

Naylor, R.H.

R.H. Naylor (1889–1952) worked as the assistant of Cheiro (William John Warner, who also went by the name of Count Louis Hamon) – the biggest name in astrology in the 1920s. Because of Cheiro's unavailability, Naylor was asked by the editor of the *Sunday Express* to cast the horoscope of the newly born Princess Margaret Rose, daughter of the future King George VI. He did so, and its popularity led to the newspaper's editor inviting Naylor to contribute the following week. In this horoscope, Naylor suggested that British aircraft might be in danger. On the day of publication, the airship R-101 crashed in northern France. The newspaper gave Naylor massive publicity, and he became famous overnight. It was also Naylor who invented the Sun-sign column on 31 August 1930. He had to find a way of writing so that each reader could feel involved, and chose to divide his essays into 12 paragraphs, one for each person born when the Sun was passing through a particular zodiac sign. The idea caught on and most newspapers and magazines now have regular horoscope columns.

❖ *see* SUN-SIGN ASTROLOGY p30

Adams, Evangeline

Various dates are given for Evangeline Adams's birth, but it is known that she died in 1933. Her astrological career began after she made a successful prediction in 1899. After this she became extremely well known, giving advice to some 100,000 people during her 40-year career. She taught astrology to John Pierpoint Morgan and was consulted by Enrico Caruso. In addition to her huge clientele, Adams wrote newspaper columns, published four books and presented a daily radio show. She was arrested in 1914 on a charge of fortune-telling. She came to court with a pile of reference books and illustrated the practice by reading a chart of the judge's son. The judge was so impressed by her that he ruled in her favour, concluding that astrology was a science.

❖ *see* REINHOLD EBERTIN p21

Ebertin, Reinhold

Members of the Ebertin family – Elsbeth (Reinhold's mother), Reinhold himself, and his son Baldur – have been a major force in both German and international astrology since the early years of the twentieth century. Ebertin was born in 1901 in Goerlitz, Germany, and was initially a student of the Witte System, but he later abandoned the Trans-Neptunian (hypothetical) planets. Throughout the 1920s he researched and developed a streamlined version that focused on the midpoints and which he named cosmobiology. The system was taught around the world and he wrote 60 books on the subject. The best known of these is *Combination of Stellar Influences*. Ebertin advocated a scientific approach, throwing out many of the time-honoured techniques of traditional astrology and concentrating on planetary and angular relationships. House systems were discarded in this system as they were not considered sufficiently reliable. Ebertin died in 1988.

❖ *see* COSMOBIOLOGY p31

Gauquelin, Michel

Michel Gauquelin (1928–91) was born in Paris, France. Originally a statistician, he attempted to repeat work done by previous researchers to establish the relationship between certain planets and types of profession. He began with a test list of 576 physicians, finding that Mars and Saturn appeared in the horoscope in a manner that could not be dismissed as chance. Extending his work gave equally positive results and he became convinced his theory was correct. He demonstrated that certain astrological principles held true to a high degree of statistical validity. The most striking example was the Mars Effect – in which they found that the charts of sports champions tended to have Mars within 10 degrees of one of the four angles of the chart. The results inflamed the scientific community, who went to great lengths to disprove the results. Gauquelin died in 1991.

❖ *see* MARS p64

PLACES

People have studied the skies since ancient times, and astrology grew up in many disparate ancient civilizations. It fell out of favour during the eighteenth century, and when it was revived at the end of the nineteenth century it was no longer an academic subject, but was practised by those versed in occult arts. Since the twentieth century it has become an adjunct to psychotherapy and a form of popular entertainment.

Babylonian Astrology

Babylonia is seen as the original home of astrology as we know it. Around 2000 BC it was deduced that the changing seasons were produced by the movement of astronomical bodies. From there proceeded the observation that there was a high and low point in summer and winter as well as in the seasons. After more sophisticated observations were made, by 1700 BC the planets, Sun, Moon and zodiac were incorporated into the developing system. Gradually the system was developed away from a simple chronology to that of mapping the future on a general scale. Later, the individual's fate dominated interest. Both were linked to the concept of measuring time. Mundane astrology saw human affairs were being predicted on a broad scale and by 600 BC the personal horoscope had come into being. Astrology has remained unchanged in its essentials since this date. It is unknown what changes occurred in these centuries to cause new skills to emerge – although the first appearance of Venus is one theory among many.

❖ see MUNDANE ASTROLOGY p28

Chaldean Astrology

Chaldean astrology is attributed to priests and is based on the finding of tablets dated about 670 BC, which reported astrological information. The location of Chaldea is subject to speculation. Chaldeans are seen as the magi of Babylonia, astrologers and diviners and 'the wise men from the East'. The chief object of their worship was the Sun, Belus. They did not worship the stars as God but worshipped those they believed He had appointed as mediators between Himself and man. In the time of Alexander the Great (around 356 BC) the Chaldeans alleged that their astrology had existed for 473,000 years.

❖ see EGYPTIAN ASTROLOGY p22

Egyptian Astrology

After the fall of Babylon in 538 BC, astrology experienced a decline. At this time in Egypt a system of magic had been developed which included telling the future through dreams. Between the second and first centuries BC two occult works were developed. The first was an astrological work attributed to the pharaoh Nachepso and his priest Petosiris. These were supposed to have been the secrets revealed after studying the stars. There also appeared the books known as the work of Hermes Trismegistus. These were a compendium built up from the library at Alexandria. Claudius Ptolemy next drew together elements of astrological theory in one logical whole. Much of our understanding of Egyptian astrology is contained within the Cairo Calendar, which consists of a listing of all the days of an Egyptian year. The listings within the calendar are broken up into favourable and unfavourable. Many Egyptian astrologers followed Ptolemy.

❖ see CLAUDIUS PTOLEMY p11

ABOVE: *As well as displaying an interest in astrology, the Aztecs were obsessive time-keepers*

CTractato contra li Aftrologi

ABOVE: *The Bible opposing astrology: an astrologer holds up a celestial sphere as proof of his claims, but the monk refutes him from the Holy Book*

Bible and Astrology

There are numerous references to astrology in the Bible. The most popularly known is that of the Three Wise Men following the star to discover the Christ child: 'Saying, Where is he that is born King of the Jews? For we have seen his star in the east, and are come to worship him' (Matthew 2:2). In some passages astrology is condemned: 'There shall not be found among you any one … that useth divination…' (Deuteronomy xviii, 10–11). Christianity and astrology had an uneasy truce in the past, but coexisted, particularly in England where many priests were students and covert practitioners of astrology. Most of the objections cited in opposition to astrology today are from the King James version of the Bible and many have been proven to be based on mistranslations. Several Christian groups state that the Bible clearly opposes astrology and often make the case that astrology is unscientific, but there are arguments to the contrary. The largest astrological library in the world is that held at the Vatican.

❖ see THOMAS AQUINAS p13

Aztec Astrology

The Aztecs and Mayans were obsessed by time and so became accurate calendar keepers. Their astrology appears to have developed in the Yucatán or Peru and spread from there; however, much of their knowledge was destroyed when the Spanish invaded their lands in the sixteenth century. Their calendar comprised 365 days – just short of the solar year. Their astrological system features circles within circles. The largest circle is the 52,000 years it takes for our Solar System to go around the Pleiades and the smallest the 'Tzol'kin', or Sacred Calendar. This is a combination of 13 numbers and 20 'day names'. In one sense there is no beginning day and no end day, because a circle is in continuous flow. Each day has basic and predictable characteristics that can be calculated. Energies go through cycles described in terms of north (direction of winter and rest), west (direction of autumn and harvest), south (direction of summer and rapid growth) and east (direction of spring and beginnings).

❖ see EGYPTIAN ASTROLOGY p22

Byzantium

Byzantium is the name given to the state and culture of the Eastern Roman Empire in the Middle Ages. After the fall of the Roman Empire in AD 410, there was a decline of learning in western Europe. With the loss of the Greek language, in which most astrological texts had been written, knowledge of astrology survived only as a passing reference. In the Byzantine East a high culture and civilization continued to flourish for another 1,000 years. Despite successive injunctions against divination, the ongoing usage of the Greek language ensured the production and survival of new astrological works. Many scholars emigrated to Persia and India where astrological writings were translated and preserved. By the seventh century, the practice of astrology had declined, but texts were still available. It was the Islamic world that was responsible for transmitting the legacy of the Babylonian astral religion to medieval Europe. The revival began around 1000, when some European scholars began to study at Islamic universities. There they rediscovered Aristotle, Ptolemy and astrology.

❖ see CLAUDIUS PTOLEMY p11

Medieval Astrology

The medieval period is generally defined as the years between 1000 and 1450. After several hundred years of being in its heyday, astrology in the West, although never totally dying out, became very quiet during the Middle Ages. Although there was doubt about astrology's use on a personal level, it continued to be used in meteorology and agriculture, and most scholars took the view that it was an important part of general knowledge, but not a scientific discipline. Boethius's sixth-century book *The Consolation of Philosophy* was influential in reinforcing what astrological knowledge remained in Britain in the tenth century. One area where astrology was particularly powerful was that of medicine. Throughout the medieval period and until the eighteenth century, it would be impossible to qualify as a doctor without passing an examination in astrology at some universities.

Arabian astrology flourished from about the tenth century and was eventually to have an incredible influence on the discipline in the West. One of the most notable of English scholars, Adelard of Bath, was born in the eleventh century and translated several Arabic astrological works. Through his work, as well as that of other writers, many Arabic texts found their way into Europe, where they formed the foundation of an astrological revival.

❖ see ABUMASSAR p12

Renaissance Astrology

By the turn of the eighteenth century, scientific interest in astrology was at a lower ebb than it had been for hundreds of years. By 1720 the last of the notable astrologers of the previous century were dead. The few that remained fell far below the expertise of their predecessors. There had been attempts to bring the study of astrology in line with the new scientific age, and the eighteenth century set off on a course of scientific empiricism and ignored the efforts of astrologers to gain their work scientific credence. Almanacs continued to sell, however, and some were brought out specifically for women. Towards the middle of the century, there was a turn towards religion, increasing the opposition to astrology. Popular interest still brought clients, but they took astrology far less seriously. By the 1790s the astrological *Conjurers Magazine* appeared – but lasted only seven issues. Astrology would not begin its recovery until the 1820s.

❖ see RAPHAEL p19

ABOVE: *Johannes Vermeer's* Astronomer, *painted in 1668 at a time when interest in the stargazing sciences was at an all-time low*

FIELDS

There are many different forms of astrology, and each practitioner will have preferred methods and systems of casting and interpreting horoscopes. These fields have different emphases – from predicting the weather, through medical diagnosis, to answering questions an individual might have. Some have been around for centuries, while others have grown up with the twentieth-century renaissance of the practice.

Relocation Astrology

In relocation astrology, the birth time and date of the person whose chart is being considered is used, but it is recast for either the place they are living at that time, or a place that they are considering living. The new chart describes the likely experiences they will have in that location. This tool is used when someone is deciding whether or not to make a move. The most important factor in a relocated chart is when planets become angular,

that is, placed near the cusps of the first, fourth, seventh or tenth houses. More specific techniques such as astro*carto*graphy and local space charts are used to give the same information in a diagrammatic form. Relocation of charts is a traditional technique that has been used for so long in the history of astrology that there is no record of when it was first devised. It is held that predictions based on a relocated chart will be more accurate for an individual as the house placements and ascendant and midheaven may potentially be different to the birth chart.

❖ see LOCAL SPACE p33

Natal Astrology

Natal astrology is the study of the personal characteristics, traits, strengths, weaknesses and talents that an individual is given at birth, based on the planetary patterns at the time, date, and place of birth. This is what most people think of as serious astrology. The ancient Greeks are given the credit for developing natal astrology and it has been studied and practised since 250 BC. Applying forecasting techniques to the natal chart enables the astrologer to offer guidelines on what is likely to happen and in what way a person is likely to cope. Although there are many fields of application for astrology, natal astrology remains the most popular.

❖ see ESOTERIC ASTROLOGY p30

LEFT: *Aristotle, who recorded the story of Thales of Miletus, a man who used his knowledge of the heavens to make money*

Financial Astrology

Financial astrology has been around for centuries. Traders in grains and precious metals in ancient India used it to set trading times in the markets. Aristotle recorded the story of Thales of Miletus (699–635 BC), who used his knowledge of heavenly cycles to predict a bumper olive crop, and turned a handsome profit. Financial astrology can refer to the practice of predicting cycles on the stock markets by allying them with planetary cycles or by casting a horoscope for a person's financial institution and analyzing it in terms of finances. Many of the theories used today are based on the work of W.D. Gann, who developed a reputation for using astrology successfully to predict market trends and was said to have calculated exact price movements in correlation with planetary movements. The banker J.P. Morgan consulted astrologer Evangeline Adams in timing some of his most important business and investment moves.

❖ see EVANGELINE ADAMS p21

Herbalism

The ancient Chinese, Indians, Egyptians and Babylonians were all herbalists, as were the ancient Greeks and Romans. Throughout the Middle Ages, herbalism was preserved in the monasteries of Britain and mainland Europe. Each physician gardener who wrote a new herbal sought to standardize the use of plants. Paracelsus (1493–1541) emphasized the importance of experience with patients and railed against blind faith. Although he distrusted traditional herbalism he revived the first-century 'doctrine of signatures'. According to this, each herb has its own 'sign'; the appearance of the plant, its colour, scent or living environment governed its use. A century later Nicholas Culpeper revitalized astrology and herbalism. Astrological herbalists connected herbs to different planets

ABOVE: *The nativities of Louis XVI and Marie Antoinette reveal their tragic destiny.*

and used astrological affinities to decide which herb to prescribe. Culpeper broke with other herbalists, as he believed they were only guessing. With the transformation of science from a speculative emphasis to that of experimentation, herbalism began to separate from medical science.

❖ see NICHOLAS CULPEPER p17

Decumbiture

Medical diagnosis by astrology. The name decumbiture comes from the Latin word *decumbo*, meaning 'to lie down' or 'to fall'. In this traditional form of astrology, a chart is cast for the moment that a patient falls ill or goes to bed. It was used in times when herbal physicians such as Nicholas

Culpeper made their diagnoses, prognoses and choice of herbs. There are a number of possible moments on which to base a decumbiture. Firstly, the moment when the patient feels so overcome by their illness that they have to lie down. This is the truest moment in time to judge a decumbiture; however, not everyone takes to their bed when unwell, even if they would like to. Alternatively, if a disease starts suddenly following an accident or some other specific event, this moment in time can also be used. In the past a chart was often cast for the moment that the physician/astrologer received a urine sample from the patient.

❖ see MEDICAL ASTROLOGY p28

Medical Astrology

Medical astrology deals with the workings of the human body. The astrologer analyzes the person's birth chart and determines bodily strengths and weaknesses, proneness to various disease states, and nutritional deficiencies. In the event of illness or disease, a medical astrologer will use predictive methods to try to determine the severity and duration of the disease. Sometimes a medical astrologer can help determine the course of a disease by the use of a chart called a decumbiture – one that is cast for the time of the onset of the illness. Medical astrology is also used in choosing the best time for surgery. The practice has very ancient roots, but it reached its peak in Europe in the late medieval and early modern periods, about 1450–1700.

❖ see DECUMBITURE p27

Mundane Astrology

Mundane astrology is the application of astrology to world affairs, taking its name from the Latin *mundus*, meaning 'the world'. In the Middle Ages it was more commonly known as the study of revolutions, meaning the study of the revolutions of the planets in their apparent orbits around the Earth. This is the origin of the idea of the political revolution – the rise and fall of states in line with celestial revolutions. Mundane astrology was used to explain history and predict the future. Originally developed in Babylon, the

ABOVE: *The celestial influx acting on the body of a woman, one of the main ideas behind medical astrology*

fundamentals were laid down by Claudius Ptolemy. In the ninth and tenth centuries Arabic astrologers added many more techniques. The twentieth century saw techniques based on the use of planetary cycles rather than the interpretation of individual horoscopes. In 1951 Charles Carter wrote a book called *Introduction to Political Astrology*. He used the term political astrology to differentiate from the traditional practice of mundane astrology, although the terms are often used interchangeably.

❖ see CLAUDIUS PTOLEMY p11

Horary Astrology

Horary astrology is the name given to the branch of astrology that casts a chart for the moment that a question is asked and provides an answer for that question by examining the chart. The rulerships of the planets, signs and houses are taken into consideration.

Only those parts of the chart that have direct relevance to the question in hand are studied. With its strict rules, horary astrology can be a very speedy way of using astrology for someone who is adept at it. It is unnecessary to know the birth time of the person asking the question as the chart is cast for the question alone. The practice reached its height in the seventeenth century, but fell out of popularity until it had almost disappeared by the beginning of the twentieth century.

❖ see ELECTIONAL ASTROLOGY p29

Electional Astrology

The astrology of electing, or choosing, the best time to go ahead with a project or activity. There are two types of electional charts – universal and particular. Universal elections do not use a specific nativity, while particular elections do. Universal election can be used, for example, to elect a time for building structures, planting crops or moving to a new location. Particular election examples are undergoing surgery, marriage, going on a journey or purchasing property of any kind. The rules of electional astrology are broadly similar to those of horary, and it is another traditional form of astrology that does not require a birth time. To cast an electional chart it is decided what needs to be achieved and what planets and houses are associated with the event. With practical considerations taken into account, the astrologer examines the positions of the planets and chart points over a given period and seeks to cast a chart that gives the most auspicious moment for the event to take place.

❖ see HORORY ASTROLOGY p28

Astrometeorology

Predicting the weather through astrology is one of its oldest uses. During the mid-nineteenth century the struggle between scientific weather prediction and more traditional forms was highlighted. A number of nineteenth-century astrologers, including Zadkiel, were members of the London Meteorological Society. It ceased to be fashionable at the end of the century and is rarely practised today. It is the science of forecasting weather, fierce storms, floods, droughts, freezes, hurricanes, earthquakes and volcanic eruptions. Astronomers in the past had observed that when the planets in geocentric longitude moved through the various constellations or zodiacal signs, seismic activity occurred and weather patterns differed according to the influence of that particular sign. Using the Sun, Moon and planets, their angular positions in relation to each other and to the Earth, astrometeorology seeks to predict the time, location and severity of weather or seismic activity at any given time, for any geographical location on the planet.

❖ see ZADKIEL p19

ABOVE: *The term 'judicial astronomy' was used to separate the work of astrologers from that of astronomers*

Esoteric Astrology

Esoteric astrology is a system that is used to analyze spiritual factors in someone's life. It reveals the soul's intention and indicates how the soul seeks to express itself in one's outer life. This form of astrology was developed out of the Theosophical Society, formed by Helena Blavatsky in the late nineteenth century. According to this system, each person has certain rays predominant in their personal chart. These rays correspond to the chakras or energy centres. Esoteric astrologers also use the Earth and a hypothetical planet, Vulcan, as objects in the chart. The astrologer Alan Leo began to popularize this form of astrology in the late nineteenth century. From 1936 the theosophist Alice A. Bailey wrote a series of books entitled

Esoteric Astrology and these form the main texts in this field. This type of astrology reached the general public with popular works such as Alan Oken's *Spiritual Astrology*.

❖❖ see HOROSCOPE p138

Psychological Astrology

The study of the personality; one of the primary applications of astrology. Psychological astrology is carried out by examining the birth chart. Throughout the twentieth century astrology became more popular, reflecting the rise in popularity of psychology. Psychoanalyst Carl Jung was interested in astrology and began to examine it in the context of his theories of synchronicity and the collective unconscious. Alongside this development, belief in human progress through technology and evolution made the predictive nature and supposed fatalism of astrology seem absurd. To adapt, some astrologers followed Jung's example and used his framework to explain the natal chart as a reflection of an individual's connection to archetypes in the collective unconscious. Psychological astrology remains hugely popular today although prediction is used within the field.

❖❖ see CARL JUNG p20

Sun-Sign Astrology

Sun-sign astrology is what most people think of when hearing the term 'astrology'. It is based on assuming that the sign on which the Sun falls on the date of birth is the first house of the chart. The other planets are placed around this chart and it is interpreted accordingly. It was not until the beginning of the twentieth century that the Sun gained prominence over the other planets in the horoscope. The astrologer R.H. Naylor invented the Sun-sign column in 1930. Other newspapers followed suit and Sun-sign columns are a regular feature of most newspapers and magazines all over the world and remain extremely popular.

❖❖ see R.H. NAYLOR p21

LEFT: *Helena Blavatsky*

Cosmobiology

The word 'cosmobiology' was first coined in 1914 by the medical scientist Feerhow and was adopted by Reinhold Ebertin and his associates in Germany during the 1920s. The discipline is concerned with the possible correlation between the cosmos and the individual, and the effects cosmic movement and stellar motions have on the individual in a given environment. Ebertin published *The Combination of Stellar Influences* in 1940, and this remains the standard guide to this method. Cosmobiology does not make use of the houses as traditional astrology does. Instead, cosmobiology relies on using the positions of the planets by signs and in relation to one another, and relies heavily on the use of midpoints. It also emphasizes the need to consider the person's background and environment. It is particularly popular as a system in Europe.

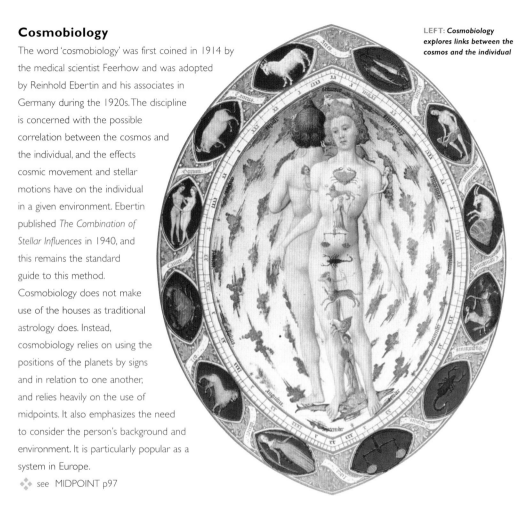

❖ see MIDPOINT p97

LEFT: *Cosmobiology explores links between the cosmos and the individual*

Hamburg School

The astrology promoted by Alfred Witte started the trend in the 1920s in Germany and evolved into what was to be known as the Hamburg School. Witte spent his life investigating the interpretation of symmetries and patterns of relationships using a moveable dial. He was a surveyor by profession and was employed by the city of Hamburg. Through the examination of thousands of charts, Witte was able to predict many precisely timed events, for example, the moment of artillery barrages and explosions on the Western Front. In 1928 he published a summary of his findings in their major systematized dictionary *Rules for Planetary Pictures*. Despite Witte's desire to simplify and rationalize astrological interpretation and to bring astrology into the twentieth century, his ideas appeared too radical and too technical for the mainstream traditionalists. His work was ignored by most students until well after World War II and his concepts only really began to penetrate the astrological establishment in the 1950s and 1960s.

❖ see HARMONICS p32

LEFT: *Manuscript showing the seven stages of the Sun and the signs of the zodiac*

Creative Astrology

Creative astrology is an astrological interpretation technique closely allied to psychological astrology. It came into being during the 1970s, developing out of humanistic psychology, in which the client is empowered to enter into a dialogue with their unconscious. The horoscope is often seen as an aid to psychology. Creative astrology also has strong links with esoteric astrology. Techniques such as guided imagery and drama are used extensively. The person whose horoscope is under discussion is encouraged to participate in the chart reading. Unlike in other forms of astrology, the horoscope is treated as a means to self-discovery, and it is assumed that it is not possible to read the birth chart and predict specific events.

❖ see PSYCHOLOGICAL ASTROLOGY p30

Harmonics

Although the use of harmonics is generally attributed to the publication of John Addey's book *Harmonics in Astrology* in 1976, similar techniques have been used in Vedic astrology for many centuries and were also used by Hellenistic astrologers around the time of Ptolemy. Harmonics is a method for investigating specific themes within the horoscope. They are a universal way of describing the shape and form of a wave, or of talking about the various kinds of energies that blend together to form that wave. In astrology, these harmonics correspond to the common idea of aspects, the various ways that planets can combine their energies, even though they lie in different parts of the zodiac. A harmonic chart is calculated by multiplying the positions of the planets by the number

Uranian Astrology

Uranian astrology was an invention of the German astrology school which had its heyday in the 1920s. It is notable for its number of Uranian or Trans-Neptunian points – hypothetical planets located far beyond the orbit of Pluto. Uranians also developed a system of midpoints, similar to the Greek formulae for Arabic Parts. The midpoints are degrees sensitive to transits and the presence of other points in that location. A configuration of midpoints, a planetary picture, shows a complex of traits, issues and likely events. Because the effects of the planets on human behaviour are considered more plausible than the divisions of life into 12 regions of the sky (houses), the use of houses fell out of favour with Uranian astrologers. This was compatible with their attempt to pare astrology down to the essentials. Harmonious aspects such as trines and sextiles are also typically eliminated in favour of more difficult aspects which are considered more intense.

❖ see COSMOBIOLOGY p31

of the harmonic. A fifth harmonic chart, which is associated with creativity, is derived by multiplying the positions by five and drawing the new positions in the chart.

❖ see CLAUDIUS PTOLEMY p11

Local Space

Local space astrology is similar in its application to Feng Shui. It tells where the best and worst areas are for a person and can be applied to a house, room or country. The horoscope is cast for the place that needs to be considered, based on a person's time and date of birth. Local space charts can be applied to such things as safe travel and business because they will show the direction of best and worst potential. The spaces where there are no lines are considered neutral. The places where the lines of particular planets fall are interpreted in accordance with that planet. Local space astrology can be used for designing a room or house so that it develops your maximum potential or help to decide if a certain location is suitable to move to.

❖ see RELOCATION ASTROLOGY p26

Astro*carto*graphy

Astro*carto*graphy is based on the traditional astrological tool of relocating a chart for where the person lives at that time, involving recalculating the chart. The resulting chart shows what the person's life would have been like if they had been born in the new place. The most important factor in a relocated chart is when planets become angular, or placed near the cusps of the first, fourth, seventh or tenth houses. In this field a computer calculates the places on Earth where each planet would be on those points. The nature of the planet concerned describes the type of experience a person could be expected to have in that location.

❖ see LOCAL SPACE p33

Sidereal Astrology

The sidereal zodiac is a star-based zodiac that uses a fixed star as a reference point. It is more commonly used in the East. There is now a gap of about 24 degrees between the two zodiacs. A planet in the sign of Aries under the tropical zodiac falls in Pisces in the sidereal. Many of the 700 million people in the Indian subcontinent use a form of sidereal astrology. The sidereal zodiac is held by many to be more astronomically correct.

❖ see ARIES p36

Tropical Astrology

In Western astrology the start of the zodiac begins with the spring equinox, when the Sun enters the sign of Aries. Owing to the astronomical phenomenon called precession, this starting point moves backwards about one degree every 72 years. Originally both sidereal and tropical zodiacs coincided. Since the third or fourth century the two zodiacs have been separating from one another. There is now a gap of about 24 degrees between the tropical and sidereal zodiacs. In the West the zodiac is used as it originally was. This means that although a planet may be spoken of as being in the sign Aries, for example, astronomically it is actually in Pisces. The sidereal zodiac, a star-based zodiac that uses a fixed star as a reference point, is more commonly used in the East although a minority of Western astrologers also use the sidereal zodiac.

❖ see PRECESSION p131

Vedic Astrology

Vedic astrology is the form of astrology most commonly used in the East. It uses the sidereal (star-based) zodiac, rather than the tropical zodiac. Charts are drawn in a square, rather than circular form and the most important planet is the Moon, rather than the Sun as in Western astrology. Dasas, routinely called planetary periods or cycles, are intervals during which the person's life corresponds to the energies of individual planets and is used as a predictive tool.

❖ see SIDEREAL ASTROLOGY p33

UNDERSTANDING THE ZODIAC

The term 'zodiac' is derived from the Greek *zodiacus*, which means 'little animals' or 'little creatures'. The zodiac is a small band of the sky, about eight degrees on either side of the ecliptic, which contains the motions of most of the planets. This band is divided into 30-degree sections called signs, which are defined and described in the study of astrology. There are 12 signs in the zodiac: Aries, Taurus, Gemini, Cancer, Leo, Virgo, Libra, Scorpio, Sagittarius, Capricorn, Aquarius and Pisces. Each sign of the zodiac has a particular graphical representation called a glyph that relates to an animal or a part of the human body. Each of the 12 signs is a unique combination of one of the four elements and one of the three qualities.

THE ZODIAC

SIGNS OF THE ZODIAC

The word 'signs' refers to the division of space on the zodiac belt into 12 sections to create a frame of reference by which the positions of celestial bodies can be identified. Each of the 12 divisions of 30 degrees is called a sign and given a name: Aries, Taurus, Gemini, Cancer, Leo, Virgo, Libra, Scorpio, Sagittarius, Capricorn, Aquarius and Pisces. These names refer to the constellations, or groups of stars, that rise and set within the path of the ecliptic, although, due to a phenomenon known as the Precession of the Equinoxes, the signs and constellations no longer coincide.

Aries

The first sign of the zodiac, a member of the cardinal triplicity, masculine and of the fire element. A bestial sign, the symbol for Aries is the ram; its ruling planet is Mars, traditionally by day. The Sun enters the sign of Aries around 21 March, the vernal or spring equinox, and exits around 19 April. This is the first month of spring and the nature and qualities of Aries are closely associated with the awakening energy that follows the hibernation of winter.

In physical terms, Aries rules the head and all the organs of the head including the brain. The mental facilities of the sign, however, are more intuitive and instinctual rather than intellectual, and manifest themselves as a rush of activity to fulfil the thought. Aries rushes headlong at its goal with sometimes little more than the initial spark of an idea as motivation. This can occasionally result in regrettable situations, due to premature actions, and because of a lack of logical forethought. But Aries is a courageous sign, so Aries is soon off again expressing a new energy.

Aries represents a search for self through activity that reaffirms existence as an individual, set apart from the rest of the crowd. Aries experiences and understands the world from a totally subjective position and judges all that is presented for consideration entirely from a personal perspective. This can be perceived as egotistical, arrogant

and selfish, as Aries is oblivious to all outside thoughts and ideas. There is a constant need to test the limits of selfhood by taking the initiative whenever the opportunity arises and by engaging in competition with other individuals. For this reason Aries is seen as the sign of the sportsperson and soldier.

The leadership qualities in Aries are considerable, as is a pioneering spirit and an apparent self-confidence – all of which mean that others are attracted to this charismatic energy. For the same reasons Aries is not comfortable in a position of obeisance, resenting those in authority. There is a distinct inability to listen to and consider the advice of others. The enormous rush of energy that propels Aries in its quest for leadership is impulsive, leaving little room for diplomacy. Aries does not respond well to routine and repetition; once a task has been completed and mastered, there is an inbuilt need to move on to the next. There is a constant desire for spontaneity and the freedom to pursue new goals, so any chosen career path should offer up plenty of opportunities to follow new areas of activity that will not require going over the same old ground.

It is important that Aries carries through and brings to completion any creative project or pursuit once it has

RIGHT: *The two faces of Mars, the ruling planet of Aries*

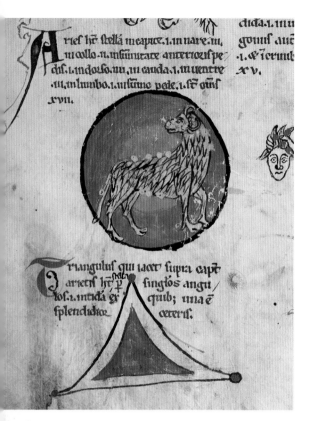

Arief he stellä meapice.i.in nare.iii.
iii collo.ii.infumitate anterioris pe
dif.i.indorfo.iiii.in cauda.i.in uentre
.iii.in lumbo.i.in fumo pede.i.fc ouf
xvii.

Trianguluf qui iacet fupra capt
arietif he p fingtos angu
lof.i.incida gr quib; una e
fplendidior ceterif.

LEFT: *The Sun is in Aries during the first month of spring*

Whatever part of the horoscope in which Aries is found is the arena of life in which there will be an aggressive and opportunistic need for action. For example, Aries on the third house cusp suggests the manner of speech and communication will be approached with the fire of initiative and an enthusiastic, forceful energy.

In its most positive expression, Aries is direct, decisive and enthusiastic with an ability to use personal initiative, courageous, and inspirational to others. In its negative expression, Aries is egotistical, combative and lacking in subtlety; there is an inability to be objective and a foolhardy, zealous approach to goals.

❖ see BESTIAL SIGNS p58

Taurus

Taurus is the second sign of the zodiac, a member of the fixed triplicity, feminine and of the earth element. A bestial sign, the symbol for Taurus is the bull; its ruling planet is Venus. The Sun enters the sign of Taurus around 20 April and exits around 20 May. This is the second month of spring and the qualities of Taurus are closely associated with this period when the beauty of nature is visible.

In physical terms, Taurus rules the neck and throat; it is also connected to the lymphatic system of the human body, and the metabolizing of energy. The neck connects the head, and therefore thought, to the rest of the body, which must respond and use the skills inherent in the body to fulfil its desires. Taurus is a sensual sign and is prone to indulging the senses of the body.

Taurus represents a search for self through an instinctive understanding of the physicality of life. There is a need to experience reality through the sense of touch. That is not to say that Taurus has no sympathy with spiritual matters, rather that there is an intuitive understanding of how the spirit manifests itself through nature, as though there is a deep understanding that for any dream to be realized there must first be a solid object with which to work. Taurus is concerned with the material world – possessions offer

been instigated. It is only through achieving the individual goals set by the self that Aries feels secure and vital.

In personal relationships Aries likes to make a conquest and can be powerfully romantic, although it can also be selfish and demanding. Aries is fiercely protective towards its nearest and dearest and exhibits strong passionate feelings towards lovers and marriage partners.

Any planet in a horoscope found in this sign will operate through the energies connected with it. The Moon in Aries, for example, suggests that all emotional and instinctive responses are subjective and focus on the need to be assertive and self-starting in the pursuit of emotional security. Saturn in Aries operates as a tendency towards the setting up of rigorous ego structures and boundaries through which the enthusiastic creative energies must pass or else remain unexpressed and stagnant.

security that is obvious and not merely ephemeral.

Taurus does not rush at anything without forethought, or decide on a course of action without first being sure that it will work out as expected; once the course is decided then the bull will steadily follow it to conclusion. Equally, Taurus is slow in forming opinions; again once the opinion is formed it is almost impossible to shift it. This is a quality inherent in all the fixed signs of the zodiac, and the one that gives Taurus its reputation for stubbornness.

Being ruled by Venus, Taurus has a great love of beauty, luxury and over-abundance. Taurus likes to surround itself with *objects d'art*, and indulge in the pleasures of fine wine and dining. In love there is a need for romance, and as an earth sign, a need for the constant demonstration of physical affection; although Taurus may be slow in trusting another enough to give their heart, once they do, it is given with loyalty and devotion. Taurus is ambitious and will patiently pursue any task that is seen to have a worthwhile outcome. Taurus is very productive, and can take any seed project or idea and turn it into a practical and working concern.

Through determined and steadfast effort, Taurus will make the most of the inherent potential in any occupation.

Any planet in a horoscope found in this sign will operate through the energies connected with it. Mercury in Taurus, for example, suggests that communication will not be frivolous or ill considered and there will be little waste of words. Whatever part of the horoscope that Taurus is found is the arena of life in which there will be a concern for pleasurable physical experience and a need for material rewards that can be possessed.

In its most positive expression, Taurus is determined, sensitive and understanding; loyal with a love of beauty in all its forms. In its negative expression, Taurus is stubborn, possessive and over-indulgent in sensual appetites.

❖ see VENUS p63

Gemini

Gemini is the third sign of the zodiac, a member of the mutable triplicity, masculine and of the air element. A human sign, the symbol for Gemini is the heavenly twins

BELOW: *Taurus the bull*

and its ruling planet is Mercury. The Sun enters the sign of Gemini around 21 May and exits around 21 June. This is the third month of spring, and the nature and qualities of Gemini are closely associated with this time of year as the days lengthen towards the summer solstice.

In physical terms, Gemini rules the hands and arms, which it likes to use in conjunction with the mind to explore one idea after another. Because of the bi-corporeal nature of the sign it is also true to say of Gemini that sometimes the left hand does not know what the right hand is doing. As Gemini also rules much of the body's nervous system, this sign reacts to almost every

BELOW: *Gemini, the twins, tends to be changeable*

form of stimulation in its immediate environment; Gemini is eager for excitement and experience, a thrill-seeker. This can lead to restlessness and fickleness in the direction that energy is channelled, occasionally resulting in a dissatisfaction that lasts only until the next mental interest is stimulated.

Gemini represents a search for self through the mental process and understanding the dualistic nature of what is observed and experienced. The Gemini mind is constantly examining the many sides of any situation in order to discover all aspects to gain greater understanding.

Gemini is an intellectual, experimenting with ideas, analyzing data, systemizing information and drawing conclusions. There is an imperative to reason through every thought and experience, which then must be communicated to those in the immediate environment.

There is an insatiable curiosity and a passion for seeking knowledge. Gemini is not content to sit in one place for long but must be out and about gathering more information, more mental stimulus, making connections with others who can help feed the hungry mind. Gemini is a social butterfly, alighting here one minute to gather information, then flying off somewhere else the next, cross-fertilizing as they gather more and move on again.

Gemini is the sign of the teacher, writer, traveller and graphic artist; as long as there is plenty of scope in daily life to take in information and pass it on, Gemini is fulfilling the innate talents and skills of the sign. The communication skills of Gemini are enormous. On the flip side this mental trickiness has a tendency to tie themselves and others up in mental knots.

Relationships, friendships and associations are important to Gemini as they provide exchange of thoughts and ideas; it is often easy to find an immediate rapport that is light, entertaining and full of excitement. However, the connection with Gemini is always mental and rarely does it carry any depth of emotion. Although Gemini has feelings, emotions are processed through the intellect and can occasionally remain unexpressed. There is a flirtatious manner about Gemini that is sometimes perceived as indiscriminate and insincere.

Any planet in a horoscope found in this sign will operate through the energies connected with it. Mars in Gemini, for example, suggests a keen understanding of strategy, a strong passion for ideas, and a need to express them forcefully, perhaps even aggressively. Whatever part of the horoscope that Gemini is found is the arena of life in which there will be a concern for rationalization on the mental level.

In its most positive expression, Gemini's value lies in a clever intellect, versatility, a fun-loving nature, and the ability to look at life from many different perspectives. In its negative expression, Gemini is a dilettante, nervous, unemotional, fickle and silly, unable to find a unifying strength of purpose.

❖ see BI-CORPOREAL SIGNS p58

Cancer

Cancer is the fourth sign of the zodiac, a member of the cardinal triplicity, feminine and of the water element. The symbol for Cancer is the crab, its ruling planet is the Moon. The Sun enters Cancer around the time of the summer solstice on 22 June and exits around 23 July. This is the first month of summer and the nature and qualities of Cancer are closely associated with the maturing life energies that were in its early creative growth stages through the spring. This is the time when life needs tending and nurturing to maximize the potential of its yield.

In physical terms, Cancer rules the chest and breasts, which symbolize in both sexes the protective and nurturing qualities connected with this sign. Cancer operates on emotional instinct and, just as its ruler the Moon is constantly going through phases of full, half, crescent, new and back again, so do the emotional moods of Cancer pass through an ever-changing cycle. There is enormous sensitivity to atmosphere and environment in Cancer, being receptive to vibrational energy that is then interpreted through the personal and subjective feeling senses. Cancer has a strong instinctive nature and is

ABOVE: *Cancer's ruler, the Moon, perceived as a boat by Egyptians*

extremely intuitive. There is an inability to regulate and control the thoughts and emotions; Cancer is subject to the mood of the moment and behaves accordingly.

Cancer represents a search for self through what is felt on an emotional level. In order for any information to be absorbed it must first be intuited and processed through the senses. Initially Cancer has a problem with being pinned down, scuttling sideways in order to avoid being trapped. The strong need for self-protection ensures that a lot of effort must be made to pierce the outer shell and touch the gentle centre. However, once the powerful emotions have been engaged, Cancer embraces with full attachment and then finds it very difficult to disengage. Home and family are very important to Cancer, which is often seen as the sign of Mother the nurturer. In all ways, that which is familiar and offers comfort assists in the feeling of security – a much sought-after commodity by Cancer.

The theme of nurturing runs strongly through Cancer, whether it be as the one giving or receiving, and it operates on many levels. Cancer is happiest when feeling loved, protected and well-fed, and they would like to offer the same to their nearest and dearest. Cancer is not above playing emotional games in order to test those that profess to love and want them, but the rewards for passing the test are great and partners and friends are offered the gentle, cosy and loving private world of home sweet home.

Cancer can be found in any career pursuit where the financial rewards are potentially great. Due to the cardinal qualities of the sign, Cancer is also extremely active and very resourceful; the ambitious nature can be seen in the tenacity that Cancer displays when searching for and holding on to a secure income. Financial and material wealth are important as they provide the stable outer security necessary to assist in the fostering of inner emotional security.

BELOW: *Leo, the lion, from a sixteenth-century Turkish treatise*

Any planet in a horoscope found in this sign will operate through the energies connected with it. Venus in Cancer, for example, suggests a love and artistic ability related to the domestic environment, an indulgence in beautiful surroundings and luxury, the mark of a good interior designer. Saturn in Cancer might operate as a harsh disciplinarian attitude around the home, demanding exacting standards in the search for a safe and secure environment.

Whatever part of the horoscope in which Cancer is found is the arena of life in which there will be a concern for emotional comfort and security. For example, should Cancer be found on the eleventh house cusp, there is a strong need for making emotional connections with friends and associates of like mind, and a desire to nurture humanity as a whole rather than just those in the immediate environment.

In its most positive expression, Cancer is imaginative, sensitive, caring and gentle, understanding of the human condition, nurturing the best qualities in those of close connection. In its negative expression, Cancer is moody, selfish, irritable, over-sensitive to imagined insults, excluding others that are not members of their personal clan.

❖ see SUN-SIGN p59

Leo

Leo is the fifth sign of the zodiac, a member of the fixed triplicity, masculine and of the fire element. A feral sign, the symbol for Leo is the lion, and its ruling planet is the Sun. The Sun enters Leo around 23 July and exits around 22 August. This is the second month of summer and the nature and qualities of Leo are closely associated with the time of year, when the heat of the Sun is ripening the fruits of the Earth brought forth during the nurturing time of Cancer. It is a time of abundant growth and glorious warmth.

In physical terms, Leo rules the heart, connecting the sign to the virtues of man such as courage, love, loyalty and generosity. Leo responds to life's stimuli with an enthusiastic but steady spirit, offering a constant strength to any pursuit. Leo exudes a natural nobility and inner confidence that inspires trust, devotion and loyalty.

Leo represents the search for self through the creative urge and a desire to affect the immediate environment so that it reflects favourably the individual identity of the ego. Leo demands to be seen as a benefic leader, a stable centre around which others revolve, much like the sign's ruling planet the Sun. There is a tendency to occasionally lie back and lazily bask in the glory that Leo feels is its due. There is a robust and handsome element, and a pride in appearance; however, this pride can easily turn to vanity and a capricious need for attention, making Leo easily won over by flattery. But Leo offers much in return for the attention and adulation: Leo is open, loving, warm and generous. Leo is passionate about love and intensely romantic. Possessive, territorial and completely loyal, the power of the emotions that Leo feels for their partner is tremendous.

The sign is closely connected with creativity and individual creative ideas are developed by Leo; they become the children, the work of art or the pet project to be played with, explored, and led through the paces that encourage maximum expression of innate potential. Leo has an exceptional talent for the dramatic, is keenly aware of the importance of making a favourable – even sensational – impact in every situation. The lion is a consummate actor and performer who seeks to be admired as a star, and in this way Leo remains a little apart from the crowd, keeping a distance from any threat that may damage the well-protected ego. This is where Leo is vulnerable.

The creative arts are an area where the lion can fulfil not only the inherent talent of the sign, but also achieve the fame and admiration so important to them. Whatever the chosen career, it is important that there is enough scope for Leo to be congratulated and appreciated for the effort that is put into any pursuit.

Any planet in a horoscope found in this sign will operate through the energies connected with it. The Moon in Leo, for example, suggests a strong emotional need to be liked, and an appreciation of drama, ostentation and glamour in everyday affairs. Mars in Leo would express itself as a powerful and energetic creative urge as well as

ABOVE: *The Sun is Leo's ruler*

an inclination towards taking risks and gambling with life. Whatever part of the horoscope in which Leo is found is the arena of life in which there will be a concern for individual creative expression.

In its most positive expression, Leo is confident, warm and generous, with an artistic flair and a refined manner, affectionate, romantic and loving, with a happy disposition. In its negative expression, Leo can be a vain show-off, egotistical and demanding, overly extravagant and hedonistic, an attention-seeking dictator.

❖ see FERAL SIGNS p58

Virgo

Virgo is the sixth sign of the zodiac, a member of the mutable triplicity, feminine and of the earth element. A human sign, the symbol for Virgo is the virgin maid; its ruling planet is Mercury. The Sun enters the sign of Virgo around 23 August and exits around 22 September. This is the second month of summer and the nature and qualities of Virgo are closely connected with this time of harvest.

In physical terms, Virgo rules the stomach and digestive system, and the mental facilities of the sign operate in a similar fashion. There is a huge mental hunger in Virgo, but all information taken in must be processed through an analytical and critical system. Virgo has an abundance of nervous energy which can result in anything from mild butterflies in the stomach to full-blown hypochondria. As an earth sign, Virgo is connected to physical reality, and the vehicle or human body must also operate at maximum

ABOVE: *The sign of Virgo, the virgin maid*

efficiency. Virgo represents a search for self through the acquiring of knowledge and practical talents, affirming their validity by putting them to use. Virgo is referred to as the sign of service; there is an instinctive knowledge that all individuals must operate within a system, using unique talents for the good of the whole. The development of a talent or idea, taking it to its highest potential, is of importance to Virgo – perfection is the goal in any pursuit. Virgo rejects that which is faulty or imperfect, and manifests intellectual skill into a skill of labour.

There is something of the craftsman in Virgo – the patient attention to detail, and the developing of routines that hone skills and perfect ability come under this sign. Virgo can be very humble and does not really require recognition for being helpful. The ego is served by affirming its own usefulness in the community. Virgo needs to be needed, and will stand up for others less fortunate in a way that they would not stand up for themselves. One way in which Virgo will measure their contribution is by reaping material benefits in direct correlation to the amount of energy invested. Virgo has a reputation for being an excellent employee. Should the benefits not fit the high quality of service and expenditure of talent, however, Virgo will move on to another employer or environment more deserving of their skills.

In human relationships Virgo is thoughtful, solicitous and kind. Even the manner in which Virgo criticizes is meant to be helpful and constructive, for Virgo wants their loved ones to be the best and as pure as they can. Virgo is devoted, but not sentimental; highly sensual, but not given to dramatic, passionate display; their charm is subtle and alluring. Sometimes Virgo is guilty of manipulating those around them by setting up a feeling of obligation on another's part for all that is done by Virgo in the name of service.

Any planet in a horoscope found in this sign will operate through the energies connected with it. Venus in Virgo, for example, might suggest a talent for perfecting artistic ability, excelling in the techniques of creating beautiful objects. Whatever part of the horoscope that

Virgo is found is the arena of life in which there will be a concern for performing a service.

In its most positive expression, Virgo is precise, dependable, helpful and kind, with an exceptional intuitive intellect and thirst for knowledge. In its negative expression, Virgo is critical, manipulative and nervous.

❖❖ see MUTABLE p57

Libra

Libra is the seventh sign of the zodiac, a member of the cardinal triplicity, masculine and of the air element. A human sign, the symbol for Libra is the scales; its ruling planet is Venus. The Sun enters Libra around 23 September and exits around 22 October. This is the first month of autumn, following the autumn equinox when the hours of daylight become shorter than the hours of night. The nature and qualities of Libra reflect this time of year, when the leaves begin to turn in readiness to drop and re-enrich the Earth to balance that which has been taken in harvest.

In physical terms, Libra is linked to the skin and the organs that regulate and filter the intake of the body, such as the kidneys and liver. Like its symbol the scales, Libra is immediately aware of imbalance and channels its energy to bring about balance and harmony.

Libra represents the search for self through active cooperation with another; relationship is sought in order to gain self-knowledge by having a reflection from which an objective point of view is acquired. Libra is unlikely to be cruel or to deliberately injure another; the innate sense of justice understands the dynamic of giving and receiving. Libra learns and grows by paying attention to the quality of the experience received in relationship with others, continually adjusting behaviour in order to create a more harmonious environment for all concerned. Libra, as a cardinal sign, is active in achieving their own ambitions, but uses the talent of diplomacy and gentle persuasion to implement their wants and desires. Libra makes a good counsellor, negotiator and mediator, due to a strong sense of democracy and the ability to see value in both sides of

ABOVE: *Mercury, ruler of Virgo*

any argument; however, this also highlights the difficulty that Libra has in making decisions, as every aspect needs to be measured and weighed before the passing of judgement. It can sometimes take so much time for Libra to make up their mind that the opportunity is lost.

As an air sign ruled by Venus, the mental facilities of Libra are intellectual, imaginative and artistic, with a predisposition towards romance and beauty. By keeping these as goals of the mind, Libra endeavours to promote them in each sphere of life in which they participate. The need for harmony and balance is displayed in Libra's personal domain by creating an aesthetically pleasing space that calms the senses. Libra dislikes crude, sloppy and unsophisticated behaviour, and is perceived by others as refined, orderly and elegant.

Any planet in a horoscope found in this sign will operate through the energies connected with it. The Moon in Libra, for example, might suggest an intuitive and emotional imperative towards making close connections with another

or an inability to display intense feelings for fear of reprisal from outside. Saturn in Libra could operate as a cautious and conservative approach to relationships and a dispassionate need to affect a sense of justice in all dealings with others. In its most positive expression, Libra is loving and romantic, charming, pleasant and cooperative with a natural artistic flair and sense of fair play. Libra is highly intelligent and an excellent listener and communicator. In its negative expression, Libra can be incapable of making a decision, superficial and insincere.

❖❖ see HUMAN SIGNS p59

Scorpio

Scorpio is the eighth sign of the zodiac and a member of the fixed triplicity, feminine and of the water element. A fruitful sign, the symbol for Scorpio is the scorpion; its traditional ruling planet is Mars, particularly by night, and its modern ruler Pluto. The Sun enters the sign of Scorpio around 23 October and exits around 21 November. This is the second month of autumn and the qualities of Scorpio are closely associated with that time of year. When the trees drop their dead leaves, they bring a promise of new growth.

In physical terms, Scorpio rules the reproductive organs and excretory functions, and is connected with regeneration and new beginnings, but only after the old has been thoroughly explored. Scorpio is referred to as the sign of death and re-birth, and its connection to the reproductive organs illustrates how sex is a process which makes new life possible, as death makes room for new forms of life to develop.

Scorpio represents a search for self through discovering the hitherto unexplored depths of that which is hidden and internal, determining the motivating force behind action and reaction to stimulus from the outside world. Scorpio is fascinated by mystery and is an excellent detective looking for truth, meaning and the purpose behind all existence. Scorpios are surrounded by an air of mystery themselves,

jealously guarding their privacy, rejecting any encroachment of the inner world from the outside. Scorpio will not expose any personal weakness and is loath to display any sign of vulnerability. This does not stop Scorpio from attempting to uncover the secret depths of others. For Scorpio knowledge brings power, and knowledge of another's secrets brings the power of control. This is a self-defence mechanism for Scorpio, insurance against any threat by being in a position to do damage first before suffering the humiliation of attack and defeat. The symbol for the sign, the scorpion, has been observed stinging itself to death rather than be subject to annihilation from an outside attacker.

There is a seductive quality to Scorpio that draws others in; their powerful self-control alludes to a strength of character and an intensely passionate nature which is extremely attractive to the opposite sex. The desire to merge completely with another is a powerful imperative and intimate relationship is often the arena in which Scorpio looks to satisfy that desire. Scorpio can go to extremes in the power of emotions – love and hate are felt forcefully. Scorpio takes a long time to accept another into their personal territory, testing the prospective lover or friend to determine their worthiness, but once a commitment has been made the love and devotion of

BELOW: *The night sky of Mars, Scorpio's ruler*

LEFT: Ruled by Venus, Libra is predisposed towards romance

Scorpio is complete and all-consuming. Equally, if Scorpio is betrayed then the full force of hate and fury is unleashed on the betrayer.

Any planet in a horoscope found in this sign will operate through the energies connected with it. Venus in Scorpio, for example, might display a desire to experience love and relationships with a life-or-death intensity, or a taste for emotionally powerful and evocative art forms. Whatever part of the horoscope that Scorpio is found is the arena of life in which there will be a concern for deep understanding, connection and transformation.

In its most positive expression, Scorpio is tenacious, strong, passionate and sensitive, loyal and creative, inspiring faith with an ability to help others transform themselves through a deep understanding of the human psyche. In its negative expression, Scorpio is destructive, manipulative and jealous, sadistic, secretive and vindictive; totally ruthless.

❖ see WATER SIGNS p55

Sagittarius

Sagittarius is the ninth sign of the zodiac, a member of the mutable triplicity, masculine and of the fire element. A feral sign, the symbol for Sagittarius is the centaur archer and its ruling planet is Jupiter. The Sun enters the sign of Sagittarius around 22 November and exits around 21 December. This is the last month of autumn and the nature and qualities of Sagittarius are closely associated with this time of the year prior to the winter solstice, the time for thanksgiving and reflection of past blessings and misfortunes.

In physical terms, Sagittarius rules the thighs and legs, the very tools needed to venture out and travel, see the world, looking for life's adventures. Sagittarius is restless, a traveller keen on exploring and understanding life from a broader perspective, needing to know what is on the other side of the horizon. Like the symbol, the archer, Sagittarius sends out energy like arrows in all directions, following to see where they land.

Sagittarius represents a search for self through activity that reaffirms humanity's place in both the physical and spiritual worlds; it does not limit this search to gratify the individual ego but is inclusive of all people. The other aspect of Sagittarius's symbol is the centaur; through the upper human part there is a soaring intellect, seeking inspiration from the heavens, while the lower animal part keeps its legs firmly on the ground, connected to the needs of physical reality. Sagittarius is concerned with the philosophy, ideas and concepts upon which human society is built; religion, law and higher education come under the precepts of this sign. Sagittarius has a great need of freedom and independence, both physically and mentally, in order to undertake the journeys of body and mind.

As one concerned with higher religious and spiritual matters, and how they can be implemented in society, there

BELOW: *Sagittarius, the centaur archer*

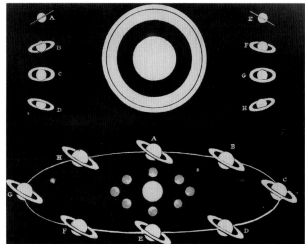

is something of the religious zealot in Sagittarius. Once an idea takes root in the mind, Sagittarius will be fanatical about the method by which it is communicated. This can sometimes be perceived as dogmatic and self-righteous.

The ruling planet, Jupiter, gives Sagittarius an optimistic and jovial character. There is a touch of good luck connected to this sign, as though the natural good spirits of Sagittarius attract abundance and good fortune. The Sagittarian approach to life is straightforward, rarely subtle, boldly going after many goals, hoping each will turn up a reward. If one does not, then Sagittarius will be momentarily disappointed, grateful for the experience and move on to the next with positive expectations.

Sagittarius always wants more of what is pleasurable, evident from the lower, animal nature of the sign: more food, more wine, more sex. It is very difficult for Sagittarius to put a limit on desire, which can often lead to their own undoing. In relationships with others, Sagittarius tries to avoid heavy emotional responsibility, and must have the freedom to come and go as the whim takes them.

Any planet in a horoscope found in this sign will operate through the energies connected with it. The Moon in Sagittarius, for example, might suggest an instinctive feeling for philosophical and religious ideology and a desire to be around many diverse people from all walks of life, but an aversion to deep emotional intimacy. Whatever part of the horoscope that Sagittarius is found is the arena of life in which there will be a concern for experience of an expansive nature. In its most positive expression, Sagittarius is straightforward, magnanimous and adventurous with an expansive and inspirational mind, an excellent teacher. In its negative expression Sagittarius is tactless and coarse, fanatical, dictatorial and never satisfied.

❖ see FIRE SIGNS p54

Capricorn

Capricorn is the tenth sign of the zodiac, a member of the cardinal triplicity, feminine, and of the earth element. A bestial sign, the symbol for Capricorn is the mountain goat, its ruling planet is Saturn. The Sun enters the sign of Capricorn at the time of the winter solstice on 22 December and exits around 19 January. This is the first month of winter and the nature and qualities of Capricorn are closely associated with this time of year when the attention of nature is turned inwards and energy goes into the plans that must be laid down for the coming spring. There is hope in this apparently barren season, as the hours of daylight are getting longer.

In physical terms, Capricorn rules the knees, that part of the body which must be strong so as not to buckle under the weight of a heavy load, and the bending of which allows the body to climb upwards towards the goals of the mind. As a cardinal sign Capricorn is goal-oriented and puts enormous energy into achieving personal objectives, but the earthy nature of the sign requires that each step along the way be perfectly planned and grounded in the reality of the physical world. Like its symbol, the mountain goat, Capricorn makes sure of each foothold before looking for the next, as it steadily advances higher up the mountain.

Capricorn represents a search for self through activity that puts in place the structures and supports necessary to manifest its aspirations and affirm its place in the hierarchy of society. Capricorn works within the structures it creates and is keen to utilize these as frameworks to achieve solid and measurable advancement upwards. Traditional values and inherited resources are the building blocks for growth in Capricorn's world.

Capricorn is pragmatic and patient in achieving ambitions, disciplined enough to wait and plan for the right opportunity before making a move and seizing advantage. Once set on a course of action Capricorn will not be deterred, being precise and methodical in the execution of a task, working hard to achieve recognition and status for a job well done. There is a persistent desire in Capricorn for the attainment of worldly power; if wealth and fame are important, respect and position are paramount. The link to time through the sign's ruling planet Saturn means that many Capricorns must wait until later life before acquiring the position and success to which they aspire.

There is an intense physical energy connected to Capricorn; calm and self-assured on the outside, it seems that just beneath the surface is a well-contained explosion just waiting to happen. But it never does – Capricorn conserves this energy until it can be channelled in the right direction for maximum impact and the achievement of ambitions, whatever form they take.

In personal relationships Capricorn appears cool and dispassionate. There is a touch of the social climber about them. Although there is an intense physical desire in the sign, Capricorn is not given to emotional display and has been known to choose a mate based as much on the prestige the match will bring as on love. Capricorn has a wonderful appreciation for the absurd and ironic, however, and makes an engaging companion and a steadfast and trustworthy friend.

Any planet in a horoscope found in this sign will operate through the energies connected with it. Mercury in

Capricorn, for example, suggests a logical, orderly mind, slow to take things in but with an excellent retentive memory and a reluctance to speak unless sure of a good impact. Jupiter in Capricorn might operate as a need to push the boundaries of career, obtaining enormous pleasure and great knowledge through pursuing ambitions.

Whatever part of the horoscope that Capricorn is found is the arena of life in which there will be a concern for patient discipline in the attainment of ambitions. Capricorn on the eleventh house cusp, for example, might suggest a need to join with others of like mind and create a framework for the advancement of the group as a whole.

In its most positive expression, Capricorn is industrious, trustworthy and loyal with good organizing skills and a deep

RIGHT: *People born between 20 January and 18 February are said to be Sun-sign Aquarius, the sign of the water bearer*

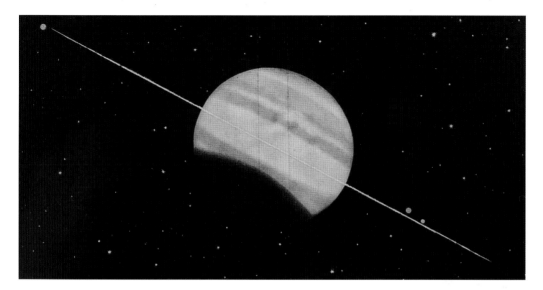

ABOVE: *The sign of Aquarius is ruled by Saturn*

spiritual understanding. In its negative expression, Capricorn is demanding, dictatorial, miserly and cold, opportunistic for position and prestige, pessimistic and brooding.

❖❖ see BESTIAL SIGNS p58

Aquarius

Aquarius is the eleventh sign of the zodiac, a member of the fixed triplicity, masculine and of the air element. A human sign, the symbol for Aquarius is the water bearer. Its traditional ruling planet is Saturn, particularly by day, and its modern ruler Uranus. Often both planets are used as co-rulers. The Sun enters Aquarius around 20 January and exits around 18 February. People whose birthdays fall between these dates are said to be Sun-sign Aquarius. This is the second month of winter and the nature and qualities of Aquarius are closely associated with this time, when rain and snowfall level all and wash clean the past, the days grow longer and there is a certainty that the future will bring warmer weather.

In physical terms, Aquarius rules the ankles and circulatory system. It is the ankles that lend grace and fluidity of movement to the way in which thoughts move around the Aquarian mind. The circulatory system distributes oxygen to the body, reflecting the manner in which Aquarius is impelled to distribute consciousness to the rest of humanity.

As an intellectual air sign, Aquarius is primarily concerned with thought. Enormous amounts of energy are channelled into performing complex mental gymnastics, which can lead to such a preoccupation with the world created inside the mind that Aquarius often loses perspective of earthly limitations. As a fixed air sign, Aquarius will pursue intuitive thoughts until a principle or theory is reached, then keep it as a building block for further ruminations; in this way Aquarius occasionally displays a stubbornness of mind. However, if conflicting information is brought to light which destroys this theory, Aquarius will happily adjust the concept to accommodate the new perspective. Intellectual ability combined with intuitive inspiration makes Aquarius an original thinker, a natural scientist, inventor and innovator.

Aquarius is co-ruled by the planets Saturn and Uranus. In the case of Saturn this operates as a connection to the past and tradition, cold reasoning and logic. In the case of Uranus, it operates as aspirations towards the future and a new order, flashes of inspiration and innovation. Rarely does the sign concern itself with the here and now.

Aquarius has a reputation for being the bohemian of the zodiac, searching for the unusual in people, ideas and experience. They demonstrate an impetus towards experimentation and an eagerness to gather food for thought. Aquarius will try anything once. Aquarius is friendly, kind and compassionate; however, they are also quite impersonal in their dealings with others, treating everyone fairly and rarely playing favourites.

The social visionary qualities of Aquarius are considerable, and the desire to communicate these visions and concepts to others is very strong. Occasionally, however, what starts out as a sharing of inspiring thought can sometimes turn into a verbal diatribe. The need Aquarius feels for equality amongst humanity operates as an imperative to rebel against authority, dragging down hierarchical structures and a championing of the underdog. Aquarius has a revolutionary spirit, with high ideals for a human utopia and a true democracy. Sometimes the eagerness to cause revolution has Aquarius concocting eccentric ideas which work well intellectually but are inappropriate to the conditions of society in the real world.

In close personal relationships Aquarius is first and foremost a friend – gregarious and social. They love being in the company of others, but due to the constant and exhaustive mental activity Aquarius also needs space to be alone and will at times appear aloof, cold and unfeeling. Despite a strong loyalty, partners will rarely be made to feel special, as Aquarius treats all equally.

Any planet in a horoscope found in this sign will operate through the energies connected with it. Venus in Aquarius, for example, may operate as an interest in modern and futuristic art forms, computer graphics, kinetic sculpture and electronic music, or as a romantic attraction to unusual, unconventional partners. Mars in Aquarius suggests a strongly opinionated person with an enthusiasm for intellectual debate or a desire to be a leader fighting for social reform. Whatever part of the horoscope Aquarius is found in will be the arena of life in which there will be a concern for innovation and humanitarian ideals.

In its most positive expression, Aquarius is friendly, gregarious and humanitarian, able to love all equally, an innovative and original thinker with an excellent ability to communicate ideas. In its negative expression, Aquarius can be cold, aloof, mentally chaotic and overly talkative, dictatorial in trying to impose their own ideas on others.
❖ see AIR SIGNS p55

Pisces

Pisces is the twelfth and last sign of the zodiac, a member of the mutable triplicity, feminine and of the water element. A fertile sign, the symbol for Pisces is the fish, its traditional ruling planet is Jupiter, particularly by night and its modern ruler Neptune; often both planets are used as co-rulers. The Sun enters Pisces around 19 February and exits around 20 March. This is the last month of winter and the nature and qualities of Pisces are closely associated with this receptive time of planting for the coming spring.

In physical terms, Pisces rules the feet, which sustain the whole and connect it to the world; the feet also leap and dance and are able to carry the body to other realms. Pisces is a collection of all the energies that have gone before; there is an innate empathy and understanding of all the thoughts, actions, feelings and physical needs that have been expressed in the previous 11 signs of the zodiac.

Pisces represents a search for self through internal emotional activity that assimilates and processes all experience of the intuitive consciousness, affirming connection to the source of all life. This ability to receive, absorb and empathize with all views makes it difficult for Pisces to choose a specific path for individual self-expression.

A bi-corporeal sign, the symbol for Pisces is two fish swimming in opposite directions joined by the thread of consciousness; this illustrates the dualistic nature of the sign, and the two ways the energy is expressed. One fish swims towards Aquarius, representing the impetus towards sacrifice of the self for the sake of others, while the other fish swims towards Aries and the need to use all the resources gathered by others in order to attain personal goals.

Pisces is often referred to as the mystic of the zodiac, with a keen ability to develop the higher spiritual mind. There is a sensitivity to emotional vibrations and thought waves in the environment, so Pisces often exhibits talents as a medium or clairvoyant. Pisces feels a strong imperative to connect with and become absorbed into something bigger than themselves, beyond accepted reality. If this desire is not channelled constructively, Pisces may be prone to taking drugs and alcohol to free themselves from the limitations of the material world.

Pisces frequently exhibits the other energies of the sign, and is able to take advantage of the reservoir of intuitive, perceptive knowledge they contain and do well in the material world as artist, musician and actor. Others are drawn to Pisces because of the sympathetic, altruistic and non-judgemental qualities they exhibit. On the surface there is a feeling of delicate vulnerability and sensitive self-sacrifice, yet Pisces also exudes a feeling of quiet inner strength. Pisces is incredibly romantic, and a little shy, with an otherworldly quality of magic and fantasy. When Pisces feels the threat of being pinned down or their freedom inhibited, they escape into the imaginative world and become elusive, offering up passive resistance by being impossible to reach.

Whatever part of the horoscope Pisces is found is the arena of life in which there will be a concern for spiritual involvement and intuitive emotional understanding. In its most positive expression, Pisces is spiritual, romantic, imaginative and creative, unselfish, trusting and not in the least judgemental. In its negative expression, Pisces is dependent, gullible, deceptive, with a difficulty in keeping a grip on reality, and prone to temperamental escapism.

❖❖ see FEMININE p56

RIGHT: *Pisces is the final sign of the zodiac*

DIVISIONS OF THE ZODIAC

The signs of the zodiac can be divided or categorized in a number of ways. These divisions reflect the properties of that sign according to certain concepts and astrological methods.

Element

Western and Vedic astrology divide the zodiac into four elements: fire, earth, air and water. Because each of the elements contains three signs, they are also referred to as 'triplicities'. Each element symbolizes a specific way of manifestation or a manner of perception. The active fire element, consisting of Aries, Leo and Sagittarius, is concerned with the initial spark of inspiration, creativity and future vision. The receptive earth element,

containing Taurus, Virgo and Capricorn, concerns itself with maintaining, organizing and regulating the material aspects of life. The active air element collects and logically analyses information and develops a theoretical understanding in Gemini, Libra and Aquarius; while the receptive water element experiences, maintains and expresses the emotional, nurturing and caring component of life.

❖ see EARTH p63

Fire Signs

The signs expressing the element fire are Aries, Leo and Sagittarius, ruled by Mars, the Sun and Jupiter respectively. The active fire element lends these signs the primal force of creative expression and the force of spirit. In the case of Aries, the cardinal fire sign, the energy that this element brings is channelled into the act of initiating activity. Leo is the fixed fire sign and channels the fiery nature into acts of creation; there is a desire to remain in a central position. Sagittarius, the mutable fire sign, is a double-bodied sign, and, as such, has two expressions of fire – the higher ideals of spirit and civilization and the lower, primal nature – endeavouring to meld the two into a united whole. Modern astrology associates the fire signs with the animating force of the spirit, which is focused on self-assertion and creativity.

❖ see AIR SIGNS p55

LEFT: *The four elements – fire, air, earth and water – with zodiac signs and alchemical symbols*

Earth Signs

The signs expressing the earth element are Taurus, Virgo and Capricorn, ruled by Venus, Mercury and Saturn respectively. They represent the realm of matter, which has given them the reputation of being purely materialistic. Taurus represents fertile plains, Virgo symbolizes valleys, which can hold shadows of sadness, while Capricorn is associated with majestic mountain peaks. Taurus, the fixed earth sign, is said to stay in one place and to secure the rhythmic repetition of daily life. Virgo, the mutable earth sign, deals with the organization of everyday occurrences. Capricorn is associated with a slow but steady climb on the social ladder. Psychological astrology regards the earth signs as representing the different facets of the perceptive type, who focuses on the perceptions of the five physical senses.

❖ see AIR SIGNS p55

Air Signs

The signs expressing the element air are Gemini, Libra and Aquarius, ruled by Mercury, Venus and Saturn/Uranus respectively. Traditionally, the active air element is connected with the thought process. Just as the air we breathe connects us all, the air signs are regarded as actively promoting connections between people in different ways. Mutable Gemini is constantly on the move in order to gather and distribute information and to organize useful practical relationships. Cardinal Libra directs its energies towards unification by smoothing out conflicts, intervening diplomatically and creating harmony using logical arguments. Fixed Aquarius creates the theoretical background for social ideals and tries to realize them by connecting groups of people.

❖ see EARTH SIGNS p55

RIGHT: Capricorn is associated with majestic mountain peaks

Water Signs

The signs expressing the element water are Cancer, Scorpio and Pisces. Traditionally, the water element refers to the spiritual aspect of life, while modern astrology links it to the emotional realm, though both systems find their analogies in actual water. Cancer, the cardinal water sign ruled by the Moon, reflects its environment, keeps the memories of childhood and seeks containment within the home and the family. Scorpio, the fixed water sign ruled by Mars (traditional) and Pluto (modern) probes into every available emotional space and resembles deep water, where death and resurrection are waiting beneath the dark surface. Pisces, the mutable water sign ruled by Jupiter (traditional) and Neptune (modern), dissolves and crosses the boundaries between the physical and the spiritual realm, often through poetry or music. Modern astrology associates

the water signs with the feeling type of Jungian psychology, focusing on emotional experience which sometimes stands in the way of logic and depends on outside impulses, which may cause neediness in relationships.

❖ see AIR SIGNS p55

Feminine

The feminine signs of the zodiac are Taurus, Cancer, Virgo, Scorpio, Capricorn and Pisces – all of the earth or water element. They are sometimes labelled as 'negative' signs. The terms 'feminine' and 'negative' refer to the basic receptive mode of these signs, comparable to the 'Yin' of the Eastern tradition. The feminine earth signs first need to be presented with factual circumstances in order to function and develop their practical talents. The feminine signs of the water triplicity need an initial impulse from outside before they can react with a feeling that will lead them to a judgement of their experience. The feminine planets are the Moon and Venus. Here, the term does not only refer to the receptive and reflective basic attitude; modern and traditional astrology alike associate these planets with feminine qualities.

❖ see MASCULINE p56

Masculine

The masculine signs of the zodiac are Aries, Gemini, Leo, Libra, Sagittarius and Aquarius – all of the fire or air element. They are also called 'positive' signs, but both terms rather refer to the basic active, enterprising mode in which these signs tend to approach the world, comparable to the 'Yang' of Eastern philosophy. The masculine fire signs, Aries, Leo and Sagittarius, actively strive for future visions, creative endeavours and a synthesized philosophical view. The masculine air signs, Gemini, Libra and Aquarius, actively

LEFT: *Scorpio, one of the three water signs*

collect, analyze and distribute information and pursue the construction of a theoretical framework for the understanding of life's processes. The planets regarded as masculine by ancient astrology are Mars, Jupiter and Saturn, to which traditional astrology added the Sun. This strict division still plays an important part in horary astrology. Less well known ancient rules state that planets of either the eastern or upper hemisphere are masculine, while certain ascendant degrees are said to bestow a 'masculine appearance' on feminine individuals.

❖ see FEMININE p56

Cardinal

The signs of the zodiac and the houses of the horoscope are not only divided by elements and modes, but also by qualities, which describe the direction and distribution of energies within the signs. The cardinal signs, also known as 'initiating' or 'leading' signs, are Aries, Cancer, Libra and Capricorn. Traditional astrology also calls them 'moveable signs', because they mark the change of the seasons. The term 'cardinal' is derived from the zodiacal position of these signs on the cardinal angles (Aries – east, Cancer – south, Libra – west, Capricorn – north) and is also applied to the corresponding houses. The nature of the cardinals is activating, initiating and creating primary experience. Planets in these signs and houses are generating motivational forces. Individuals with a strong cardinal emphasis in their horoscope are often initiators of ideas and actions who seek to actively influence or direct their environment. Since their energies are so much focused on contact and exchange with the outside world, the cardinal signs are sometimes in danger of losing contact with the inner self.

❖ see FIXED p57

Fixed

The fixed signs are Taurus, Leo, Scorpio and Aquarius; the fixed or succedent houses are the second, fifth, eighth and eleventh. The term originates in the fact that the season to which each of the fixed signs belongs is firmly established by the time the Sun enters into them. Accordingly, matters signified by these signs and houses in horary charts tend to be of a lasting nature, and new undertakings will be a long time developing. Fixed types are said to be slow but determined, stubborn but dependable and persevering. Negatively, inflexibility may lead to isolation.

❖ see TAURUS p38

Mutable

The mutable signs are Gemini, Virgo, Sagittarius and Pisces; the corresponding mutable or 'cadent' houses are the third, sixth, ninth and twelfth. In horary astrology, the common signs denote connection, mediation and diversity, but also change and instability. Modern astrology regards the 'mutable type' as a 'mixed type'. Such a person is described as mobile and versatile, an open-minded mediator between impatient initiators and rigid maintainers.

❖ see FIXED p57

Commanding Signs

One of the divisions of the zodiac used in traditional and ancient astrology. It refers to the first six signs of the zodiac – Aries, Taurus, Gemini, Cancer, Leo and Virgo – and describes the nature as commanding, due to the placement of these signs on the horoscope and their connection to the developmental stages of growth centred around the projection of the self in the world and the fulfilment of the self's needs.

❖ see CANCER p41

Obeying Signs

Obeying Signs is one of the divisions of the zodiac used in traditional and ancient astrology. It refers to the final six signs of the zodiac – Libra, Scorpio, Sagittarius, Capricorn, Aquarius and Pisces – and describes the nature as being obeying due to the placement of these signs on the horoscope and their connection to the culminating stages of growth centred around the relationship of the self with others in the world and the fulfilment of joint needs.

❖ see SCORPIO p47

Northern Signs

The northern signs are also referred to as boreal or septentrional signs, and are so called because they decline from the equinoctial or celestial equator (the Earth's equator projected into space) in a northward direction. The northern signs are measured from zero degrees of Aries, the point where the Sun's path intersects the celestial equator at the spring equinox, and contain the first half of the zodiac; they are Aries, Taurus, Gemini, Cancer, Leo and Virgo.

❖ see ARIES p36

Southern Signs

Southern signs, also referred to as austral or meridional signs, are so called because they decline from the equinoctial or celestial equator (the Earth's equator projected into space) in a southward direction. They are Libra, Scorpio, Sagittarius, Capricorn, Aquarius and Pisces. The southern signs are measured from zero degrees of Libra, the point where the Sun's path intersects the celestial equator at the autumn equinox, and contain the final half of the zodiac.

❖ see LIBRA p45

LEFT: *Feminine and masculine – Yin and Yang*

Bestial Signs

Also known as quadrupedian signs; one of the divisions of the zodiac. It refers to those signs in the zodiac represented in their symbol by four-footed creatures. The bestial signs are Aries the Ram, Taurus the Bull, Leo the Lion, Sagittarius the Centaur and Capricorn the Goat. Each represents characteristics and behavioural tendencies associated with its respective creature.

❖ see ARIES p36

ABOVE: Bestial sign, Leo

Feral Signs

This refers to the signs Leo and Sagittarius. Both signs are bestial signs, represented by four-footed creatures, but they have the added description of being feral or wild beasts. This pertains to the nature or characteristics of Leo and Sagittarius as partaking of unpredictable and uncontrollable qualities as opposed to those creatures of a domesticated nature.

❖ see LEO p42

Bi-corporeal Signs

Also known as double-bodied signs; one of the divisions of the zodiac used in traditional and ancient astrology. It has also found a use in modern psychological astrology. The term refers to those signs of the zodiac represented by symbols of two bodies. These are Gemini the Twins and Pisces the Fish. The name describes the nature of bi-corporeal signs as having two modes of behaviour, or being able to express two different perspectives on one matter.

❖ see PISCES p52

Common Signs

One of the divisions used in traditional astrology, 'common' refers to the signs Gemini, Leo, Sagittarius and Pisces. It describes them as retaining a property or nature that

partakes of the signs preceding and following its position in the zodiac. Gemini therefore retains properties of Taurus and Cancer, Leo includes properties of Cancer and Virgo, Sagittarius has properties of Scorpio and Capricorn and Pisces contains properties of Aquarius and Aries.

❖ see ARIES p36

Barren Signs

One of the manifold divisions of the zodiac, used in traditional and ancient astrology. In the judging of a horary chart, when a barren sign appears of the ascendant or fifth house cusp, it suggests that any further action invested in the matter questioned will not produce any worthwhile results. There are three barren signs: Gemini, Leo and Virgo.

❖ see VIRGO p44

Mute Signs

One of the divisions of the zodiac used in traditional and ancient astrology; also known as signs of slow voice. In the judging of a horary chart, when a mute sign appears on the ascendant, it suggests that there will be little or no further news pertaining to the matter questioned, or that any news will be slow in arriving. The Mute signs are the three water signs, Cancer, Scorpio and Pisces.

❖ see MERCURY p62

Voice Signs

This refers to all the signs not considered mute or of slow voice. The voice signs are Aries, Taurus, Gemini, Leo, Virgo, Libra, Sagittarius, Capricorn and Aquarius. In the judging of a horary chart, when a voice sign appears on the ascendant or the more so if the planet Mercury should be in a voice sign, it suggests that there will be further news pertaining to the matter questioned.

❖ see MUTE SIGNS p58

Human Signs

One of the manifold divisions of the zodiac used in both traditional and ancient astrology. The term refers to the zodiac signs Gemini, Leo, Libra and Aquarius and pertains to the qualities of these signs as partaking of a manly, humane or courteous nature. Each sign represents aspects of human behaviour and a concern with energy that promotes the furthering of human ideals through the use of intellectual abilities and creativity of a progressive nature.

❖ see AQUARIUS p51

Solstice Signs

Solstice signs refer to Cancer and Capricorn. When the Sun is at zero degrees of Cancer, it is the time of the summer solstice, i.e. it appears to reach its furthest point north of the ecliptic and marks the longest day of the year in the northern hemisphere. Consequently when the Sun is at zero degrees of Capricorn, it is the winter solstice, reaching its furthest point south of the ecliptic.

❖ see CAPRICORN p49

Equinoctial Signs

Equinoctial or solstice signs refer to Aries and Libra. When the Sun is at zero degrees of Aries, it is the time of the spring or vernal equinox, and day and night are of equal length all around the Earth. From this date the hours of daylight are longer than the hours of night. When the Sun is at zero degrees of Libra it is the autumn equinox. Day and night are of equal length again, but from this date the hours of daylight gradually become less than the hours of night.

❖ see ARIES p36

Sun-Sign

Sun-sign refers to the zodiac sign that the Sun was passing through on the date of birth. The Sun passes with regularity through each of the 12 signs in the period of one year. The Sun, at the centre of the Solar System and around which all other celestial bodies rotate, is the source of life and growth; therefore the Sun-sign represents the qualities and behavioural nature that an individual feels happiest and most comfortable projecting.

❖ see SUN p62

ABOVE: *The Sun rises above the stones of Stonehenge, Wiltshire, at dawn on the summer solstice*

PLANETARY CHARACTERISTICS

The word 'planet' is an astronomical and astrological term, derived from the Greek word for 'wanderer'. Astronomy applies the term to a celestial body of a certain size, circling a star and with no light of its own. Astrology applies the same term to the wandering stars of our Solar System, whose positions and interactions are believed to reflect life on Earth. Although not planets in the astronomical sense, the Sun and the Moon are included in this group and even given special importance as 'lights' or 'luminaries'. Each astrological planet has its own characteristics. They were believed to radiate their own light and to be floating in a multi-layered celestial sphere, which marked the gradual descent from spirit to matter. Some modern astrologers also work with hypothetical planets and asteroids.

PLANETS AND ASPECTS

THE PLANETS

Each of the planets in the Solar System is a focus for astrology – particularly our own planet, Earth. Although not real planets in an astronomical sense, the Sun and the Moon are also categorized as such in astrology. Taken on their own, or in groups or pairs with related characteristics, these are some of the most important elements in casting, reading and interpreting the chart.

Sun

Although the Sun is not a planet in the astronomical sense, astrology refers to it as such because astrological nomenclature was established when our Solar System was still seen as geocentric. Western solar astrology is based on the apparent annual path of the Sun around the Earth, which is divided into 12 equal parts. The Sun is the traditional and modern ruler of Leo, is exalted in Aries and in its fall in Libra. Its nature is described as masculine, hot and dry. The Sun's glyph, a circle with a point in the middle, illustrates its astrological meaning: the central, all-encompassing life force and the individual as the centre of its own universe. In the chart, a favourably placed and well-aspected Sun indicates creativity, self-reliance, courage, strength, success, a healthy physical disposition, generosity, a warmly affectionate nature, authority, grand-scale undertakings and leadership qualities. An afflicted Sun suggests a lack of self-esteem or, at the other end of the scale, over-confidence, as well as egotism, selfishness and bad fortune. In the physical body, the Sun rules the heart and the blood as carrier of life-sustaining substances.

❖❖ see LUMINARY p145

Mercury

Nearest planet to the Sun, ruler of Gemini and Virgo. Mercury, named after the Roman messenger of the gods, has a rotational cycle of around 88 days. Apart from Venus,

ABOVE: *The messenger god Mercury*

it is the only planet which rules two zodiac signs. Its nature is traditionally described as cold and dry. Mercury is neither feminine nor masculine, but takes on the nature of the planet(s) with which it is connected. Its exaltation in Aquarius and fall in Leo are not accepted by all astrologers. The key words for Mercury are movement and communication. Astrology generally equates Mercury with the ability to analyze and communicate, also with the ability to make connections between people, objects, facts and events. Therefore, Mercury rules thought, written and spoken language, telephones, newspapers, traffic, logistics, transport, shops, offices and commerce; it describes teachers, messengers, salesmen, secretaries, journalists, travel agents, etc. A dignified Mercury indicates a quick logical mind, wit, humour, eloquence, good memory, organizational talent, craftsmanship and adaptability. An afflicted Mercury may indicate learning difficulties, nervousness, fickleness, and/or speech impediments. Traditionally, Mercury rules the hands, shoulders and lungs; some modern medical astrologers also connect it with the nervous system and blood circulation.

❖ see VIRGO p44

Venus

Personal planet, night ruler of Taurus and day ruler of Libra. Venus orbits the Sun between Mercury and Earth, with a rotational cycle of 224.7 days. Venus's nature is traditionally described as feminine, moderately cold and moist. Also known as 'the lesser fortune', its influence is generally benefic. As a personal planet, Venus describes the manifestation of spiritual values in daily life. Named after the Roman goddess of love, the planet rules affections, diplomacy, harmony and beauty. In the male horoscope it describes the type of woman the native feels attracted to. Psychologically, Venus represents the need for emotional or material security and therefore indicates how the individual tends to relate to others and handles financial affairs. A dignified Venus suggests physical beauty, pleasant manners, a good sense for colours, shapes and proportions, diplomatic skills, artistic talents, warm affections, popularity and financial success. An afflicted Venus may indicate

laziness, debauchery, unfaithfulness, jealousy, selfishness, emotional coldness and an excessive need for entertainment and the 'good life'. Physically, Venus rules the kidneys, bladder and sexual organs.

❖ see RETROGRADE p150

Earth

Astrology is still based on an Earth-centred (geocentric) model of the Universe because psychologically and practically speaking the geocentric model still works for the purposes of astrology. In the past the Earth was believed to lie at the centre of the Universe with the planets and stars rotating around it. The entire system was set up and put in motion by God, and it was by His will that the planets influenced life on Earth in a regular way. The planets (the Moon, Mercury, Venus, the Sun, Mars, Jupiter and Saturn), the stars and the heavenly regions rotated around Earth (and man). The Earth in the birth chart is always 180 degrees from the natal position of the Sun. Thus, if the Sun is at one degree of Scorpio, the Earth will be found at one degree of Taurus. The Earth is the esoteric ruler of Sagittarius and represents the physical location of a person's spiritual path.

❖ see NICOLAS COPERNICUS p13

Moon

Luminary, ruler of Cancer. Although the Moon is not a planet, but the Earth's satellite, it is the second most important celestial body in astrology. It rules zodiacal Cancer, is exalted in Taurus, in its fall in Scorpio and has a rotational cycle of 27 days 7 hours 43 minutes. Its nature is feminine, cold and moist. The Moon rules women, fertility, marriage, motherhood, emotions, the family, the home and cyclic or routine activities. It also rules the growth cycles of plants, food, all natural bodies of water and matters pertaining to them, history, the past and the general public. In the natal chart, the Moon describes the imaginative, reflective side of the individual, unconscious impulses, emotional reactions, childhood experiences, the mother–child relationship and the native's need for emotional comfort. A dignified Moon indicates a highly sensitive, caring and compassionate nature, the ability to give shape to one's ideas and plans, public success, artistic talents or paranormal abilities. An afflicted Moon often indicates emotional or material instability, self-absorbance, over-sensitivity, weakness, confusion, fear or the failure of one's plans. In the body, the Moon traditionally rules the breast, but is also connected to the womb, the digestive system and glandular secretions by some.

❖ see RULER p145

Mars

Fourth planet from the Sun; ruler of Aries. The red planet Mars, named after the Roman god of war, circles the Sun between Earth and Jupiter with a rotational cycle of roughly two years. Before the discovery of Pluto, the modern ruler of Scorpio, it was the traditional ruler of that sign. Mars is exalted in Capricorn, in its fall in Cancer, and its nature is masculine, hot and dry. Modern astrology interprets Mars as the inner drive for action, self-manifestation and both positive and negative aggression, as well as the male sex drive. A dignified Mars indicates courage, pride, physical strength, decisiveness, healthy sexual appetites and a sense of fair competition. An afflicted Mars may signify rashness, uncontrolled anger, violence, egocentricity, tyranny, ruthlessness, obscenity, dishonesty or rebelliousness. Mars rules all matters, objects and people connected with warfare, bloodshed, conquest and destruction. Sports people, chemists, pharmacists and physicians are Mars-ruled as well. Physically, Mars rules the primary sexual organs. The Martian person is said to be of medium stature, fair to red-haired and of a ruddy complexion.

❖ see ARIES p36

Jupiter

Fifth planet from the Sun, ruler of Sagittarius. Jupiter orbits the Sun between Mars and Saturn, in a rotational cycle of approximately 12 years. It is the biggest planet in our Solar System. Jupiter was the traditional ruler of Sagittarius by day and Pisces by night before the

18 LA LVNE

LEFT: *A 1920s Tarot card showing the Moon*
RIGHT: *The planet Mars overlooks a battle scene*

discovery of Neptune, which has been assigned to Pisces by modern astrology. Jupiter is exalted in Cancer and in its fall in Capricorn; its nature is masculine, hot and moist. Jupiter is seen as a benefic and has key words like generosity, popularity, expansion, success, optimism, happiness, honesty and justice attached to it. Jupiter describes judges, lawyers, teachers, healers, philosophers, religious leaders, industrialists and members of government. An afflicted Jupiter can signify an inability to accept limitations and may thus indicate recklessness, over-optimism, vanity or self-indulgence. The body parts ruled by Jupiter are the thighs and the liver.

❖ see PISCES p52

Saturn

The outermost of the traditional planets. Saturn orbits the Sun between Jupiter and Uranus with a rotational cycle of 29.458 years. While Saturn is the traditional ruler of zodiacal Capricorn by night and Aquarius by day, modern astrology assigns the latter sign to Uranus. Saturn's nature is traditionally masculine, cold and dry, melancholic and malefic. Astrological Saturn often represents the father, conventional views, generational conflicts and issues of fear, repression and control. Saturn rules all natural and man-made structures, be it the skeleton, any hierarchy, organization, authority, the karmic law of cause and effect, a life plan or time itself. A well-placed Saturn may denote discipline, practical and organizational talents, patience, successful ambition, reliability, responsibility, honesty, frugality and often a very dry sense of humour. Saturn's negative manifestations include rigidity, restriction, narrow-mindedness, depression, excessive limitations and fear of life. Saturn's cycle symbolizes learning through pain, with an inbuilt challenging 'examination' every seven years. Many astrologers regard a person as adult only after the first Saturn return at the age of roughly 29 years.

❖ see SATURN RETURN p140

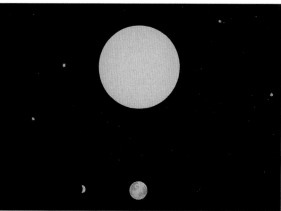

ABOVE: *A view of Uranus*

Uranus

First Trans-Saturnian planet; modern ruler of Aquarius. Originally named after the astronomer William Herschel, who discovered it in 1781, Uranus orbits the Sun between Saturn and Neptune with a rotational cycle of 84.015 years. In modern astrology, it became the ruler of zodiacal Aquarius, a sign associated with non-conformity and revolutionary tendencies, which upholds the creed of 'freedom, equality and brotherhood' of the French Revolution, which took place shortly after Uranus's discovery. Accordingly, modern mundane astrology views Uranus as an indicator of new discoveries, uprisings and revolutions and of unpredictable occurrences. It is linked with electricity and modern technology like computers, aviation or space travel. Natally, Uranus represents the individual's need for self-realization and freedom from traditional restrictions. A prominent, well-aspected Uranus suggests originality and inventiveness to the point of genius, independence, unconventionality and an interest in the latest global fashions and developments. An afflicted Uranus may indicate disruptive or anti-social behaviour, stubbornness and delusions bordering on madness. Transiting Uranus's opposition to its natal position, at about 42 years of age, often marks the beginning of the mid-life crisis.

❖ see TRANS-SATURNIAN PLANETS p69

Neptune

Second Trans-Saturnian planet, modern ruler of Pisces. Neptune was officially discovered in 1846. This planet orbits the Sun between Uranus and Pluto with a rotational cycle of 164.75 years. Mythological Neptune is the Roman ruler of the sea and brother of Zeus (Roman: Jupiter). In modern astrology, the planet Neptune rules Pisces, the traditional domain of Jupiter. Astrologically, Neptune's main characteristics are unlimitedness and the dissolution of clearly defined outlines. Positively, Neptune may indicate great sensitivity, empathy, compassion, altruism, high ideals, self-sacrifice, spirituality, psychism, clairvoyance, telepathy, a rich dream life, altered states of consciousness, artistic inspiration or musical talent. Its negative manifestations include over-idealization, delusion, deception, alcoholism, drug abuse, apathy, neediness, disappointment, irrational fear and identification with the role of the victim. On a mundane level, Neptune rules anything to do with the sea, floods, actors, movies, fashion, chemicals, gases, mass movements, chaos and hidden or secretly undermining activities or influences.

❖ see TRANS-SATURNIAN PLANETS p69

Pluto

Third Trans-Saturnian planet. Pluto was discovered in 1930. The aphelion of Pluto's orbit lies outside and the perihelion inside Neptune's path. Pluto's maximum distance from the ecliptic is 17 degrees 8 minutes 34 seconds; it has a rotational cycle of 248.4 years. The long duration of its transit through one sign has made Pluto an indicator of the evolutionary development of man, for better or for worse. It is linked to esoteric movements seeking redemption, the relentless elimination of outlived traditions and the positive transformation of lifestyles. Its undermining and disturbing side is linked to plutonium, nuclear power, political or religious fanaticism, deadly viruses and any means of mass destruction. Pluto is connected to death, hidden fears or talents, power, psychological insight, secrecy, sexuality and the unconscious. In its positive manifestation, Pluto's tremendous powers are used to heal and to regenerate; negatively expressed it may result in obsessive compulsive tendencies. Any planet in aspect with Pluto tends to manifest in extremes.

❖ see EIGHTH HOUSE p87

BELOW: *Mythological Neptune*

Chiron

Chiron, discovered in 1977, was named after the centaur in Greek mythology. Too large to be classed as an asteroid and too small for a planet, the new body inspired the term 'planetoid' ('planet-like'). Chiron's rotational cycle varies from 49 to 51 years; its orbit is highly elliptic and connects the orbits of Uranus and Saturn. This astronomical profile has given Chiron the nickname 'maverick', meaning 'outsider' or 'drop-out'. Many astrologers still dismiss Chiron as irrelevant. Mythological Chiron, an immortal healer, suffered from a fatal wound and could neither live nor die. Astrological Chiron is said to describe a physical or psychological 'wound' which may be incurable, but can lead to an understanding of similar suffering in others. In analogy with its orbit, Chiron is also said to describe the native's ability to combine traditional Saturnian limitations with the pioneering and rebellious spirit of Uranus.

❖ see ASTEROID p125

ABOVE: *Chiron takes its name from the Greek centaur*

Inferior Planet

A planet that has an orbit between the Earth and the Sun: Mercury and Venus. A superior planet has its orbit around the Sun, outside the Earth's orbit.

❖ see SUPERIOR PLANET p68

Superior Planet

A superior planet is one that has its orbit around the Sun, outside the Earth's. The superior planets are Mars, Jupiter, Saturn, Uranus, Neptune and Pluto. The planets that have orbits between the Earth and Sun – Mercury and Venus – are termed inferior planets.

❖ see INFERIOR PLANET p68

Personal Planet

Planets from the Sun to Mars. Due to their fast motion through the zodiac, the Sun, the Moon, Mercury, Venus and Mars are also known as the personal planets. They are regarded as mainly describing personal characteristics and everyday activities as, for example, likes and dislikes or the subject's ways of thinking.

❖ see TRANSPERSONAL PLANETS p69

Barren Planets

Traditionally, the planets Mars and Saturn are regarded as 'barren', that is they prevent the conception, birth or survival of children, especially when placed on the ascendant, in the fifth or eleventh houses, where they retrograde or negatively aspect the rulers of the same. In modern astrology, the Trans-Saturnians, especially Uranus, sometimes signify barrenness or artificially induced conception.

❖ see BARREN SIGNS p58

Hypothetical Planets

As the term suggests, 'hypothetical planets' are undiscovered bodies that are believed to be a part of the Solar System. Some astrologers claim the existence of more than 1,000 'Aromal planets'. There are about 35 hypothetical planets being used by some astrologers.

Attempts to ascertain the effectiveness of hypothetical planets statistically have hitherto only had negative results. One exception is the planet Pluto: intuited, named and assigned to Scorpio by the theosophist Isabelle Pagan in 1911, it was discovered in 1930 and is by now fully integrated in modern astrology.

❖❖ see ESOTERIC ASTROLOGY p30

Dark Moon

Hypothetical planet or focal point of the lunar orbit; also called Lilith. The dark moon constitutes a rather confusing issue: the name was given to a hypothetical second moon orbiting the Earth, which is said to be visible only when passing between the Earth and the Sun. The term dark moon can also refer to the focal point farthest from Earth of the Moon's elliptic path. This point has a rotational cycle of 3,232 days. French astrologer Joëlle de Gravelaine describes it as the dark, destructive side of the feminine principle, analogous to Adam's first wife Lilith in Rabbinic mythology. Both dark moons are interpreted as malevolent and relating to betrayal, obsession, stillbirth and abortion.

❖❖ see HYPOTHETICAL PLANETS p68

Trans-Neptunian Planets

Hypothetical Planets. The trans-Neptunians are the planets of the 'Neptunian Chain' in esoteric astrology. This scheme assumed that Neptune did not belong to our Solar System and that there were two other relevant planets outside its orbit. One of them may have been Pluto.

❖❖ see HYPOTHETICAL PLANETS p68

Trans-Saturnian Planets

Planets outside Saturn's orbit. The trans-Saturnian planets used by modern astrology are Uranus, Neptune and Pluto, discovered in 1781, 1846 and 1930 respectively. Also known as the 'new' or 'outer' planets, they are believed to be indicators of human evolution and of the individual's connection with the collective mind.

❖❖ see TRANSPERSONAL PLANETS p69

Transpersonal Planets

Planets outside Mars's orbit. In natal astrology, Saturn and Jupiter are seen as mediators between the individual and society, while Uranus, Neptune and Pluto are interpreted as being linked with collective tendencies, i.e. human evolution.

❖❖ see TRANS-SATURNIAN PLANETS p69

ABOVE: *The Dark Moon is also called Lilith*

Peregrine

A planet is called peregrine ('wandering') if it has no essential dignity in the horoscope. Essential dignity is given to a planet for being the ruler of the sign in question, day ruler of the triplicity in a daytime horoscope, or night ruler of the triplicity in a night-time horoscope. If none of these conditions apply, the planet is said to be weak and inclined to manifest its negative characteristics, even if it gains accidental dignity through angularity or reception.

❖❖ see HOROSCOPE p138

ASPECT PATTERNS

The term 'aspect' (from Latin for 'looking at') relates to planets facing each other at a specific angle within the horoscope. This angle is referred to as 'aspect'; the relevant planets are 'in aspect' with each other, meaning that they combine their forces and form a harmonious or conflicting relationship, depending on the angle in question.

Grand Trine

Triangular aspect pattern involving three or more planets separated by an angle of 120 degrees ('trine') each. The relevant planets are situated in signs of the same triplicity and, due to the harmonious nature of the trine aspect, cooperate in an easy flowing manner. The grand trine is regarded as an extremely fortunate asset. Because of the lack of tension the pattern may also denote laziness or inertia. Since everything goes well, there is no reason for action and hence no opportunity to stimulate growth.

❖ see TRINE p73

Yod

Triangular aspect pattern consisting of two planets in a sextile aspect (60 degrees), while both of them connect to a third planet in a quincunx (150 degrees). The resulting shape resembles a finger, which is why the Yod is also known as 'Finger of God' or 'Finger of Fate'. The apex planet at the tip of this finger is often referred to as the action point that provides clues as to the probable solution of problems or conflicts arising from this aspect combination. The quincunxes of the Yod disharmoniously connect planets in signs of opposite polarity, while the sextile combines planets in signs of the same polarity harmoniously. This contradiction characterizes the workings of the whole pattern and signifies a mixture of inner tension combined with constructive insight and the ability to act.

❖ see FEMININE p56

T-Square

The T-square is an aspect figure involving two planets in opposition, which are both squared by a third planet. The relevant planets usually occupy signs of the same quadruplicity, automatically emphasizing the cardinal, fixed or mutable quality in the chart. The T-square indicates vast energies at work within the individual, constantly searching for outlets through action.

❖ see APEX PLANET p70

Apex Planet

In some triangular aspect patterns the apex planet is the one occupying that point. Two or more planets closely grouped together in this position will combine their forces and act as the apex planet. It is the most significant of all planets involved in the pattern and represents an outlet for the configuration, a focal point towards which its energies are directed.

❖ see YOD p70

Grand Cross

The 'grand cross' is a combination of four or more planets involved in two oppositions which are separated by square aspects. They are thus forming a cross of planets in each sign of the relevant quadruplicity. Due to the tense nature of both, the opposition and the square, the grand cross implicates a lot of tension and conflict.

❖ see SQUARE p72

ABOVE: *Sepharial's geodetic prediction method found that eclipses had a particular significance on earthly events*

Kite

The 'kite' is an aspect pattern used in natal astrology. It is based on three planets forming a grand trine, one of which is opposed by a fourth planet, which is in sextile with the two remaining points of the grand trine. The pattern implies the sensitivity and creativity of the grand trine, but also contains the inner tension of the opposition and the restlessness frequently accompanying the sextile.

❖ see MYSTIC RECTANGLE p71

Mystic Rectangle

Aspect pattern containing four or more planets connected by two trines and two sextiles, with oppositions running between all four corners of the figure. The mystic rectangle does not necessarily imply mystical abilities in the individual, but the characteristics associated with it could make such tendencies possible. The trines facilitate creativity with their inherent ability to understand, while the sextiles add some restlessness and the opportunity to be productive. The oppositions promote awareness through conflicting impulses which demand integration. Thus the mystic rectangle denotes an individual with an extraordinary ability to make use of his abilities.

❖ see YOD p70

MAJOR ASPECTS

The major aspects form a group of specific angular planetary relationships, defined by Ptolemy and also known as 'Ptolemaic aspects'. Their interpretation is based on the relationship between the elements or qualities of the occupied signs. Planets in signs of the same element are in trine, i.e. considered to be in a harmonious relationship, whereas planets in signs of the same quality are squaring each other, i.e. functioning at cross-purposes.

Conjunction

The conjunction is in fact rather a position than an aspect. It entails a close gathering of two or more planets, ideally with the same zodiac degree and symbolizes close cooperation of the planets, which combine their potential and reinforce each other. Whether this has positive or stressful results largely depends on the nature of the relevant planets. The admissible orb for the conjunction is still a subject of discussion and ranges from three to as much as 10 degrees. Ancient astrology even worked with a 'conjunction by sign', which regarded planets in the same sign as conjunct, even if they were 29 degrees apart. This practice is still used in Vedic astrology. Conjunctions with the Sun have a special set of traditional rules. A planet within five degrees of the Sun is called 'combust' and is regarded as weak or even ineffective by most astrologers, while a planet within 17 minutes of arc from the Sun is called 'cazimi' and is supposedly much strengthened.

❖ see CAZIMI p147

Sextile

The sextile involves two or more planets at an angle of 60 degrees from one another. The permissible orb for this aspect is far from agreed among modern astrologers, but is mostly given as four degrees, or six degrees when the lights are involved. Although it equals half a trine and is therefore often belittled as a 'minor' or 'weaker' trine, the sextile is one of the major aspects. The aspect usually combines signs of the same polarity, though not of the same element and is symbolically related to the third and the eleventh house. It denotes the ability to turn intellectual understanding into productivity, to develop one's talents and to make use of fortunate opportunities for growth and for the fulfilment of one's hopes.

❖ see TRINE p73

Square

An aspect between two or more planets positioned at an angle of 90 degrees is called a square. The allotted orb for this aspect is usually six to eight degrees. The square

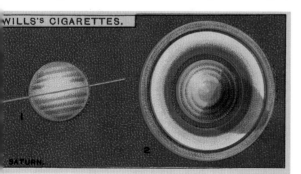

WILL'S'S CIGARETTES.

SATURN.

LEFT: *In conjunction, two planets may combine their potential*

combines planetary energies operating from different elements and from signs of opposite polarity; hence it is a tense and disharmonious aspect. Traditional astrology regards it as malefic and modern astrology regards it as an aspect of constant inner tension, urging the individual towards action in order to relieve it. Success is frequently delayed or thwarted, either by circumstances or by inconsistent behaviour on the part of the individual himself, and often demands great effort sustained over long periods. The element background of the relevant signs may give an indication as to the severity of the square in question. On the positive side, the square offers numerous opportunities for learning and personal development.

❖ see MALEFIC p143

Trine

The trine is one of the classic Ptolemaic aspects, consisting of two or more planets positioned at an angle of 120 degrees from each other. The orb given to this aspect is usually eight degrees, or 10 degrees in cases where lights are involved. The trine combines planetary energies working from the same element background as well as from the same masculine or feminine polarity. Therefore, the relevant planets are said to cooperate in the most harmonious way. Modern astrology associates the trine with inspiration and creativity. But since the trine is so completely void of friction, its gifts may be taken for granted.

❖ see MASCULINE p56

Opposition

The opposition consists of two or more planets or horoscope points separated by an angle of 180 degrees, i.e. being positioned on opposite sides of the zodiac. As the name indicates, the opposition is mostly an aspect of conflict. In horary astrology, two opposing significators may

ABOVE: *In a trine, planets like Jupiter cooperate harmoniously*

indicate a negative answer to the question or an insurmountable obstacle to the matter at hand. In modern natal astrology, the relevant planets symbolize conflicting inner impulses activated simultaneously. A person with several natal oppositions is said to literally be in constant opposition in the areas occupied and ruled by the relevant planets. At the same time the signs which are occupied by the planets in opposition form an axis that deals with similar issues from different perspectives. Therefore, the opposition also offers opportunities for integration and personal growth.

❖ see HORARY ASTROLOGY p28

MINOR ASPECTS

The group of specific planetary relationships defined as 'minor aspects' contains aspects of various backgrounds. Their interpretation is often intimately linked with that of the 'major' original and simply provided with the adjective 'weaker'.

Semi-Decile

The semi-decile is one of the lesser known and used minor aspects. It is sometimes also called vigintile and belongs to a group of aspects, known as the quintiles, which were introduced by Johannes Kepler in the seventeenth century. It covers an angle of 18 degrees, with an orb of maximum one degree. The semi-decile is regarded as positive and harmonious, indicating new beginnings, the constructive exchange of old conditions for new ones. It is said to create favourable conditions for new enterprises.

❖ see JOHANNES KEPLER p16

Quindecile

By dividing the zodiac into 15 segments, one arrives at an angle of 24 degrees; this is known as the quindecile aspect. Like the other aspects of this group, it refers to special intellectual, occult or creative talents, which are present but need to be developed by the individual. Those who consider it do not agree as to whether it is a harmonious or disharmonious aspect, but the quindecile suggests a focus on an extreme interest, pursued by the individual at all costs.

❖ see JOHANNES KEPLER p16

Semi-Sextile

The semi-sextile is an aspect of 30 degrees; the relevant planets are one sign apart. It is usually allowed an orb of no more than two degrees. The opinions about its significance and interpretation differ greatly. Whereas some

astrologers regard it as a preparatory phase for individual strengths to emerge, and interpret it as beneficially providing good opportunities, others call it 'dissociate' and connect it with disturbing, albeit minor, incidents. This could be due to the fact that some semi-sextiles operate from signs that harmonize in their expression, while others involve signs of a conflicting nature.

❖ see NOVILE p74

Decile

The decile is an aspect of 36 degrees and is generally allowed an orb of one degree or, if the lights are involved, two degrees. It is also known as 'semi-quintile'. Like the quintile, the decile is an aspect of subtle influence. It confers insight into the workings of natural forces combined with mental resourcefulness and creative talent, and is also associated with occult interests. In some instances it may resemble a Uranian influence and indicate working with groups. The innate talent, however, needs to be consciously developed by the individual.

❖ see SEMI-DECILE p74

Novile

The novile is one of the 'abstract' minor aspects and involves two planets positioned at an angle of 40 degrees. The name refers to the division of the zodiac into nine segments, which lies at the base of this aspect. Astrological literature is remarkably quiet about the novile, therefore its allotted orb is as unclear as its meaning is in most cases.

RIGHT: *Scholars observing the night sky*

Those who attempt an interpretation nowadays usually associate the novile with the ninth harmonic, which is closely linked to the navamsas in Vedic astrology and relates to the finding of one's true life purpose and connecting, as it were, to the higher octave of one's life. Accordingly, the factors involved in the novile are said to provide information as to the individual's unique earthly mission. The planets and their signs and houses indicate the key to self-realization and fulfilment through identification with one's spiritual purpose.

see VEDIC ASTROLOGY p33

Semi-Square

The semi-square is an aspect of 45 degrees. It is usually allotted an orb of no more than three degrees, sometimes five degrees if the lights are involved. Most astrologers are content to compare it to the square and simply call it 'weaker'. Both aspects do indeed manifest in similar ways. There is a difference in strength between semi-squares that stand by themselves, and may indeed be called weaker squares, and those which activate an existing square, for example, when a planet transits a square's midpoint, in which case the semi-square may work out quite explosively.

see SESQUIQUADRATE p76

Septile

The septile is one of the 'abstract' minor aspects. It is based on a division of the zodiac into seven segments, which gives it an angle of 51 degrees 25 minutes 43 sec of arc. This makes it difficult to discern in the chart, which may be one of the reasons why the septile is seldom used. Interpretations vary from 'inspiring but weak' to 'emotional and practical difficulties'. The septile appears to have a

Neptune/Uranus connotation and its positive or negative manifestations probably depend on the compatibility of the relevant planets and of the signs they occupy.

see NOVILE p74

Quintile

The quintile is an aspect of 72 degrees and is generally allowed an orb of two degrees. If one of the lights is involved, the orb may be as wide as three degrees. The quintile is one of the lesser known and less frequently used aspects, although some astrologers regard it as important.

ABOVE: *Due to interpretations of the number five and of the five-pointed star, the quintile is said to give great mental and creative powers*

It was introduced by seventeenth-century astrologer Johannes Kepler and is based on the division of the circle into five segments. Because of the numerological implications of the number five and the cabalistic interpretation of the five-pointed star, the quintile is said to denote extraordinary mental powers of invention and creation, which can be used to give spiritual principles a practical, earthly application. Although the individual is given this talent, (s)he still has to develop it through means described by the planets involved, their positions in signs and houses and by the houses they rule.

❖ see SESQUIQUINTILE p76

Sesquiquintile

The sesquiquintile, also known as tredecile, is part of the aspect group also known as quintiles or Keplerian aspects.

It involves two or more planets positioned at an angle of 108 degrees from each other and is given an orb of two degrees. Most textbooks ignore this aspect, possibly because it may interfere with the trine, depending on the orb given to either aspect. Lilly interpreted it as mildly beneficial, similar to trine and sextile, while others regard it as an 'almost major' aspect, indicating the laying of mental or practical foundations for further personal growth.

❖ see WILLIAM LILLY p17

Sesquiquadrate

The sesquiquadrate involves two planets positioned at an angle of 135 degrees from each other. It is usually given an orb of three degrees, sometimes five degrees if the lights are involved. The sesquiquadrate is one of the 'minor squares', which is an indication of its disharmonious nature.

Whereas the square itself, and also the semi-square (the other 'minor square') in many cases, hold the possibility of turning their tension into productivity through a conscious act of will, the sesquiquadrate does not seem to hold this option. Natally, it often indicates dangerous over-impulsiveness, domineering tendencies and a propensity towards anger and irritation. Some mundane astrologers relate it to radicalism and even terrorist activities, when Mars and Neptune are involved. It has even been suggested that a sesquiquadrate transit to the ruler of the eighth house may imply danger of death when supported by other aspects.

see SEMI-SQUARE p75

Bi-Quintile

The bi-quintile is one of the aspects introduced by Johannes Kepler and it is based on the division of the circle into five segments. The bi-quintile (double-quintile) covers an angle of 144 degrees and is generally allowed an orb of two degrees or, if one of the lights is involved, three degrees. Like the other Keplerian aspects, it is seen as relating to the subtler functions of the human mind. The planets involved can be used in the development of creative or occult abilities far above the ordinary. The bi-quintile is associated with clairvoyance, magic and a general interest in hidden or occult forces. When separating, it denotes almost genial powers of creative self-expression. In both cases, the 'tools' used by the individual are described by the planets involved, their placement in signs and houses and by the houses they rule.

see JOHANNES KEPLER p16

Inconjunct

In traditional astrology, the term may sometimes indicate the sextile and is at times wrongly used instead of 'disjunct', pertaining to an unaspected planet. Commonly, though, the inconjunct, also known as 'quincunx', is an aspect of 150 degrees, with an orb of three degrees. It frequently manifests itself as a crisis, in which several urgent and contradicting demands are placed upon the individual, who is forced to set priorities and to choose between desire and necessity. When approached positively, this may lead to a redefinition of the individual's goals or to a reassessment and improvement of working methods. Negatively, the individual may be tempted to use occult methods or public resources with selfish motives, which will result in even more problems in the areas indicated by the relevant planets and their position in the houses they rule. The inconjunct is also part of the significant aspect figure called 'Yod'.

see YOD p70

RIGHT: *An inconjunct aspect may have incited these witches to experiment with occult practices*

CASTING THE CHART

Charts are one of the most important aspects of the practice of astrology. It is from these that astrologers can intepret and predict the events that will happen to an individual or even a country. There are various methods of casting and intepreting a chart, including a number of different house systems. Each house hosts planets and other indicators relative to the

that reveals information about the area of life described by that house. For example, the first house represents personality, the second money and possessions, etc. Certain points on the chart have a particular significance. The shape of the chart can also reveal much about the person or people to whom it relates, and areas of life such as marriage, love. home life, illness, friends, sex

HOUSE SYSTEMS

A house system is the method used whereby the horoscope is divided into 12 sectors, each representing a different area of life. Each house system is different, so the house a planet is in for any given chart depends on the house system used in constructing the chart. Some astrologers favour a single house system, whereas others argue that different systems suit particular purposes, and may use one system for natal charts and another for predictive work.

Equal House System

The Equal house system is the oldest system in use, dating from the first century BC. In this system, each house is exactly 30 degrees, starting with the ascendant as the cusp of the first house. In most cases, this means that the midheaven will not be the cusp of the tenth house, but a separate point instead. The cusp of the tenth house, also

ABOVE: *Ptolemy, who advocated the Equal house system*

called the nonagesimal, is exactly 90 degrees from the ascendant, as measured along the ecliptic. Many astrologers in the United Kingdom and India use this house system, largely because astrological schools in those countries have promoted this system. It is commonly held that this is the house system advocated by Ptolemy in his *Tetrabiblos*. However, it is now believed that attribution of Equal houses is a misunderstanding of the text and that what is in fact referred to is whole-sign houses, in which the whole of the sign that the ascendant falls in is counted as the first house, the following as the second house, and so on.

❖ see ECLIPTIC p134

Lunar Mansions

A series of 28 divisions of the Moon's travel through one complete circuit of 360 degrees, each mansion representing one day's average travel – roughly 13 degrees – beginning at zero degrees Aries. Lunar mansions were originally sidereal, based on the movement of the Moon relative to certain stars. In Vedic astrology they are called asterisms or nakshastras. Only 27 are used in Vedic astrology – the twenty-second is omitted. Lunar mansions were used in Arabic, Chinese and Indian astrology. The cusps of the mansions were known as crucial or critical degrees and the days on which the Moon formed inharmonious aspects to the Sun – seventh, fourteenth, twenty-first and twenty-eighth days – were said to be critical days, coinciding with the cusps of the first, eighth, fifteenth and twenty-second mansions.

❖ see MOON p63

Porphyry House System

The Porphyry system dates from the third century AD. It is named after the neo-Platonist Porphyry (AD 233–305), who wrote on Pythagoras, Plotinus and Ptolemy. It is possible that Porphyry derived this system from a little-known astrologer called Orion (c. AD 150–175). He reintroduced the system in his book *Introduction to Ptolemy's Tetrabiblos*, written in around AD 295. This makes it one of the earliest quadrant house systems. It is similar to the Equal house system but uses the midheaven as the tenth house cusp. The remaining houses are determined by trisecting each quadrant in thirds. This means that the ascendant does not form the first house cusp, and may not even fall into the first house, in a similar fashion to the midheaven in the Equal house system. The simplicity of this system makes it popular but it has never reached the levels of the Equal house system because its teaching is not so widespread.

❖ see EQUAL HOUSE SYSTEM p80

Alcabitius House System

The Alcabitius house system is a time-based system. To derive the house cusps the portion of the circle made by the ascendant above the horizon (the diurnal arc of the ascendant) is divided into three. This circle runs parallel to the equator. This is done by dividing the time (in sidereal time) that it takes for the degree of the ascendant to reach the midheaven into three equal parts. The next three cusps are derived by adding these divisions to the sidereal time at birth and the houses below the horizon are calculated in reverse. This system was commonly used in medieval times

ABOVE: **Nostradamus, a user of the Alcabitius house system**

and is the house system used by Nostradamus. It is attributed to Alcabitius, a Syrian astrologer c. AD 950, who wrote a book on astrology. This was translated into Latin in the thirteenth century and became one of the most popular astrological works. However, Alcabitius did not actually invent this house system, but merely promoted it. As it does not cause distortion at high latitudes, it is occasionally used where Placidus would be unsuitable.

❖ see PLACIDUS HOUSE SYSTEM p82

LEFT: *Johann Müller, known as Regiomontanus*

Regiomontanus House System

Regiomontanus is one of the house systems most commonly used by horary astrologers. The method is named after Johann Müller (1436–76), more commonly known by his Latin name Regiomontanus. The system is a modification of the Campanus system, in which the celestial equator is divided into equal 30-degree arcs and used as the primary reference instead of the prime vertical. These segments are then projected on to the ecliptic, with the degrees at which they cut the ecliptic marking the house cusps. The cusps are regarded as the centre of the houses. The popularity of Regiomontanus came about because the house cusps are fixed for an observer at a particular latitude, and can be inscribed on an astrolabe plate, making it possible to calculate the houses quickly, and Müller developed a comprehensive set of tables, called the *Tabulai directionum profectionumquem*, for the system.

❖ *see* ALCABITIUS HOUSE SYSTEM p81

Campanus House System

The Campanus system is a space-based system. The thirteenth-century mathematician Johannes Campanus designed this system using the prime vertical, a great circle which passes through the east and west points of the horizon as well as the zenith and the nadir. He divided it into equal 30-degree segments and the great circles, which passed through these points, and the north and south points of the horizon, became the house cusps. The main drawback of the Campanus system manifests in higher latitudes, where the angle of the ecliptic to the prime vertical becomes more acute, causing the longitudinal position of house cusps in relation to the ecliptic to become unequal and the houses markedly distorted. Campanus also believed that the cusp should mark the centre of a house, rather than its start.

❖ *see* ZENITH HOUSE SYSTEM p83

Placidus House System

The Placidus system is a time-based system, based on trisections of arcs. The eleventh and twelfth house cusps are calculated by trisecting the time it takes any degree of the ecliptic to travel from the ascendant to midheaven (or semi-diurnal arc). This provides the degrees for the opposite house cusps as well. Similarly, the time it takes for any degree to travel from the immum coeli to the ascendant (or semi-nocturnal arc) is trisected to produce the second and third house cusps. It is named after its assumed creator, the seventeenth-century astrologer monk Placidus di Tito. Some sources state that he derived the system from the eighth-century Arabian astrologer Ben Djabir. It has been the most popular house system for many years because its tables are readily available, but it cannot be used for high latitudes.

❖ *see* IMMUM COELI p91

Zenith House System

Method of chart division. The zenith house system was proposed by the astrologer Zariel (David Cope) and is also known as the horizontal system. The zenith system divides the horizon into 12 equal sectors and has great circles passing through the zenith and nadir. Thus, instead of being based around the north–south axis, or midheaven and immum coeli, it is based around the zenith–nadir axis. The cusp of the first house will not be the ascendant as the houses are divided equally from the zenith, similar to the division from the midheaven in the Porphyry system. This point is also known as the anti-vertex. The anti-vertex and vertex (the opposite point to the anti-vertex) are used by astrologers, who do not use this house system, to describe how a person relates to others and conducts their relationships. Because the system bears a relationship to the Campanus system, tables used for Campanus may be used to find Zenith system cusps with minor alterations. The Zenith house system is also sometimes used to describe the Equal house system.

❖ see CAMPANUS HOUSE SYSTEM p82

Koch House System

The Koch, or birthplace, system was introduced by the German astrologer Dr Walter Koch in the 1960s. It is based on dividing the quarters of the chart formed by the ascendant and midheaven axes into three equal time segments. This results in individual calculation of the intermediate house cusps for the birth location, using the ecliptic, the ascendant and place of birth as reference points. It has been described as a variation on the Alcabitius system. The specific 'Tables of Houses' was only ever calculated to 60 degrees latitude, as the system did not work in polar regions. For example, there can be a difference of almost a complete sign between Koch and Placidus cusp calculations in high latitudes. Some practitioners claim that the intermediate cusps in this system are powerful points that respond to transits and progressions.

❖ see ECLIPTIC p134

Topocentric House System

The Topocentric house system was derived from the timing of events, in the 1960s, by South American astrologers Anthony Page and Vendel Polich. Their research was established entirely through practical experiments focused on the nature and timing of events, the naibod arc and use of primary directions to determine house cusps that related to those events. They found that the cusps lay on a great plane passing through the birth location rather than a great circle that they labelled a 'cone of rotation'.

❖ see PLACIDUS HOUSE SYSTEM p82

BELOW: *Several house systems are believed to have derived from early Arabic practices*

HOUSES

Houses are one of the four essential tools of astrology. Their 12-fold division is one of the fundamentals of astrological interpretation. Although there is a tendency amongst modern astrology to ally the house meanings with the signs – the first house being similar to Aries, for example – houses and signs were originally completely separate concepts. Planets placed in the sector, or house, are effective in the area of life described by that house.

First House

The first house is that which begins with the ascendant and it is therefore an angular house. In modern astrology the first house represents the personality and its expression. It is associated with the appearance, general behaviour and general tendencies in relationships with others. It can also indicate the level of personal vitality and strength. The first house is the house of the individual. In mundane astrology it represents the common people or the general state of a nation. In a chart for an event it represents whoever makes the first move. It is associated with pale colours and white. It is diurnal, masculine and cardinal. It represents the direction east. Mercury is said to have joy, or be happily placed, in the first house. Saturn and Aries are traditionally associated with the first house.

❖ see MERCURY p62

Second House

In modern astrology the second house is associated with money and possessions, income and expenditure. It shows what constitutes personal security. In horary astrology it represents the finances and assets of the person asking the question. In political astrology it refers to the nation's assets and financial status. It represents the treasury, revenue and all places and activities concerned with

money-making, such as banks. In event charts it represents the friends and allies of whoever initiates the action. In medical astrology it represents the throat and neck, as far down as the shoulders. It is associated with the colour green. It is succedent, feminine and nocturnal in nature. It shows the direction east-north-east. It is associated with Jupiter and Taurus and it is considered particularly unfortunate in traditional astrology if the Sun or Mars are in the second house.

❖ see MARS p64

Third House

In modern astrology the third house represents communication, short journeys, siblings, cousins and neighbours. It is associated with early schooling and our attitude and relationship with knowledge itself. In horary astrology it represents the ability of the person asking the question to communicate well. In political astrology it represents rumours and propaganda, the media and all means of disseminating news and information. In lawsuits or conflicts it represents all written statements and the ability to affect the situation through correspondence. In medical astrology it represents the shoulders, arms, hands

RIGHT: *Claude Vignon's* Treasure, *represented by the second house*

and fingers. It is associated with orangey-yellow or rusty colours. It is a cadent, masculine, nocturnal house. It represents the direction north-north-east. The Moon is said to have joy, or be happily placed in the third house. It is associated with Gemini and Mars.

❖ see GEMINI p39

Fourth House

The fourth house is that which begins with the immum coeli and it is therefore an angular house. In modern astrology the fourth shows our roots and past, and it is usually held to represent the father. In traditional astrology it always represented the mother. It also represents grandfathers, hidden treasure, land and property. In political astrology it represents land and the workers on it. A planet representing a lost object in this house suggests that it will be found. In medical astrology it represents the breast or lung area. It is an angular, feminine and nocturnal house. The fourth house is associated with Saturn as well as Cancer and the Sun.

❖ see IMMUM COELI p91

Fifth House

In modern astrology the fifth house represents creative expression, sports and recreation, gambling and speculation. Romance and sexual expression also fall under the fifth house. Conception, promiscuity, scandal and over-indulgence are shown by this house. Places of entertainment are also included here. In horary astrology the fifth represents the children of the person asking the question and the sex of the unborn child. In mundane astrology it represents ambassadors and diplomats as well as all public places of enjoyment. In medical astrology it represents the stomach, liver, heart and back, the back of the shoulders and sides of the body. It is associated with the colours black, white and honey. It is a masculine and succedent house. It represents the direction north-north-west. Venus is happily placed there, and it is also associated with Leo.

❖ see VENUS p63

Sixth House

In modern astrology the sixth house is the house of service. It represents the day-to-day routine of work, employment in general, pets and employees. It is also the house of health. Illness and disease, their causes and curability and health-industry workers are shown by this house. In horary astrology it represents these issues related to the person asking the question. In political astrology it represents the nation's food reserves and those who keep public records. It represents the working classes generally, public employees and services such as the civil service, the armed forces and the police. In medical astrology it represents the nature of illness and whether it is physical or psychological. It rules the lower part of the belly and small intestine, the guts, liver and kidneys. It is associated with the colour black and is a cadent and feminine house. It represents the direction west-north-west. Mars has joy here and Virgo and Mercury are associated with it.

❖ see HORARY ASTROLOGY p28

LEFT: *An astrologer, represented by the seventh house*

Seventh House

The seventh house has the descendant on its cusp and is an angular house. In modern astrology it is the house of marriage, as well as of relationships in general and of open enemies. It is associated with any sort of partnership, including business partnerships and litigation. It represents the person against whom action is taken, the spouse or lover. It also represents fugitives, runaways and thieves. In horary astrology this house represents the astrologer. In political astrology it shows the marriage and divorce rate and issues pertaining to them. It describes public enemies to the nation and whether war or peace may be expected. In medical astrology it shows the doctor treating the ailment and their ability to cure the disease. It rules from the navel to the top of the legs, including the buttocks, bladder, womb and reproductive organs. It is a masculine, angular and western house. It is also called the angle of the west.

❖ see MEDICAL ASTROLOGY p28

Eighth House

In modern astrology this is often known as the house of other people's values. It describes that which is shared, how we unite with others and sex. It is the house of death, inheritance and any activities concerned with the dead. Financial obligations, debts, taxes, losses and loans are also represented. Traditionally, it is related to crisis, hidden matters and deadly fears. Psychological astrology regards it as a house of inner transformation and growth. In political astrology it represents the national debt, collector of taxes and financial relations with other countries. In conflicts and legal matters it represents the friends and assistants of the defendant. In medical astrology it is associated with the sex organs, haemorrhoids, gallstones, bladder and poisons generally. It is associated with the colours green and black and is a feminine, succedent house. It represents the direction west-south-west. It is associated with Scorpio and Saturn.

❖ see SCORPIO p47

Ninth House

In modern astrology, the ninth house is known as the house of the higher mind. It is associated with religious and philosophical issues and religion in general. It is the house of in-laws, higher education and long journeys, foreigners and foreign interests, law and lawyers. In traditional astrology it is associated with dreams, divination, mysticism and belief. In horary astrology, it also represents the spouse's brothers and sisters as well as grandchildren. In political astrology, the ninth house describes the Church, other religious institutions and all institutions of higher learning. Shipping, airlines and anything connected with long journeys as well as the publishing industry; universities and scientific organizations are also represented by this house. In legal matters it represents lawyers who serve the prosecution and writs or communications that affect the defendant. In medical astrology it represents the buttocks, hips and thighs. It is associated with the colours green and white, and is a cadent and masculine house. Its direction is south-south-west. The Sun joys, or is happy, in the ninth, and it is associated with Sagittarius and Jupiter.

❖ see SAGITTARIUS p48

Tenth House

With its cusp of the midheaven, the tenth house is an angular house. In modern astrology it refers to what we would like to be remembered as having contributed to the world. It is the house of ambition, associated with career and profession. It is also associated with fame, notoriety, reputation, public work and the mother. It describes the trade of a person, employers, prestige, power, and success. In political astrology it refers to those in authority over a nation, including prime ministers and presidents. In legal matters it represents the judge or magistrate and the ruling in a law court. In medical astrology it describes the curing of illness, and is also associated with the knees, calves and shins. It is associated with the colours red and white and is a feminine house. It is associated with Capricorn and Mars.

❖ see CAPRICORN p49

Eleventh House

In modern astrology the eleventh house is associated with friends, friendship, larger groups and networking. It is the house of ideals and social reform. Traditionally known as the house of good fortune, it is related to supporters, benefactors, hope, trust, praise, comfort, goals and ambitions. In horary astrology it refers to the friends of the person asking the question, stepchildren and the profit or income from a professional endeavour. In political astrology it is associated with Parliament, especially the House of Commons, Senates and other major political bodies. It represents the hopes of a nation. Places of comfort and relief are also represented here. In medical astrology it represents the legs to the ankles. It is associated with the colour yellow or saffron, and is a masculine and succedent house. Traditionally, it was regarded as a powerful house, considered equal in some sources to the fourth and seventh houses. Its direction is south-south-east, and it is associated with the Sun and Aquarius. Jupiter has joy, and is happy in this house.

❖ see HOUSES p84

Twelfth House

In modern astrology the twelfth house represents dissolution, sacrifice, withdrawal, and past lives, secret enemies, conspiracies and behind-the-scenes activities. It represents hidden, restrained and secret matters. Traditionally, it is an unfortunate house, associated with sad events, sorrow, anguish, captivity, imprisonment and persecution. It represents places that are denied access to public view. It is associated with scandal and skeletons in the closet. In political astrology it is associated with the prison system, criminals, spies and enemies of the nation, underground movements and secret societies. In medical astrology it is associated with the feet. In legal matters it is the house of incarceration. It is associated with the colour green and the direction east-south-east. It is a feminine, cadent house and reputed to be the most unfortunate in the chart. It is associated with Pisces and Venus, and Saturn joys (is happy in) this house.

❖ see FEMININE p56

ABOVE: *An engraving of Fame, associated with the tenth house*

Cadent Houses

The cadent houses are those that precede the angular houses, that is, the third, sixth, ninth and twelfth houses. These houses are considered weaker than angular houses. The word 'cadent' means 'fallen'; a planet in a cadent house has been carried away from the cardinal position of the angular house and symbolizes a falling from grace and weakening of power. Originally the cadent houses referred to a lack of familiarity and the fear and danger that can arise from it. The most afflicted are the sixth and twelfth houses as they have least relationship with the ascendant. When timing an event from a chart, a cadent planet indicates that it is likely to take months, rather than weeks or days. Although the distinction is particularly important in horary astrology, modern astrology does not distinguish between the houses in this manner.

❖ see SUCCEDENT HOUSES p89

Angular Houses

The angular houses are those that have one of the angles – ascendant, midheaven, immum coeli or descendant – on the cusp. That is the first, tenth, fourth and seventh houses. Planets placed in one of these houses are strengthened, though whether positively or negatively depends on the nature of the planet itself as well as any aspects it makes. A planet in the first house is stronger than one in the tenth, followed by the fourth and seventh houses in that order.

❖ see CADENT HOUSES p89

Succedent Houses

The succedent houses are those that follow the angular houses. That is, the second, fifth, eighth, and eleventh houses. A succedent planet is one that occupies a succedent house. These are houses of stability, where the ideas developed in the angular houses can be administered. All succedent houses are connected with possessions. Succedent houses are said to be in the middle ground and succedent activities are aimed at managing and controlling things. There is a correspondence between succedent houses and the fixed signs. The succedent houses are related to the accumulation of resources, developing stability and reserves, maintaining or developing things. In Western astrology the eleventh house is considered the strongest whereas in Vedic astrology the fifth house holds more strength. Traditionally, the eleventh house was regarded as a powerful house, considered equal in some sources to the fourth and seventh houses.

❖ see ANGULAR HOUSES p89

CHART POINTS

The points on a chart play an important role for the astrologer in defining and interpreting the horoscope. Angles such ascendant, descendant and midheaven reveal information about an individual's reactions and preferences to life experiences. They can also reveal information about compatibility between individuals when charts are compared.

Cardinal Points

The four cardinal points are at 0 degrees of the cardinal signs Aries, Cancer, Libra and Capricorn. The annual passage of the Sun over these points marks the astrological beginnings of the seasons and in ancient astrology they were used to mark the four quarters of the heavens. They also refer to the four main directions and some astrologers regard planets in these degrees as especially powerful.

see ANGLES p90

Angles

The four cardinal points in the horoscope. The angles are the ascendant, descendant, midheaven and immum coeli, or the cusps of the first, fourth, seventh and tenth houses. Planets placed near these points are extremely potent positively or negatively, depending on the nature of the planet and the aspects it makes in the chart. The signs found on these points reveal much about the individual's orientation to the basic experiences in life. As they are calculated according to the date, time and place of birth, these points are highly personal. In predictive work the angles are often moved forward, or directed, to describe what is likely to happen in the particular areas of life that they relate to.

see MIDHEAVEN p91

Ascendant

Sign rising in the east, and the degree of the zodiac that appeared on the eastern horizon at the moment for which the chart is cast. It is often loosely applied to the whole of the rising sign and sometimes to the entire first house, as well as specifically to the exact degree on the horizon. Planets close to the rising degree are said to be in the ascendant. It is the first point on the chart wheel and forms the cusp of the first house.

see FIRST HOUSE p84

LEFT: *Birth charts contain points called angles*

Descendant

The western angle or cusp of the seventh house represents our relationships with those around us and what we project on to others. Calculated for the time, date and place of birth, the descendant moves about one degree every four minutes. Because the descendant is one of the four angles of the chart, any planet in conjunction with it is regarded as having a strong influence in the chart. Planets that make an aspect to the descendant have an influence on relationships. The descendant is one of the main points to consider in synastry and if your partner's ascendant is in the same sign as your descendant it shows an exceptionally close bond.

see ASCENDANT p90

Midheaven

The midheaven is the cusp of the tenth house in the chart, and one of the four angles opposite the midheaven. It is the point where the Sun is at midday at the time and place you were born. A planet placed near it is extremely potent negatively or positively, depending on the nature of the planet and the aspects it makes in the chart. In predictive work it may be moved forward, or directed, to describe what is likely to happen. This point represents the public persona, and differs from the ascendant in that it is not exactly about the way a person is initially perceived, but more about how their career and social standing reflects upon their place in the world.

see ANGLES p90

Immum Coeli

The immum coeli, or IC, is the cusp of the fourth house. It is the north angle of the chart. A planet placed near it is extremely potent negatively or positively, depending on the nature of the planet and the aspects it makes in the chart.

It is a highly personal point as it is calculated according to date, place and time of birth. It is most closely associated with issues relating to the home, past, family and domestic concerns. In horary astrology it indicates the end of the matter in question.

see FOURTH HOUSE p86

Aries Point

The first degree of the chart. Another word for zero degrees Aries, or vernal point. This is the point where the celestial equator intersects the ecliptic in the east. This marks the vernal equinox and the beginning of the tropical zodiac. It is considered significant when working with midpoints, especially if a birth time is not available.

see TROPICAL ASTROLOGY p33

ABOVE: *The cardinal points*

East Point

The east point is a symbolic point showing where the ascendant would be if we were born at the Equator. It lies directly opposite the point where the ecliptic intersects the prime vertical. This point is known as the vertex. The east point is therefore also known as the vertex and the anti-vertex (opposite to vertex) is known as the west point.

❖ see ECLIPTIC p134

West Point

The west point is where the western horizon intersects the prime vertical and the celestial equator. It is an unfortunate place for the Moon to be.

❖ see EAST POINT p92

North Node

The Moon's nodes are points that indicate where the orbit of the Moon around the Earth crosses the ecliptic. The nodes form an axis, rather than separate points being exactly opposite each other, although are generally interpreted separately. Often only the north node is entered on the chart. The ancients held that the Moon's north node partook of the nature of Venus and Jupiter.

❖ see TRUE NODE p92

True Node

The nodes do not move at a predictable speed and vary from day to day. The mean node is the position based on average speed. With the assistance of computer software it is now easy to calculate the position of the true node.

❖ see NORTH NODE p92

Antiscion

Mathematical point. To find the antiscion, a line is drawn from zero degrees of Cancer to zero degrees of Capricorn on the chart, and planets are reflected across that line to the corresponding degree on the other side. The opposite point is called the contra-antiscion.

❖ see CANCER p41

Arabian Part

Mathematical point. Arabian Parts (or Lots) are significant points that are arithmetical constructs of two or more components such as planets or house cusps. There are endless Parts including Parts of death, illness, marriage, treachery, journeys, etc. When aspected by natal or transiting planets they are sensitive points in the chart. They are used when a specific issue is being examined in the chart. Although it is possible to use Parts in any form of astrology, only the Part of Fortune is generally used today.

❖ see PARS FORTUNA p92

Pars Fortuna (Part of Fortune)

An Arabian Part that bears the same relationship to the rising degree as the Moon does to the Sun. The Part of Fortune is derived from adding the longitude of the Moon to the ascendant and subtracting the longitude of the Sun. The formula is reversed for night births. It is symbolized by a cross within a circle. It shows an area in the chart where benefit can be gained.

❖ see ARABIAN PART p92

Degree Symbol

A system of degree symbols assumes that each zodiac degree has a special meaning, which is expressed by the symbol assigned to it. Hellenistic astrology used the monomoira, a system in which each zodiac degree was assigned to a specific planet. Scottish astrologer Wemyss constructed a system of degree symbols that includes the meanings of hypothetical planets. Other systems of degree symbols have been devised by psychic methods.

❖ see SABIAN SYMBOL p92

Sabian Symbol

The system attaches a specific meaning to each degree of the zodiac, which is expressed and summarized by a symbolic image. The symbols for immum coeli and midheaven provide information as to the 'how?' and 'why?'.

❖ see DEGREE SYMBOL p92

Critical Degree

The cusp degrees of the lunar mansions. Days on which the Moon passes over such a point are called 'critical degree days' and usually mark a change in the course of events. Some astrologers only regard the cusps of the first, eighth, fifteenth and twenty-second lunar mansion as critical.

❖❖ see CUSP p93

Cusp

The cusp of a sign or house is the point at which it begins. Therefore, zero degrees of Aries is the cusp of Aries. The cusp of a house is generally regarded as the most powerful part of the house. Therefore, a planet up to five degrees before the cusp may be regarded as being in that house.

❖❖ see ARIES p36

Nonagesimal

The nonagesimal is the ninetieth degree of the ecliptic, the middle or highest point which is at any given moment

ABOVE: *The Moon is said to be oriental when moving to full*

above the horizon. The nonagesimal represents a more personal point of accomplishment than does the midheaven. Relating directly to the ascendant, it shows what we are willing to do to attain our personal goals.

❖❖ see EQUAL HOUSE SYSTEM p80

Vertex

In astronomical terms the vertex is the point where the prime vertical intersects the ecliptic in the west. The anti-vertex is the same point in the east. It is usually viewed as an axis, comprising the vertex and anti-vertex. It is usually found in the fifth, sixth, seventh or eighth house. By combining the meaning of turning point with those of the houses, the vertex is related to meeting people. It is a sensitive point on the chart and often relates to a compulsive yet fortunate experience. It is mainly used for examining issues connected with relationships.

❖❖ see FIFTH HOUSE p86

INTERPRETATION

There are as many ways to interpret a chart as there are astrologers, but there are also very clear rules pertaining to the interpretation of different kinds of horoscopes. Above all, however, the astrologer has to learn to apply the many rules of the art without bending or stretching them before applying his/her intuition and creativity to the interpretation.

Chart Shape

Some visually distinctive planet configurations or aspect patterns are referred to as chart shapes. The distribution of planets in the horoscope gives the astrologer an impression of what kind of chart he is dealing with. Certain chart shapes have always been looked upon as special, for example, the five- or six-pointed star, the kite or the mystic rectangle. In addition to the traditional chart shapes, Marc Edmund Jones (1888–1980) introduced and named several planetary patterns and described the personal characteristics they signify. These chart shapes, also known as 'Jones patterns', are quite popular among modern astrologers.

❖ see CONFIGURATION p96

Tripod

The 'tripod' is one of the so-called 'Jones patterns', a distinctive planetary formation which tells the natal astrologer about basic characteristics of the individual at first glance. In this pattern the planets are placed in three separate groups and each group is connected to the other by at least one trine aspect. A 'group' may also consist of only one planet, which is why this pattern is sometimes confused with the 'bucket'. The tripod suggests a focus on spiritual growth through understanding, the ability to blend opposites and to transcend the dualities inherent in life on Earth.

❖ see CHART SHAPE p94

Bucket

The 'bucket' – also known as 'wedge' or 'funnel' – is an easily recognizable chart shape. It consists of a tight group of planets within 180 degrees of one hemisphere ('bucket') and a singleton planet ('handle') in the opposing hemisphere. Two planets in close conjunction may also be counted as a singleton. The closer the planets of the 'bucket' are grouped together, the more energies are being generated in the areas defined by their house position. These energies are then focused towards the singleton and released through it, in a manner according to its position in sign and house.

❖ see CHART SHAPE p94

See-Saw

The 'see-saw' is one of the so-called 'Jones patterns' – a distinctive planetary formation which informs the natal astrologer about certain characteristics of the individual in question at first glance. The 'see-saw' consists of two groups of planets, which are separated by at least two empty houses on each side. There should be no more than one empty house in each group and the pattern should contain at least one opposition. This chart shape suggests a strongly dualistic individual nature. The subject is constantly aware of antagonistic views or conflicting possibilities which should be considered.

❖ see TRIPOD p94

Locomotive

The 'locomotive', also known as the 'open-angle pattern', is one of the so-called 'Jones patterns'. In this configuration, all planets are found within 240 degrees or less, with no more than one empty house between them and leaving one-third of the chart empty. Visually, this pattern slightly resembles a train on its anticlockwise journey through the chart. The leading planet is seen as a strong driving or motivating force. The pattern as a whole suggests an open mind, unconventionality and great powers of self-motivation. Negatively, it implies restlessness and the continuous search for individuality.

❖ see CHART SHAPE p94

Composite Chart

One of the methods of analyzing a relationship is the composite chart. This is an artificial horoscope, based on the natal horoscopes of the persons involved and must be distinguished from the relationship chart. It is erected by calculating the midpoints between the charts for each planet. For example, if person A's Sun is at 10 degrees Aries, and person B's Sun is at 10 degrees Gemini, the composite Sun will be at 10 degrees Taurus. The composite houses are calculated either on the basis of the midheaven midpoint or the ascendant midpoint. The results of either method are only slightly different, but may affect the timing of events by solar-arc progression or

ABOVE: The Hireling Shepherd in William Holman Hunt's painting could have his relationship analysed in a composite chart

transits to the angles. The location for the chart is the one where the relationship takes place. The idea behind this method is that two or more people combine their forces and blend their energies to create an artificial third entity, the relationship, which then starts to lead a life of its own.

❖ see MIDPOINT p97

Sunrise Chart

When the time of birth is unknown, a chart is cast for an arbitrary time and the house cusps ignored. Although it is common to use noon for the time of such a chart, it may also be cast for any other time. Sunrise is often used, as people are statistically more likely to be born early in the morning than at midday. If the birth is assisted, e.g. by caesarean, this is unlikely to apply.

❖ see CUSP p93

Configuration

The term 'configuration' has various meanings. It is mainly applied to certain important aspect patterns, like the grand trine, the grand cross, the T-square or the mystic rectangle – all of which focus the horoscope's energies in special ways. Sometimes the term is used to describe certain planetary patterns or chart shapes, such as the 'locomotive', the 'see-saw' or the 'bucket'. Traditional astrology at some point referred to all aspects as configurations.

❖ see CHART SHAPE p94

Considerations Before Judgement

Technique to ascertain whether a chart is fit to be judged. The considerations are applied to horary charts before they are judged. If any of them are present then the chart is deemed unfit. They are also termed 'strictures' or 'cautions'. The chart is valid if the ruler of the hour and ascendant are of the same triplicity or nature, a factor which is frequently ignored. When less than three or more than 27 degrees rise, the chart is considered unfit. If the Moon is in the later degrees of a sign, the chart is unsafe – often ignored. If the Moon is in via combusta (between 15 degrees Libra and 15 degrees Scorpio) or void of course (cannot form an exact aspect before changing sign) the chart is unfit. If Saturn is in the first or seventh houses or the seventh cusp is afflicted, the chart is unfit. If the ruler of the seventh is badly placed or ruler of the ascendant combust, the chart is unfit. These definitions do not apply to birth-chart analysis.

❖ see MOON p63

Hemisphere Emphasis

A strong emphasis on any of the hemispheres gives a chart a basic theme. Eastern hemisphere: focusing on the self, exerting control and shaping one's own destiny. Western hemisphere: search for identity and meaning, dependency on approval from others, difficulty to affect inner change. Upper hemisphere: socially and success-oriented, searching for the meaning of all experience, treating others as 'objects'. Lower hemisphere: focusing on personal experience, subjective approach, experiencing relationships as obstructive.

❖ see LORD OF CHART p97

Derived Houses

Derived houses are usually used in horary astrology, although some people apply the technique to natal astrology. It is a method whereby the

LEFT: **Libra is associated with the twelfth house**

ASTROLOGY

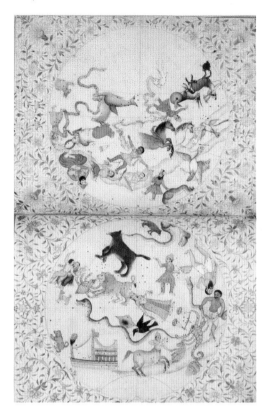

ABOVE: *The Eastern and Western hemispheres, which focus on the self and a search for identity, respectively*

astrologer turns the chart and uses another house as the first house. For example, if there is a question about a spouse, the person asking the question is represented by the first house and their spouse by the seventh. If the question is about the spouse's employer, the seventh house is used as the first and the employer is represented by the tenth house from the first or, in other words, the fourth house of the chart.

❖❖ see HORORY ASTROLOGY p28

Lord of Chart

The lord of the chart, also known as almuten in Arabic astrology, has special significance in that it is said to 'colour', i.e. determine, the whole chart. It is found by weighing the strength of all planets by sign, house, triplicity, term and face. Traditionally, the lord of a chart was the strongest planet by house position, while the most emphasized planet by sign and aspect was known as the ruler of the horoscope. In a rather simplistic fashion, modern astrologers often refer to the ruler of the ascendant as both – 'chart ruler' or 'lord of chart'. A feminine planet such as the Moon or Venus may be referred to as 'lady of chart'.

❖❖ see FEMININE p56

Midpoint

The use of midpoints dates back to Ptolemy's work where he stressed them as helping to locate places of power in a chart. Midpoints were also used before and after the Middle Ages, the most popular form being that of Arabic Parts. Early in the twentieth century, midpoints as a technique were re-invented by a group of astrologers living in Hamburg, Germany. Planetary pictures are a form of midpoints activating midpoints. The midpoint of two planets is the exact halfway point between them. There are two midpoints for each pairing, one of long arc and one of short. It is the midpoint of shorter arc that is usually referred to. The meaning is based on the combination of meanings of the planets involved. Midpoints are written with/between the planets concerned, for example, Sun/Jup, for the Sun Jupiter midpoint. If that point makes an aspect to a planet or chart point, it is followed by =. So Sun/Jupiter = Ascendant means that the Sun Jupiter midpoint is aspected by the ascendant.

❖❖ see COSMOBIOLOGY p31

Midpoint Tree

Midpoint trees display, in diagrammatical form, the list of midpoints connected, by aspect, to a planet within a selected orb. The midpoint, planet or chart point under consideration is written at the top and a vertical line drawn downwards. Horizontal lines are then drawn across this vertical line. Any two factors that give a midpoint that

makes an aspect to the chart point being considered are listed on these horizontal lines, placed on the right and left respectively. The closest aspect is listed first. This allows the astrologer to see all factors involved in the pattern at one time.

❖ see MIDPOINT p97

Synthesis

To arrive at a detailed judgement, the astrologer has to consider all horoscope factors and weigh them against each other. Beginning and advanced students alike are often overwhelmed by the volume of information and turn to so-called 'cookbooks' or interpretational computer software. But whereas these tools may be of great help in memorizing the different rules and ways of interpretation, they do not and cannot provide a synthesized analysis. This task remains with the astrologer who has to combine strict adherence to the framework of rules with intuition and sensitivity.

❖ see HOROSCOPE p138

Home Life

Matter of the fourth house and the Moon. Questions concerning a person's home life are answered by planets in the fourth house, position and aspects of its ruler, and by the position and aspects of the Moon. The fourth house is traditionally connected to the father but has become the modern domain of the mother, because of its Cancerian undertones. In either case it describes early family experiences, which shape the subject's domestic behaviour as an adult. The Moon provides information about the individual's caring qualities and emotional needs, which are likely to express themselves in the intimacy of the home.

❖ see CANCER p41

Sex

Fifth-house matter. There are many horoscope factors pertaining to sexuality. For example, a strongly placed Mars

LEFT: *The Fountain of Eternal Youth under the influence of Venus, who can trigger sexual appeal in individuals*

or Sun may indicate great sexual appetites in a male horoscope, while females with a strong Venus often exude a sex appeal befitting the goddess of love. Among the signs, Scorpio is especially noted for its interest in sex. Accordingly, modern astrology looks at eighth-house factors in this context, because of the psychological connection between sex and death. But traditionally, the main indicators for 'venereal sports' are all horoscope factors of the fifth house, the area associated with creation, recreation and procreation.

❖ see LOVE p99

Children

To answer questions concerning children, the astrologer will look at the fifth house, an area of the natal horoscope connected to recreation, procreation and, in psychological astrology, to the child within. Planets in the fifth house – as well as the general condition and aspects of its ruler – will provide information about children and the relationship with them. Traditional astrology uses more elaborate methods and looks at the ascendant and its ruler as well as the condition of the Sun and Moon. If the ascendant or fifth house has a barren sign on the cusp or contains a barren planet, the chances of having children are considered to be slim. The same judgement applies if the Sun, as representative of the individual's creative powers, is considered to be in bad shape or if the Moon, significator of female fertility, is weak or afflicted. On the other hand, fruitful signs on the relevant cusps, benefics involved with the significators and Sun and Moon dignified promise numerous happy and healthy offspring.

❖ see BARREN SIGNS p58

Love

Even beginners in astrology would agree that feelings of love are symbolized by Venus or, in the case of motherly love, by the Moon, but there are as many differentiations concerning the significator of this human condition as there are forms of love. Traditionally, love matters are

BELOW: *This seventeenth-century quack doctor's cures would be located, astrologically speaking, in the tenth house*

chronic illnesses are ruled by Saturn. A connection between the sixth and the twelfth house may indicate illness as a result of self-destructive behaviour or hospitalization. The modern planet Pluto appears to be connected with major surgery.

❖ see CRITICAL DEGREE p93

Occupations

Matter of the sixth and tenth houses. The planets, and the rulers of the signs on the cusps of the sixth and tenth houses, have special significance when considering occupations. Traditional astrology reserves the sixth house for one's 'servants' (i.e. employees) and looks at the tenth house and its ruler to find out about the most likely bread-winning activity. In modern astrology, the idea of 'service' as a basic theme of the sixth house remains intact, but is now connected with one's daily work and the circumstances under which this is carried out. Therefore, the factors connected with the sixth house may describe one's profession and give information about the working environment, colleagues, one's own attitude towards work, etc. The tenth house covers another area of the occupational theme. Psychologically, it describes what the subject identifies with and how he perceives his role in society. Factors of the tenth house describe the individual's ambitions, aspirations and, consequently, his most likely choice of career, as well as his chances of failure or success.

❖ see LOVE p99

Marriage

Subject of the seventh house. Marriage matters are generally described by planets in the seventh house and its ruler by position and aspect. Since these astrological rules were first laid out, our attitude towards traditional marriage has drastically changed, so nowadays relationships resembling marriage are also included. Traditional astrology

described by planets in the seventh house and the position and aspects of its ruler. Infatuations and mainly physical romantic adventures belong to the fifth house. While love is generally perceived as positive, even malefic planets rule certain forms of love: Saturn rules love of the body and of property.

❖ see MARRIAGE p100

Illness

Matter of the sixth house. The basic theme of the sixth house is service, and because the body is seen as serving the soul it also describes the subject's health. Planets in this area and the condition of its ruler are factors to be considered when assessing the basic health disposition. Afflictions, which may possibly result in illness, can be triggered by transit or progression. Traditional astrology also considers the ascendant, its ruler and first-house planets as indicators of illness or health, since they describe the physical manifestation of the native. In a horary chart concerning an illness, the ninth house gives information about its outcome, while the cure is to be found in the tenth house. Transits of the Moon over critical degrees mark turning-points in the course of an illness. Long and assigns Libra and the Moon as cosignificators of this subject, because Libra is the sign of relating and the Moon rules emotional matters and domestic affairs. Planets in the seventh house describe the psychological tools we bring into the partnership or the expectations we project on to our partner; they therefore give an indication of the type of partner we will choose or how the marriage is going to develop. For example, the planet Jupiter in this house shows a generous attitude towards others and the choice of an equally generous partner; hence a marriage will be prosperous, provided that the planet and the ruler of the seventh house are both in good shape. Since the seventh house also represents public enemies and lawsuits, afflictions may still end in divorce.

❖ see LOVE p99

Friends and Enemies

Matter of the seventh, eleventh or twelfth house. In analogy with the seventh sign Libra, allies and associates are described by the seventh house. However, since this chart area is just concerned with the principle of relating, a malefic in this house or its afflicted ruler may signify an open enemy, for example in a lawsuit. The eleventh house relates to one's hopes and dreams, which can only be fulfilled through the cooperation of like-minded people, hence its connection with friendships. The twelfth house signifies secret enemies, often in the sense of a person being their own worst enemy.

❖ see ELEVENTH HOUSE p88

Travel

Astrology divides the subject of 'travel' into two parts: short and long journeys. Short journeys, like the daily trip to work, a weekend visit or any travel inside the country, are described by planets in the third house and by its ruler; also by Mercury or Gemini. A (temporary) affliction may indicate traffic jams, train strikes and the like, as is often the case during Mercury's retrograde periods. International travel and 'travelling in the spirit', as in watching travelling programmes or reading about foreign countries, belongs to planets in the ninth house and the ruler thereof.

❖ see GEMINI p39

BELOW: *Journeys undertaken in Rickman's helicopter could belong to the third or the ninth house, depending on their extent*

PREDICTION METHODS

There are many different techniques that can be used for prediction, some of them based on the actual movements of the planets and others that are more symbolic. In traditional forms of astrology, definite and extremely specific predictions are made, often outlining events throughout a person's life. In the more modern forms of astrology, predictions take the form of outlining trends – good and bad periods – which the person can deal with as they see fit.

Direction

The term 'direction' refers to numerous different ways of moving the planets in the chart and judging their new positions in relation to their birth chart. Generally, the term is used to describe a method whereby a special measure is added to the position of all planets, related to a period of life. There are a number of forecasting methods that can be called directions.

❖❖ see PRIMARY DIRECTION p102

Primary direction

In general terms direction means any method of moving the planets and chart points forward so that predictions may be made. Usually the term is used to refer to primary directions. In this system a calculation of the four-minute intervals during which a given planet will move from its birth position to the place where it conjoins or aspects (makes an angular relationship to) a sensitive degree is made. As each four-minute arc represents

a year of life, it is assumed that in a given year there will be in force a directed aspect between these two bodies. Primary directions are based on the first motion, the Primum Mobile of Aristotle, the apparent nightly trek of the planets across the sky from east to west. This means that calculations are made in Right Ascension along the Equator, and that an error of four minutes in the actual birth moment makes a difference of one year in the timing of a prognosticated condition or event. Owing to difficulty in calculation they fell out of favour for many years.

❖❖ see DIRECTION p102

RIGHT: The direction method refers to the ways of moving the planets in a chart, as the planets move around the zodiacal system and change our fortunes

ABOVE: *A plan of a geocentric universe*

Converse Direction

The term 'direction' refers to various ways of moving the planets around the horoscope according to a certain key formula and then judging their new positions in relation to the natal chart. One of these methods of direction is the so-called secondary progressions, which use the daily motions of the planets to describe a whole year. Thus, the first day after birth describes the first year of life, the second day the second year and so on. Converse directions use the same formula but, instead of moving forward, the planets are progressed backwards through the zodiac.

❖ see DIRECTION p102

Progression

Progressions are based on the actual movements of the planets after birth, symbolically related to a time period or cycle of life. This method involves using the ephemeris for the year of birth and counting forward one day to represent a chosen time period. Usually a day is held to represent a year of life. In minor or tertiary progressions, one day can be held to represent a month or week of life. As the planets from Saturn and beyond move comparatively slowly, only the planets from Mars inwards are progressed. House cusps, including the ascendant and midheaven, may also be progressed.

❖ *see* SECONDARY PROGRESSION p104

Secondary progression

Secondary progressions are based on the formula of: one day = one year. In this system the astrologer casts a chart for the year in question by casting it for that many days after birth using the ephemeris of the year of birth. Secondary progressions are based on the actual motions of the planets along the ecliptic, on the assumption that the conditions encountered on the second day of life will be those which will govern the second year of life; hence an error of four minutes in the actual birth moment makes a difference of only one day in the timing of the prognosticated condition or event.

❖ *see* TERTIARY PROGRESSION p104

Tertiary progression, minor progression, lunar progression

Tertiary progressions are based on the lunar return cycle. Following the day of birth, each return of the Moon to its zodiacal position is equal to a year of life. One day in the ephemeris represents one lunar month of life. Usually a day is held to represent a year of life as in secondary progressions. In minor or tertiary progressions, one day can be held to represent a month or week of life. There are numerous variations on this theme. In one form of minor progressions a month in the ephemeris represents a year of life. This gives faster motion than with tertiary progressions but slower than the actual movement of the planets. With secondary progressions the outer planets

move too slowly to be considered. However, with minor or tertiary progressions additional trends from these planets may be considered. Whatever method is used a chart is cast and may be read as a stand-alone chart as well as in comparison to the birth chart.

❖ *see* DIRECTION p102

Transit

Transits are based upon the actual motions of the various planets. The transits in effect at any time are the actual positions the planets occupy, considered in relation to the places they occupied on a given date of birth. Apart from very detailed work only the planets lying outside the orbit of Mars are considered in transits. As there is no actual calculation involved – an astrologer simply looks up the positions of the planets for a given date and places them around the outside of the birth chart – this is the easiest and most popular prediction technique. Transits are considered to be more event-oriented than other forms of direction, such as secondary progressions. Particular attention is paid to the returns of the planets to their original positions and to the halfway points in their cycles. They are often used in conjunction with other techniques to provide more comprehensive information as, in this way, all of the planets in the chart may be moved and considered from their new vantage points.

❖ *see* PROGRESSION p103

Naibod

Naibod refers to a table of times for calculating an arc of direction. Named after Valentine Naibod (1510–93), a sixteenth-century professor of mathematics who wrote a number of books on astrology, Naibod tables are used to calculate primary directions, a form of forecasting. Primary directions are a calculation based on the number of four-minute intervals during which a given planet will move from its birth position to the place where it joins or aspects a sensitive degree. To use them, the right ascension (the distance measured along the celestial equator eastwards from the spring equinox) of the body concerned is calculated and subtracted from its longitude. This is then reduced to time, counting each degree as one year, five days and eight hours, and each minute to six days and four hours. Naibod tables save hours of tedious calculation when working with this predictive method. However, as primary directions such as these have fallen out of fashion, few people nowadays use the method. With better computer software, directions are gaining in popularity once more.

❖ see DIRECTION p102

Planetary return

 A return chart is constructed for when the transiting planet in question returns to the exact position it held in the birth chart. A chart is drawn up for then and examined as a chart in its own right as well as in comparison to the original birth chart. A return chart can be calculated for any of the planets, including the Sun and Moon. A solar return relates to the following year – the time it takes the Sun to move around the whole chart. A lunar return relates to one month, Mars return twenty-two months, Jupiter twelve years, Saturn return 29 and a half years. Because of retrograde motion, it takes a year for Mercury and Venus to travel around the chart. Each type of return chart refers to the issues relating to that planet. So a Venus return chart is primarily about relationships, as well as providing a picture for the following year. Only the solar and lunar return charts are commonly used except when a definite focus on an issue is needed.

❖ see VENUS p63

Profection

This is the moving of a chart point or planet at the rate of one sign per year (in the case of annual profection), 13 signs in 12 months (monthly profection) or one sign every two-and-a-half days or one sign a day (depending on method used). This was a common method in ancient

times and was used frequently by medieval astrologers, after which it fell out of favour. By the seventeenth century this ancient method of prediction had taken on the quality of a continuous rate of direction or progression. It has recently been revived.

❖ see PROGRESSION p103

Geodetic

The theory of geodetic equivalents was first put forward by the astrologer Sepharial (1864–1929). His work showed how to calculate charts for any place on Earth and how eclipses can trigger events at these locations. An eclipse falling on the meridian geodetic equivalent of any place is seen as highly significant. Geodetic equivalents is a house system structure into which you can place any chart. A geodetic chart has zero Aries rising if cast for zero degrees of latitude.

❖ see ECLIPSE p134

RIGHT: *Transits are placed around a birth chart*

MEASUREMENT AND TIME

Both astronomy and astrology make use of
different types and forms of measurement. In
astronomy, they help to work out the positions,
luminosity and distances between planets and
other space bodies. In astrology such
measurements serve an equally important
purpose, helping practitioners to correctly cast
and interpret an individual's horoscope. The
accurate measurement to find positions of

planets and chart points are all significant
indicators for interpretation and prediction.
Perhaps most important of all are
measurements of time. Whether applied to the
Earth or celestial objects, everything is defined
by time – orbits, relationships between celestial
bodies, and how an individual reacts to certain
life experiences. Understanding different time
zones, for example, is imperative in astrology.

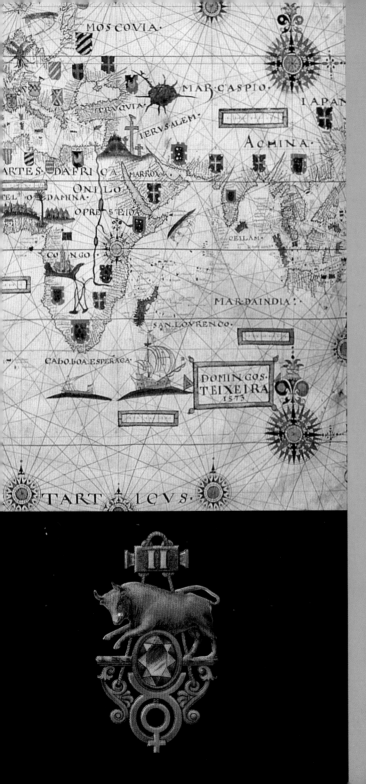

MEASUREMENT

ASTRONOMY MEASUREMENTS

Many measurements used in astronomy are drawn from geographical measurements, thus latitude, longitude, meridian and others have counterparts and applications within the celestial sphere. As well as these, astronomers make use of special measurements such as elongation or magnitude to gauge the distance, positions or brightness of bodies in space.

Latitude

Astronomical latitude is the angle between a line down from the plane of the Equator and that plane itself. It is measured in degrees north or south of the ecliptic. There are three types of celestial latitude. The one that parallels the horizon is called altitude; the one that parallels the Equator is called declination; and the one that parallels the ecliptic is called latitude. As the path of the Sun forms the ecliptic, the Sun can have no latitude. In geography it is the angular distance north or south of the Equator.

❖ see DECLINATION p110

Longitude

Geographical longitude is the distance of any point on the Earth's surface measured east or west of Greenwich. Celestial longitude is the distance between the first point of Aries and any celestial body, measured along the ecliptic. Geocentric longitude figured from the Earth as the centre is used by astrologers to express the zodiacal positions of the planets, but is rarely used by astronomers. The search for longitude originally began with navigation and it was a number of years before a reliable system was defined.

❖ see LATITUDE p108

ABOVE: *The Equator is the line of latitude which spans the centre of the planet*

RIGHT: *Tropic of Capricorn*

Equator

The Equator is the line of latitude that passes through the centre of a planet at the greatest distance from its rotational axis, splitting the planet into northern and southern hemispheres. The Equator is the longest line of latitude on Earth, the line where the Earth is widest in an east-west direction. It is 40,075.16 km (24,901.55 miles) long.

❖ see LATITUDE p108

Tropics of Cancer and Capricorn

The Tropic of Cancer and the Tropic of Capricorn each lie at 23.5 degrees latitude. The Tropic of Cancer is located at 23.5 degrees north of the Equator and the Tropic of Capricorn lies at 23.5 degrees south. They mark where the Sun is overhead at noon on the solstice around 21 June and on the Tropic of Capricorn around 21 December.

❖ see SOLSTICE p117

Meridian

Circle of longitude that passes through the south point of the horizon, through the zenith, to the north point of the horizon. It coincides with geographical longitude. Each point on Earth has its own meridian which passes through its zenith. The point in the heavens where the projection of this circle intersects the ecliptic marks the midheaven in the horoscope. The Sun is at the meridian at noon.

❖ see MIDHEAVEN p91

Obliquity

Obliquity is the angle between the plane of a planet's orbit and that of the planet's equator. The apparent path of the Sun – the ecliptic – intersects the celestial equator at an angle of 23 degrees. The inclination of the ecliptic to

the celestial equator is termed the obliquity of the ecliptic. The cause of the seasons is the obliquity of the Earth's rotational axis to its orbital plane. The hemisphere of the Earth that is tilted towards the Sun receives a greater flux of solar energy than the hemisphere tilted away, resulting in higher temperatures.

❖ see ECLIPTIC p134

Horizon

The circle around the Earth that separates the visible and invisible hemispheres or an extension of the plane of the observer. The astronomical horizon, called the rational horizon, is obtained by drawing a line from the Earth's centre parallel to the horizon. The terms 'visible' or 'physical' horizon describe the line that terminates our vision where the celestial bodies appear and disappear.

❖ see EARTH p63

Zenith

Highest point in the sky relative to a position on the Earth. The zenith lies directly opposite the nadir, the lowest point in the sky. Astronomically it is situated at the intersection of the meridian and the prime vertical circles.

❖ see MERIDIAN p109

Celestial Sphere

When viewed from the Earth, the sky resembles an inverted bowl and the stars and other bodies appear to be on the inside of a large sphere with the Earth at its centre. This large imaginary globe forms the celestial sphere. Within this, the Earth rotates on its axis from west to east, and to an observer on Earth the celestial sphere appears to move westwards. This apparent movement causes the Sun and other bodies to appear to rise east of the observer's meridian.

❖ see EARTH p63

Celestial Equator

The celestial equator is Earth's equator projected into space. Just as Earth's equator divides the sphere of the earth into two hemispheres the celestial equator divides the apparent sphere of the sky into a northern and southern celestial hemisphere.

❖ see EQUATOR p109

Celestial Latitude and Longitude

Celestial longitude is measured east or west along the ecliptic and celestial latitude north or south of the ecliptic. They are the equivalent of geographical latitude and longitude projected out into space. The celestial latitude lines represent the celestial coordinates known as

declination. The corresponding coordinate to longitude in the sky is called right ascension. Unlike longitude, which is measured in degrees and minutes, right ascension is usually measured in hours and minutes.

❖ see DECLINATION p110

Elevation

Elevation is equivalent to altitude, as it measures the distance of a planet or body above the horizon. Elevation of the pole is equivalent to latitude. If a planet has more latitude than another, it is said to be in elevation by latitude. If they have the same, the one with most declination is the most elevated. In astrology it refers to a planet close to the midheaven. It is one of the accidental dignities.

❖ see LATITUDE p108

Declination

Declination is the equivalent of latitude in the sky. It reports how far a star is from the celestial equator. To find the declination of a star, follow an hour circle straight down from the star to the celestial equator. The angle from the star to the celestial equator along the hour circle is the star's declination. It is the angular measurement of a celestial object north or south of the celestial equator.

❖ see LATITUDE p108

Right Ascension

One element of the astronomical coordinate system on the sky; this can be thought of as longitude on the Earth projected on to the sky. Right ascension is usually denoted by the lower-case Greek letter alpha (α) and is measured eastwards in hours, minutes and seconds of time from the vernal equinox. There are 24 hours of right ascension and the 24-hour line is taken as 0 hours. Right ascension may be expressed in degrees, in which case there are 360 degrees of right ascension to make a complete circuit of the sky.

❖ see LONGITUDE p108

RIGHT: *A fifteenth-century representation of the Celestial Sphere*

qui puirtutes ei pcepit ei ut fieret & factu est & quieno & man
dauit sup ipsu postea. xii. uirtutib; que eu uoluero de oriente inoc
cidentia desup & subter & de puyrio eas nenroch quonñ flant oms
in una parcem ad firmandu quod locutus est.

eium in circuitu

mb; que flant
vii. errantium.

o dum audisset ioancon a magistro suo q septem errancia nsõ firma
ta in celo dicit ioancon magist' meus uideo celum uoluens in mensura
irecta & cognoui æ ista sñ currencia nsõ firmata in celo ut cetere

LEFT: *A medieval astronomer puzzles over some measurement*

Coordinate

Celestial coordinates specify which direction something is in respect to the Earth, but not distance from it. For objects inside the Solar System (comets, planets, moons, asteroids) distance is often specified in Astronomical Units (AU). An AU is the average distance from the Earth to the Sun or 149,597,870 km (92,955,730 miles). Any of two measurements that determine position – for example, longitude and latitude – can be referred to as a coordinate. Coordinates used in astronomical measurement include declination, right ascension, celestial latitude and longitude and altitude. They are usually measured in degrees, although right ascension is often measured in units of time.

❖ see DECLINATION p110

Degree

The 360th part of a circle. The entire sky spans 360 degrees. Up to about 180 degrees of sky is visible from any given point on Earth with an unobstructed horizon. The degree is used to make measurements of distance or position.

❖ see CELESTIAL SPHERE p110

Arc

An arc is a portion of a curved line, such as a circle or ellipse, and is thus the orbital distance separating two bodies, or between two points. The diurnal arc is the arc that the Sun passes through from sunrise to sunset. The nocturnal arc is what remains after subtracting the diurnal from 360 degrees. The arc of direction is the distance between a significating planet and the point where it forms an aspect to a promittor.

❖ see SIGNIFICATOR p144

Azimuth

Measurement to help locate celestial objects. Azimuth is a measurement used to map the position of astronomical objects. It is the angle from the observer's north point projected on to the horizon. If an object is at due north its azimuth is 0 degrees. If it is due east its azimuth will be 90 degrees. By using altitude along with azimuth an object can be located in the sky.

❖ see ALTITUDE p112

Altitude

Altitude is a measurement in mapping astronomical objects on the celestial sphere (the sky as visible from Earth). It is the angle of the object from the observer's horizon, measured against the plane of the horizon. If an object is on the horizon, its altitude is 0 degrees. If it is at the observer's zenith (directly above), its altitude is 90 degrees. Altitude is used to locate objects in the sky.

❖ see CELESTIAL SPHERE p110

Prime Vertical

The prime vertical is the great circle that intersects the horizon at the east and west points, passing through the zenith at right angles to the meridian. All other vertical circles, which also pass through the zenith and nadir, do not pass through the east and west points of the horizon. The plane of the prime vertical corresponds to the points of the intersection of the horizon and Equator.

✧ see ZENITH p110

Elongation

Elongation is the angle between a planet (or moon or other object) and the Sun, as seen from the Earth. In standard ephemerides, this is usually denoted by the Greek letter epsilon (ε). A celestial object's (an object within the Solar System) phase angle is the elongation of the Earth from the Sun, as would be seen by an observer. It is, however, not a term in general use in astrology.

✧ see SUN p62

Hour Angle

The hour angle is the angle between the great circle that passes through the North and South Poles and bisects a specific point in the heavens. It is expressed in hours as indicating an interval of time before or after it passes over the meridian at the rate of 15 degrees an hour. If the vernal equinox is at the observer's local meridian and sidereal time is 0H, the hour angle is equivalent to local sidereal time.

✧ see SIDEREAL TIME p121

Magnitude

In astronomy, the measure of the brightness of a star or other celestial object. The stars catalogued by Ptolemy in the second century AD – all visible with the unaided eye – were ranked on a scale of brightness such that the brightest stars were of 1st magnitude and the dimmest

stars were of 6th magnitude. The modern magnitude scale was placed on a precise basis by N. R. Pogson in 1856. The modern magnitude scale permits a precise expression of a star's relative brightness and extends to both extremely bright and very dim objects. Thus, an object 2.512 times as bright as a 1st-magnitude star is of 0 magnitude; brighter objects have negative magnitudes. The Sun's magnitude, for example, is −26.8.

✧ see FIXED STARS p127

BELOW: *An early astronomer views bodies in space*

ASTROLOGY MEASUREMENTS

Measurement is as important in astrology as it is in astronomy. The positions of planets and chart points, the strength of the planets, and various cycles – celestial and seasonal – all play a part in correctly casting and intepreting the chart.

Logarithms

Logarithms are proportional parts of a quadrant, expressed in numbers, whereby calculations of the planets' places at a given time can be made by addition and subtraction instead of by multiplication and division. They were invented by John Napier (1550–1617) in 1614 to help in his astrological calculations. Until the advent of computers astrologers commonly used logarithms to help in chart calculation. Many continue to do so, although they are nowadays not commonly used in schools.

❖❖ see TABLES OF HOUSES p114

Absolute Longitude

Term used to describe the position of a planet or chart point in the horoscope. Usually positions are given as degrees of a sign, for example, seven degrees of Gemini. Absolute longitude expresses this as part of the horoscope circle and, as Gemini begins at 60 degrees, in this case would be 67 degrees. It is sometimes necessary to convert to absolute longitude.

❖❖ see LONGITUDE p108

Tables of Houses

Sets of tables that show the degrees of the signs which occupy the cusps of the houses in different latitudes for every degree of right ascension, or for every four minutes of sidereal time. Each different house system requires a different set of tables, although the ascendant and midheaven remain consistent whatever system is used.

Astrologers use them when calculating charts and, as the most readily available for a number of years were Placidus tables, this tended to be the most used system. As most astrologers now use computers there is more variance in house systems used.

❖❖ see PLACIDUS HOUSE SYSTEM p82

Culmination

Positional measurement. A celestial body culminates when it meets the upper meridian. In astrology the term describes when a planet arrives at the midheaven, or the cusp of the tenth house, by direction, progression or transit. It is sometimes used as a term to indicate the completion of an aspect – the arrival of a planet at an exact degree. 'Culminator' is a term used to describe a planet that reaches such a critical position.

❖❖ see TENTH HOUSE p88

Solar Arc

The angular distance between the Sun in the birth chart and the Sun moved by secondary progression. This value is used for a method of direction called solar arc directions. A solar arc direction is when the Sun is first progressed as in a secondary progression – that is, one day after birth is equivalent to one year of life. The position of the Sun in the birth chart is subtracted from this position. This figure, called the solar arc, is then added to all the bodies and chart points to give new positions that are then used for prediction.

❖❖ see SUN p62

Detriment

The detriment of a planet is in the sign that is opposite to the one that it rules. Being in detriment weakens a planet and is considered a debility. A person represented by a planet in detriment may feel outclassed or obliged to work. A planet in detriment may also indicate loss or difficulty. The planet generally functions at a disadvantage. It cannot operate at full strength and may indicate a need to adhere to rules. Describing a planet as being in detriment is not a moral judgement of the value of the planet, or the individual whose chart it is, but is rather an aid to balancing the differing factors of the horoscope. The Sun is in detriment in Aquarius, the Moon in Capricorn, Mercury in Sagittarius and Pisces (Jupiter-ruled signs), Venus in Aries and Scorpio (Mars-ruled signs), Mars in Taurus and Libra (Venus-ruled signs), Jupiter in Gemini and Virgo (Mercury-ruled signs) and Saturn in Cancer and Leo (Moon-ruled signs).

❖ see DEBILITY p116

Almuten

Meaning 'the strong holder', the almuten of any degree of the zodiac is the planet having most essential dignity at that degree. Some degrees may have more than one almuten (i.e. if two planets are equally dignified in that degree, they are both almuten). Because signs may have both day and night rulers, almutens may vary for the same degree of the zodiac, depending on whether it is a day or night chart. The chart itself can have an almuten, which is often referred to as Lord of Chart. It is this meaning that is generally used today.

❖ see DIGNITY p115

Dignity

There are two kinds of dignity – essential and accidental. Essential dignity refers to a planet being in a degree of the zodiac where it is in a strengthened position. The essential dignities are those of rulership, exaltation, triplicity, term and face. A planet in its rulership is completely comfortable there, as if it were at home and can set its own agenda. A planet in its exaltation is like a welcomed guest - things are done for them. In its triplicity it is comfortable as a neighbour popping round for coffee would be and is considered fortunate. In its term it is an acquaintance invited indoors and in its face it is accepted. The precise zodiac degrees where planets are in dignity can vary depending on the system used. An accidental dignity occurs when a planet is placed in the first, fourth, seventh, tenth or eleventh house, is moving quickly or is within seventeen minutes

RIGHT: *Mars is in its detriment when in Taurus, the Bull*

of the Sun's position (cazimi). Other positions can also give accidental dignity. A planet may have essential or accidental dignity, both or neither. The more dignity a planet has, the stronger it is, and essential dignity is always stronger than accidental dignity. The opposite to dignity is debility.

❖ see DEBILITY p116

Azimene

A planet is said to be azimene when it is placed in certain weak or lame degrees which, if rising at birth, is said to make the subject blind, lame or otherwise physically afflicted. If the ruler of the chart or the Moon falls in one of these degrees it is said to have a similar effect. The degrees are 0 Aries, 6–10 Taurus, 0 Gemini, 9–15 Cancer, 18, 27, 28 Leo, 0 Virgo, 0 Libra, 19, 28 Scorpio, 1, 7, 8, 18, 19 Sagittarius, 2–29 Capricorn, 18, 19 Aquarius and 0 Pisces. This traditional judgement of planetary strength has now fallen out of popular use.

❖ see MOON p63

Debility

Measure of planet's strength. A planet is said to be debilitated when it appears in certain signs and houses which are considered to be incompatible with the energy or characteristics of the planet. It is weakened by an adverse aspect, being in the sign of its detriment or fall, or by being in a cadent (third, sixth, ninth, twelfth) house. Being retrograde is also a debility. Often the term is simply used to refer to a planet in the sign opposite that of its rulership (detriment) or exaltation (fall). The Sun is in detriment in Aquarius, fall in Libra; the Moon is in detriment in Capricorn, fall in Scorpio; Mercury is in detriment in Sagittarius and Pisces, fall in Pisces; Venus is in detriment in Aries and Scorpio, fall in Virgo; Mars is in detriment in Taurus and Libra, fall in Cance; Jupiter is in detriment in Gemini and Virgo, fall in Capricorn; Saturn is in detriment in Cancer and Leo, fall in Aries. The outer planets – Uranus, Neptune and Pluto – are not part of this traditional system and therefore cannot be said to be debilitated.

❖ see DETRIMENT p115

ABOVE: *The Sun, whose position in relation to the celestial equator determines the two annual equinoxes*

Solstice

In the northern hemisphere the summer solstice is the longest day of the year when the Sun is furthest north. The winter solstice is the shortest day of the year. In the southern hemisphere, winter and summer solstices are reversed. The summer solstice marks the first day of summer. At the time of the solstices (around 21 June and 21 December) the maximum and minimum periods of daylight are experienced. The Sun is above the horizon for different lengths of time at different seasons. At the June solstice in the north the direct rays produce about three times as much heat as at the December solstice.

❖ see EQUINOX p117

Equinox

Although it originally referred to the time of year when night and day are of equal length, the modern definition is when the Sun's centre crosses declination 0. Day and night are not quite the same length on the equinoxes. The vernal or spring equinox (near 21 March) occurs when the Sun crosses the celestial equator moving northwards. It was originally in Aries. It now occurs when the Sun is in Pisces. In astrology it is still counted as when the Sun enters Aries. The autumn equinox (near 23 September) occurs when the Sun crosses the celestial equator, moving southwards. Astrologically this is when the Sun enters Libra.

❖ see SOLSTICE p117

Long Ascension

Signs of long ascension take longer to ascend than others. Cancer, Leo, Virgo, Libra, Scorpio and Sagittarius are the signs of long ascension in the northern hemisphere. Long and short ascension are reversed in the southern hemisphere. It was previously accepted that major aspects occurring in signs of long ascension were stretched to the next largest major aspect, and that those in signs of short ascension were shrunken to the next smallest major aspect.

❖ see SHORT ASCENSION p117

Short Ascension

Speed that a sign rises. Some signs rise more quickly than others. The signs of short ascension – Capricorn, Aquarius, Pisces, Aries, Taurus and Gemini – are often found intercepted in horoscopes; in other words the cusp of the third house may be in Cancer and the fourth in Virgo. That would mean that the sign Leo was intercepted. In the southern hemisphere, long and short ascension are reversed and the signs of long ascension become the signs of short ascension. In horary astrology if the ascendant is less than three degrees, especially in a sign of short ascension, the chart is not fit to be judged. In the past aspects occurring in signs of short ascension were shrunken to the next smaller major aspect. For example, a square between a planet in Capricorn and a planet in Aries might act more like a sextile.

❖ see LONG ASCENSION p117

Metonic Cycle

The metonic cycle is named after the Greek astronomer Meton, who, in about 432 BC, discovered the Moon's 19-year period, at the end of which the new Moon occurred on the same day of the year. Based on this information, Meton corrected the lunar calendar. His calculations were two hours off the correct figure. The period had been discovered in Babylon 50 years previously, so it seems likely that he learned of it through Babylonian sources. Four metonic cycles are known as a callipic cycle, named after Callipus, who proposed it as an improvement.

❖ see CYCLE p131

Swift in Motion

A planet is said to be swift in motion when its travel in a 24-hour period exceeds its mean motion. The average daily motions of the planets are: Moon 13 degrees 10 minutes 36 seconds, Sun 0 59 08, Mercury and Venus 0 59 08 (same as the Sun), Mars 0 31 27, Jupiter 0 4 59, Saturn 0 2 1.

❖ see MOON p63

TIME MEASUREMENTS

There are two methods of time-keeping based on the rotation of the Earth. Solar time is kept with reference to the Sun and sidereal time with reference to the stars. The time required by the Sun to pass over the meridian twice is known as an apparent solar day, but as this varies with the time of year, the mean solar day is used as the average day. Time is usually now expressed in the 24-hour clock format.

Calendar

The roots of our modern civil calendar lie in ancient Rome. The original Roman calendar started on 1 March and consisted of 10 months totalling 304 days, numbering the years from the foundation of Rome. Later, the months of January and February were introduced and the year increased to 354 or 355 days. After some years, however, it was noted that the calendar year was out of sync with the solar year and an extra month was introduced in some years. In 45 BC Julius Caesar reformed the calendar, approximating the year at 365.25 days, achieved by having a leap year every four years. The Roman year now began at 1 January. There were still problems, however, and to resolve such errors the calendar was reformed again by Pope Gregory XIII in 1582. Catholic states adopted the new Gregorian calendar immediately but Protestant states took longer. In 1752 the English civil calendar was reformed; the start of the English legal year was moved from 25 March to 1 January, adopting the civil year observed in other countries.

LEFT: Pope Gregory XIII made changes to the calendar in 1582

❖ see YEAR p119

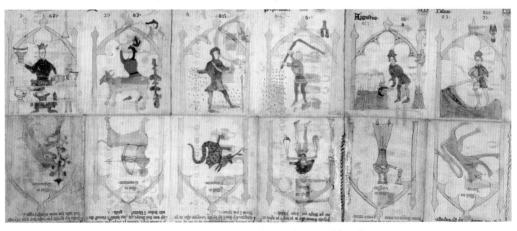

ABOVE: *A thirteenth-century calendar showing the months July to December, including signs of the zodiac*

Year

The solar, or tropical, year is a period of time in which the Earth performs a revolution in its orbit around the Sun. The sidereal year is the time in which the Sun's centre, passing eastwards from the ecliptic meridian of a star, returns to the same point.

❖ see DAY p119

Day

What is normally referred to as a day is the period of light between sunrise and sunset, the period of daylight or sunshine. The interval of time between two successive passages of a star over the meridian is a sidereal day. A lunar day is the day of the full Moon.

❖ see SIDEREAL TIME p121

Minute

The sixtieth part of one hour or degree. The Babylonians performed astronomical calculation in the sexagesimal (base 60) system. This was convenient for simplifying time division, since 60 is divisible by 2, 3, 4, 5, 6 and 10. A minute derives from the first fractional sexagesimal place.

❖ see SECOND p119

Second

The sixtieth part of one minute, derived from Babylonian mathematics. One second is the time that elapses during 9,192,631,770 cycles of the radiation produced by the transition between two levels of the caesium 133 atom.

❖ see MINUTE p119

Leap Year

Leap years occur every four years, except years ending in 00, unless that year is divisible by 400. Leap day (29 February) only occurs during a leap year. The Julian calendar assumed that the year had 365 1/4 days, with a 366-day leap year added every fourth year. The accumulated error of one day every 128 years led to the use of the Gregorian calendar.

❖ see CALENDAR p118

Greenwich Mean Time

The times of various events, particularly astronomical and weather phenomena, are often given in Universal Time (UT), often referred to as Greenwich Mean Time (GMT). The two terms are often used to refer to time kept on the Greenwich meridian (longitude zero). It is the basis for the worldwide system of civil times, and times that vary from Greenwich Mean Time are expressed plus or minus a specific number of hours. It was adopted in 1884 at the International Meridian Conference as the single meridian to replace the numerous ones then in existence. It is civil time in the UK in winter.

❖ see SUMMER TIME p119

Summer Time

Summer Time was first defined in an Act of 1916, which ordained that for a certain period during the year legal time should be one hour in advance of Greenwich Mean Time. The Summer Time Acts of 1922 to 1925 extended the period during which Summer Time was in force and, from 1916 to World War II, clocks were put in advance of GMT by one hour from the spring to the autumn. During the war, double summer time was introduced and was used when normally ordinary Summer Time would have been kept. During the winter clocks were kept one hour in advance of GMT. In 1968 clocks were advanced one hour ahead of GMT on 18 February and remained so until British Standard Time.

❖ see GREENWICH MEAN TIME p119

Standard Time

Originally time was a local matter, based on true noon, when the Sun was at its highest point in the sky for that particular location. With the coming of railways it became necessary to establish a consistent time system. Standard time-zone meridians were spaced at 15-degree intervals of longitude east and west of Greenwich in the UK, and all clocks in each zone were adjusted to the mean solar time of the midpoint of the zone. Although standard time was legally adopted on 18 November 1883, it was not in common use in many areas for a number of years.

❖ see TIME DIFFERENCES p120

Local Mean Time

Before time was standardized different times would be kept in different places. For general use time would be adjusted to an average for a certain area giving local mean time. The Earth rotates once every 24 hours, and so places to the east start their day sooner than places to the west. Until late into the eighteenth century watches and clocks were mostly for the rich, and their inaccuracy made the difference between clock and sundial less obvious. From 1792, in England, it became normal to use local mean time, rather than apparent time from a sundial. Whilst travel and communications were slow, these local time differences were of little importance, and most towns and cities in Britain used local time. But as transport and communications improved, accurate time became more essential. By the

1840s there were at least three organizations that suffered inconveniences because of the use of local times - the railways, the telegraph companies, and the Post Office. Standard time was introduced throughout the end of the nineteenth century and local mean time began to disappear, although for many years towns would observe both local and standard time.

❖ see STANDARD TIME p120

Time Differences

The primary reason for time differences at different locations is the adoption of time zones. In order to create consistency within a given area, time zones are 15 degrees apart and use the mean solar time of the midpoint of the zone. The international date line at 180 degrees longitude is the point at which, by convention, the date changes. It is a day later to the west of the line than east. Most countries also operate a summer-time system, where the clocks are moved forward in the spring and back again to standard time in the autumn, usually by one hour, although this may vary. The dates on which this is done also vary from country to country and from year to year. Prior to the establishment of the railway network, local mean time was kept in most areas. Although standard time was introduced in the late nineteenth century, for some years many places would use two different time systems, the local time and railway time.

❖ see TIME ZONES 120

Time Zones

Originally time was a local matter, based on true noon, when the Sun was at its highest point in the sky for that particular location. With the coming of railways it was necessary to establish a consistent time system. Standard time zone meridians were spaced at 15-degree intervals of longitude east and west of Greenwich and all clocks in each zone were adjusted to the mean solar time of the midpoint of the zone. The present system employs 24 standard meridians of longitude (lines running from the

ABOVE: *The Royal Observatory at Greenwich, from which time zones are measured, with the park in the foreground and ships on the Thames to the left*

North Pole to the South, at right angles to the Equator) 15 degrees apart, starting with the prime meridian through Greenwich. These meridians are theoretically the centres of 24 standard time zones. Time is the same throughout each zone and differs from the international basis of legal and scientific time, Greenwich Mean Time, by an integral number of hours; minutes and seconds are the same. In practice, the zones have in many cases been subdivided or altered in shape for the convenience of inhabitants.

see GREENWICH MEAN TIME p119

Sidereal Time

Sidereal time is time measured relative to the stars (the period between successive conjunctions with any star). One sidereal day – 23 hours and 56 minutes – is the period during which the Earth completes one rotation on its axis (this is the same as the time it takes to come into alignment with a particular star). Because the stars are so distant from us, the motion of the Earth in its orbit makes a negligible difference in the direction to the stars; hence, the Earth rotates 360 degrees in one sidereal day. Sidereal time may be considered the same as right ascension when seeking to align star maps to the sky. The right ascension that you find

at your zenith is the current sidereal time. Astrological tables are published using sidereal time and a conversion is necessary to give clock time in order to cast the horoscope.

see LONG ASCENSION p117

Tropical Year

The solar, or tropical, year is a period of time in which the Earth performs a revolution in its orbit around the Sun, or passes from any point of the ecliptic to the same point again. It is 365 days, 5 hours, 48 minutes and 46 seconds in length. It is about 20 minutes shorter than the sidereal year. The tropical year is what is generally meant by the term 'year'.

see SIDEREAL TIME p121

Vernal Equinox

The vernal equinox (Latin for 'equal night of spring') occurs when the Sun moves to 0 degrees Aries in March. At this point day and night are of equal length, hence the name. Seen from northern latitudes, the Sun will now be above the equatorial plane, until it moves into Libra in September, at which point the autumnal equinox occurs.

see EQUINOX p117

UNDERSTANDING ASTROLOGY

Like any specialist field, astrology and
astronomy have many specialist terms – a
language of their own. Although seen today as
two distinct disciplines, there is at times
significant crossover in the terminology used.
Sometimes expressions can mean the same
thing and simply apply to both astrology and

are accepted between the two. This section
defines and interprets some of the expressions
used earlier in the book, relating to all aspects
of astrology, from charts to signs, aspects to
planets, the positions and movement of celestial
bodies, as well as some of the tools used by
astronomers to observe and understand the
universe in which we live.

ASTRONOMY TERMS

Today astronomy is divided into two main branches: astrometry and astrophysics; the former is concerned with determining the places of the investigation of the heavenly bodies, the latter with the investigation of their chemical and physical nature. In antiquity, astronomy revolved around attempts to fix the apparent positions of the objects on the sphere and for many centuries the terms astrology and astronomy were interchangeable. Many of the terms used in astronomy are also interchangeable.

Universe

The total sum of all that exists; the physical system that encompasses all known space, matter and energy, existing now, having existed in the past or postulated to exist in the future. There cannot be more than one Universe. Most physicists and astronomers refer to the known universe as the Universe. The Universe is infinite. The observable portion which is within the grasp of our senses with the aid of technology is infinitesimal.

❖ see GALAXY p124

Galaxy

A galaxy is a star cluster, or group of stars, dust and gas, held together by the gravitational attraction between its components. The Sun and its system are contained within the Milky Way galaxy, which moves around a gravitational hub called the galactic centre. From long-exposure images made with large ground-based and space telescopes, we know today that the Milky Way is similar to countless other galaxies and we now recognize that galaxies are the major structural units of the Universe. Our galaxy was originally called the Milky Way because it was believed to have been formed from a luminous celestial fluid. Galaxies are usually classified as elliptical, spiral or irregular in shape. Only three galaxies outside the Milky Way can be seen from Earth.

❖ see SOLAR SYSTEM p125

Constellation

Astronomers officially recognize 88 constellations covering the entire sky in the northern and southern hemispheres. Our modern constellation system is derived from that of the ancient Greeks. The oldest description of the constellations as we know them comes from a poem called *Phaenomena*,

LEFT: *A spiral galaxy*

written in about 270 BC by the Greek poet Aratus. It seems likely the Greek constellations originated with the Sumerians and Babylonians of ancient Mesopotamia. In AD 150 Ptolemy published *The Almagest*, which contained a summary of Greek astronomical knowledge, including a catalogue of 1,022 stars, together with estimates of their brightness, arranged into 48 constellations. Over the years astronomers have added constellations in the gaps between Ptolemy's figures and mapped the uncharted regions of the sky near the South Celestial Pole.

❖ see GALAXY p124

Solar System

The Solar System is the planetary system that contains the Sun, the nine planets, about 90 satellites of the planets, comets and asteroids. The Sun is the focal point and the planets orbit the Sun. The planets move in regular orbits and each has a pull of gravity which varies according to its mass and size. The planets can be divided into two groups: the terrestrial planets include Mercury, Venus, Earth and Mars; these are rocky and Earth-like, rotate more slowly than the gas giants and are closer to the Sun. The gas giants are Jupiter, Saturn, Uranus and Neptune. These are large and composed of gaseous elements. Pluto has recently been reclassified as a planetoid. The orbits of the planets are ellipses with the Sun at one focus, although the orbits of Mercury and Pluto are almost circular. The orbits of the planets are all more or less in the same plane.

❖ see UNIVERSE p124

Asteroid

Also called 'planetoid' or 'minor planet' if of a larger size. More than 10,000 asteroids have orbits sufficiently well known to have been catalogued and named, but thousands

BELOW: *The ceiling from the* **Sala del Mappamondo** *fresco by G de Vecchi and da Reggio, showing the constellations*

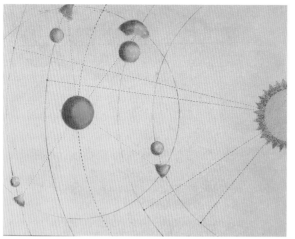

the modern picture of comets as essentially very old Solar System objects made of primordial ice and dust, generally in unstable orbits. Ideas about the true nature of comets are available from the time of the rise of Hellenistic natural philosophy in about 550 BC, when the Pythagoreans considered comets to be kinds of planets that were seen infrequently and mostly near the horizon in the morning or evening sky. For centuries they were believed to portend evil.

see ASTEROID p125

more exist. Most asteroids are irregularly shaped, unlike the spherically shaped major planets. The largest known asteroid, Ceres, has a diameter of 1,000 km (630 miles); the three next largest are Pallas, Vesta and Juno. Only Vesta can be seen with the naked eye. The orbits of most asteroids lie partially between the orbits of Mars and Jupiter. Asteroids with orbits in the outer Solar System are known as Centaurs. The origin of asteroids is unclear; one theory states that they were formed from material that could not condense into a single planet because of perturbation effects involving Jupiter. Some asteroids are actually nuclei of comets that are no longer active. The four main asteroids are used for interpretation by some modern astrologers.

see PLANETOID p126

Comet

The word 'comet' comes from the Greek *komete*, meaning 'the hairy one'. Before 1600, comets were essentially considered to be heavenly omens and were not established as astronomical phenomena. Then followed two centuries of mostly positional measurements with emphasis on the motions and the orbits, until the early nineteenth century, when the era of cometary physics was inaugurated. The next major step occurred in 1950 with the sudden emergence of

Planetoid

Celestial body generally used in reference to larger asteroids; also known as minor planets. Planetoids are made up of much of the same material as planets, but they are smaller. In astrology the most commonly used planetoid is Chiron, although there are differences of opinion over the actual classification of this body (some claim it is a comet or an asteroid). It was first sighted in 1977 on its path between Saturn and Uranus. A new planetoid was discovered in October 2000. Officially named 2000 EB173, this measures about 640 km (400 miles) in diameter or about one quarter the size of Pluto. Because of its small size, the new planet is known as a Plutino, meaning 'Little Pluto'. In the year 2000 there was much controversy about the classification of Pluto; many astronomers believe that it should be reclassified as a planetoid.

see ASTEROID p125

Satellite

Apart from Mercury and Venus, all planets have satellites, termed moons. The Moon is a satellite of Earth and both may be seen as satellites of the Sun. Minor satellites are small chunks of rock in orbit around planets, as compared with large satellites like the Earth's Moon.

see SOLAR SYSTEM p125

Fixed Stars

The fixed stars were so called to distinguish them from the planets, or wanderers. Fixed stars are those that appear to be stationary relative to the Earth, although they do advance at the rate of less than one minute a year, moving one degree in 72 years. They do not move across the ecliptic as the planets do. Those near the ecliptic and of significant magnitude have considerable influence. Fixed stars do not lie within the zodiac; they are all beyond it in the constellations, whereas planets move within the zodiac. Fixed stars have an influence when making a major aspect to a planet or significant point in the chart. They are particularly important when near the ascendant or angles, or when near the Sun or Moon. Because they move so slowly they have to be within one degree of an aspect of a chart point or body to have a relationship with it. Many astrologers only use fixed stars when in conjunction with the body or point being considered.

❖ see ALDEBARAN p158

Antares

Fixed star. Antares presently lies at almost 10 degrees of Sagittarius and is a binary star, fiery red and emerald green. Antares was originally in Scorpio and it is strongly associated with this sign, often seen as a destructive influence. Antares is one of the four key stars in the heavens, also called archangel stars.

❖ see FIXED STARS p127

ABOVE: *Morehouse's Comet, photographed from Greenwich in 1908*

Regulus

Regulus was one of the four stars of the ancient Persian monarchy when, as watcher of the north, it marked the summer solstice. It was seen as one of the four guardians of heaven, one who regulated all things in the heavens. It is now at the end of the twenty-ninth degree of Leo.

❖❖ see FIXED STARS p127

Alcocoden

Planet that determines length of life. Meaning 'the giver of years', this term refers to the planet that reveals the length of time a person is going to live. It was used extensively in medieval astrology. It is usually the almuten (the planet that holds most dignity) of the degree of the hyleg (the planet used to determine life length). It is rarely used in modern astrology, as present-day astrologers are less keen to predict the date of death.

❖❖ see REGULUS p128

BELOW: *The fixed stars, which appear to be stationary from the Earth, but which in fact advance, albeit extremely slowly*

Caput Algol

Fixed star used by astrologers. Also called simply Algol, this is a malefic fixed star representing the Gorgon, whose hair consisted of hissing snakes and who was decapitated by Perseus, which is analogous to losing one's head in a matter. It has been classed as an evil star in many cultures. Algol is now at about 26 degrees Taurus.

❖❖ see MALEFIC p143

Circumpolar

Type of star. Circumpolar literally means 'to circle around the pole' and circumpolar stars are those of the north circumpolar region, at the North Pole. They are those that circle overhead all night, without setting or dipping below the horizon. They move in an anticlockwise direction. They include Ursa Major and Minor, Cassiopeia, Cepheus and Draco constellations. Most stars are further away from Polaris, and fall below the horizon. These appear to rise in the east and set in the west.

❖❖ see CONSTELLATION p124

New Moon

The new Moon is the phase of the Moon when it is not visible from Earth, because the side of the Moon that is facing us is not being lit by the Sun. This means that the Sun, Earth, and Moon are almost in a straight line, with the Moon between the Sun and the Earth. At the time of the new Moon, the Moon rises at about the same time as the Sun, and it sets at about the same time as the Sun. In astrology a new Moon heralds a time for new beginnings, as it adds a new infusion of potential. It opens fresh new possibilities and is the perfect time to write down what you want to manifest in your life, to set goals and start new projects.

❖❖ see FULL MOON p129

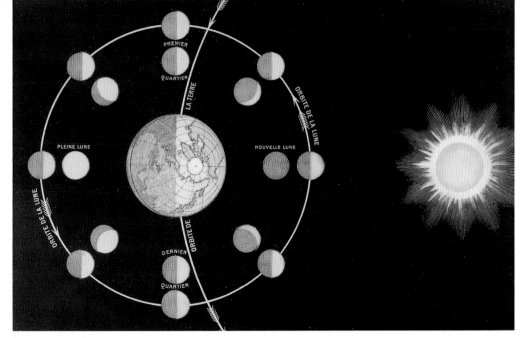

ABOVE: *The phases of the Moon. The complete cycle from one new Moon to the next is referred to as a synodic period*

Crescent Moon

The Moon forms a crescent shape twice in its cycle. The waxing crescent Moon can be seen after the new Moon. It will grow larger until it looks like the first quarter Moon. The waning crescent Moon can be seen after the last quarter Moon. It will grow smaller every day, until it looks like the new Moon.

❖ see FULL MOON p129

Gibbous Moon

One of the phases of the Moon. The waxing gibbous Moon can be seen after the first quarter Moon and before the full Moon. It grows larger each day. The waning gibbous Moon can be seen after the full Moon, but before the last quarter Moon and grows smaller each day.

❖ see MOON p63

Full Moon

The Moon is full when its lighted side faces the Earth. This means that the Earth, Sun and Moon are nearly in a straight line, with the Earth in the middle. The Moon that

we see is very bright from the sunlight reflecting off it. In astrology the full Moon represents a pinnacle point, taking things to extremes. It was commonly believed that during the full Moon people could act in an unpredictable manner, giving birth to the word 'lunacy'. The flow of blood is believed to increase around the time of a full Moon, so traditionally this is a bad time to undergo surgery. The two-and-a-half week period after the full Moon is the best time to consolidate, organize and complete that which you began earlier.

❖ see MOON p63

Waxing Moon

A waxing crescent can be seen after the new Moon, but before the first quarter Moon. The crescent will grow larger and larger every day, until the Moon looks like the first quarter Moon. The waxing gibbous Moon can be seen after the first quarter Moon, but before the full Moon. Waxing means increasing. In astrology the waxing Moon shows a time for action and growth.

❖ see WANING MOON p130

Waning Moon

A waning Moon is one that is decreasing in size from the perspective of someone on Earth. The waning gibbous Moon can be seen after the full Moon, but before the last quarter Moon. The amount of the Moon that we can see will grow smaller and smaller every day. The waning crescent Moon can be seen after the last quarter Moon and before the new Moon. The crescent will grow smaller and smaller every day, until the Moon looks like the new Moon. In astrology a waning Moon is a time to break negative habit patterns.

❖ see WAXING MOON p129

Motion

Planetary movements. The term 'motion' literally means 'movement'. In astrology, it refers to the movements of the planets through the zodiac, which are the foundation of any astrological method of prediction. Until the sixteenth century, the planets were thought to move around the Earth. Trying to improve Ptolemy's planetary system, Copernicus discovered the Earth's movement around the Sun. His assistant Kepler revolutionized astronomy by introducing the heliocentric system in his Three Laws of Planetary Motion.

❖ see JOHANNES KEPLER p16

Apparent Motion

Motion viewed from the Earth and relative to the Earth as if it were stationary. It is traditional to speak of motions in terms of how they appear, rather than what they actually are. The rotation of the Earth makes the planets appear to travel in a westerly direction, although they move in the opposite direction.

❖ see MOTION p130

BELOW: *The waning Moon over a mountainous landscape*

Proper Motion

Term used to describe the motion of any body in space, compared to apparent motion which results from the rotation of the Earth. Proper motion is loosely applied to the direct motion of a planet through the zodiac signs in distinction to the diurnal rising and setting caused by the Earth's rotation. A distinction between apparent and actual motion of a celestial body.

❖ see APPARENT MOTION p130

Cycle

The Universe has many cycles. The Milky Way turns like a wheel and all the stars within it revolve around its centre. The Solar System moves within this galaxy. The Sun spins on its axis once every 24 days and 16 hours. The planets turn on their axes and orbit the Sun. Moons orbit their planets. Astrologers are most interested in the cycles of the planets as they orbit the Sun. They each take a differing amount of time to complete an orbit, and the length of this, as well as its halfway and quarter points, are astrologically significant. For example, the Sun returns to its place in the birth chart approximately one year later, an occasion we celebrate on our birthday. The time at which a planet returns to its original place in the birth chart is referred to as a 'return' and charts are cast for these times.

❖ see ORBIT p131

Synodic Period

The synodic period is a cycle from new Moon to new Moon, lasting 29 days, 12 hours and 44 minutes. The Moon spends two-and-a-half days travelling through each astrological sign. In astronomy the term 'synodic period' refers to the length of time during which a body in the Solar System makes one orbit of the Sun relative to the Earth. Because the Earth moves in its own orbit, the synodic period differs from the sidereal period, which is measured relative to the stars. The synodic period of the Moon is called the lunar month, or lunation.

❖ see WAXING MOON p129

Precession

Movement of equinoctial points. The precession of the equinoxes is the westward motion of the equinoxes along the ecliptic. Precession is caused by the slow movement of the Earth's axis that results in the celestial poles and equator appearing to move against the background of the stars. The equinoctial points move west at a rate of about 50 seconds a year, and in 25,800 years the Earth completes one precessional cycle. The Sun crosses the Equator about 20 minutes earlier each year and 50 seconds of arc further west. This moving zodiac is known as the tropical zodiac. Because of precession there is now a discrepancy between the positions described by astrology and the actual astronomical positions in the zodiac belt; at present this is about 23 degrees. One of the foremost arguments against astrology is that its practitioners do not take note of precession in calculating charts. However, the tropical zodiac is directly related to the Sun's path and the seasons.

❖ see EQUINOX p117

Orbit

A regular, repeating path that an object in space takes around another. An object in an orbit is called a satellite. A satellite can be natural, like the Moon, or man-made. In our Solar System the Earth orbits the Sun, as do the other eight planets. They all travel on or near the orbital plane, an imaginary disc-shaped surface in space. All the orbits are circular or elliptical. In addition to the planets' orbits, many planets have moons in orbit around them. Orbits are the result of a perfect balance between the forward motion of a body in space, such as a planet or moon, and the pull of gravity on it from another body in space, such as a large planet or star. Comets are in an irregular orbit around the Sun. Most asteroids in our Solar System are orbiting the Sun in a band between Mars and Jupiter. Even our Sun is travelling around the centre of the Milky Way galaxy.

❖ see MOTION p130

ABOVE: *Halley's comet is in an irregular orbit around the Sun*

opposite of perihelion. The distance of the planets from the Sun can vary widely. For example, Mercury can be between 46 and 70 million km away from the Sun at its perihelion and aphelion respectively.

The aphelion of the Earth occurs about 4 July each year. At this point it is moving at its slowest.

❖❖ see PERIHELION p132

Perihelion

The point in its orbit where a planet is closest to the Sun; opposite of aphelion. The distance of the planets from the Sun can vary widely. Perihelion occurs around 4 January. Planets move more quickly at perihelion than they do at aphelion.

❖❖ see APHELION p132

Apogee

Apogee refers to a point in the Moon's orbit when it is at its furthest point from the Earth; the opposite to perigee. In astrology the apogee marks the point of the black Moon, or Lilith – a hypothetical body used in chart interpretation. The variety of calculation methods can lead to very different results.

❖❖ see PERIGEE p132

Perigee

Perigee refers to a point in the Moon's orbit when it is at its closest to the Earth. The combined effects of orbital eccentricity and the Sun's tides result in a substantial difference in the apparent size, with the Moon looking much brighter at perigee.

❖❖ see APOGEE p132

Aphelion

In a non-circular orbit around the Sun, the aphelion is the point at which a planet is furthest from the Sun; the

Ingress

Meaning 'to disappear behind', in astronomy ingress means that a body has just passed behind a second body or its shadow. In astrology, an ingress is when any planet enters a new sign and is 00 degrees 00 minutes of that sign. For example, when Venus enters Virgo, Venus is at the ingress of Virgo and therefore 00 Virgo 00. Ingresses are used extensively in Sun-sign astrology.

❖❖ see EGRESS p132

Egress

From the Latin *egressus* (from egredi 'to go out'), in astronomy egress means to exit from behind a second body or its shadow. Both ingress and egress are used to describe the times when, for example, the Moon enters and leaves the Earth's shadow during a lunar eclipse. Astronomically, this is the point at which a body leaves a constellation. In astrology, the term is used slightly

RIGHT: *Mercury's aphelion is 70 million km from the Sun*

differently, referring to the point at which a planetary body or luminary leaves a sign.

❖ see INGRESS p132

Ecliptic

Circle of the Sun's path. The ecliptic is so named because eclipses can only occur when the Moon crosses this great circle. It describes the centre line of the zodiac, which extends about eight degrees above and below the ecliptic. The ecliptic is the plane of the Earth's orbit around the Sun. From the Earth we seem to see the Sun moving along the ecliptic rather than the Earth. As we look into the heavens, the Sun appears to follow its path through the centre of the zodiac. In reality we are following our cyclic path around the Sun.

❖ see CELESTIAL SPHERE p110

Eclipse

An eclipse occurs when one celestial body obscures another; the term is generally used to refer to the relationship between the Sun and the Moon. A lunar eclipse occurs when the Moon passes into the Earth's shadow, and is visible over the whole night hemisphere of the Earth, lasting up to two hours. During a total lunar eclipse the Moon takes on a dark red colour. When the Moon shadows the Sun's light as viewed from the Earth, or passes through the shadow cast by the Earth, it is known as a solar eclipse. Eclipses may be total, partial or annular (a ring of the Sun is left around the Moon). In a total eclipse the surface of the Sun is completely blocked by the Moon, in a partial eclipse it is only partially blocked, and in an annular eclipse it is partial, but the apparent

LEFT: *The sun's place in the ecliptic*

diameter of the Moon can be seen completely against the apparent diameter of the Sun. A solar eclipse may be all three of the above for different observers.

❖ see OCCULTATION p134

Occultation

Occultations occur when a moving object, such as a planet or the Moon, blocks the light coming from a more distant object, such as a star. It describes when a smaller astronomical body passes behind a larger astronomical body. If the primary source of illumination of a reflecting body is cut off by the occultation, that phenomenon is also called an eclipse. When a large celestial body hides a small one from view (as when the Moon moves in front of a star or Jupiter over one of its moons), the event is usually termed occultation.

❖ see ECLIPSE p134

Superior Conjunction

The conjunction of an inferior planet (one which orbits between the Earth and Sun), Mercury or Venus, with the Sun is a superior conjunction when the Sun is between the Earth and the planet. It is an inferior conjunction when that planet is between the Earth and the Sun.

❖ see INFERIOR CONJUNCTION p134

Inferior Conjunction

The conjunction of an inferior planet (one that orbits between the Earth and the Sun) Mercury or Venus, with the Sun is an inferior conjunction when that planet is between the Earth and the Sun. It is a superior conjunction when the Sun is between the Earth and the planet.

❖❖ *see* SUPERIOR CONJUNCTION p134

Saros Cycle

Eclipses of the Sun and Moon occur in a pattern that repeats itself every 18 years, a fact that has been known since ancient times. This period is called the saros, a term taken from a Babylonian word and first used by the astronomer Edmund Halley. Eclipses of the Sun and Moon can only occur at new or full Moon respectively, and have to occur close to the nodes of the Moon. The time between successive passages by the Moon through one of its nodes is called the draconic month and equals 27.212220 days. The time between successive new or full Moons is called the synodic month and equals 29.530589 days. If we take 223 synodic months (6,585.321 days) and compare them with 242 draconic months (6,585.357 days) we can see that they are almost the same. This period is the saros and it amounts to 18 years, 10-and-a-third days.

❖❖ *see* ECLIPSE p134

Syzygy

Syzygy occurs when the Moon (or a planet) is in opposition or conjunction with the Earth and Sun. At syzygy, the Moon (or planet) is seen as new or full (from Earth). In astronomy the term refers to an alignment of three bodies of the Solar System along a straight or nearly straight line. A planet is in syzygy with the Earth and Sun when it is in opposition or conjunction, i.e. when its elongation is 180 degrees or 0 degrees.

❖❖ *see* MOON p63

Node

From Latin *nodus* ('knot'); the node of any planet is where the orbit of a planet satellite intersects the orbital plane of a planet. Mercury and Venus occasionally transit (pass in

RIGHT: *Astronomers observing an eclipse*

front of) the Sun and can be seen as a black dot on the Sun's face. This will occur if an inferior conjunction occurs within a day or two of the date at which the planet crosses the ecliptic – when it crosses a node. Transits of Venus (or Mercury) happen only when the Sun, Venus (or Mercury) and Earth exactly line up.

❖❖ *see* ORBIT p131

Galactic Centre

The gravitational centre around which the Sun revolves in the Milky Way, or the point in our Galaxy around which the Solar System revolves in a 225-million-year period

ABOVE: *The Great Galaxy in Andromeda – a collection of stars, dust and gas, held together by gravity*

known as a cosmic year. It is currently around 26 degrees Sagittarius. The Sun and stars in the Milky Way all revolve around this point. In the birth chart a planet or chart point near the galactic centre is said to indicate someone who is likely to do something on a large scale. When examining this point in the birth chart, only the conjunction and opposition are used.

❖ see GALAXY p124

Heliocentric

Centred around the Sun. The Greek Aristarchus of Samos (c. 310–230 BC) developed a heliocentric model of the Universe, in which he proposed that all the planets, including Earth, revolved around the Sun, and that the Earth rotated on its axis once a day. His ideas did not gain widespread acceptance during his lifetime. The sun-centred model was later revived by Nicolas Copernicus, around 1500. He was dissatisfied with the complexity of

the geocentric model but was later to have trouble with the Church for his ideas. Some parts of his model have been modified – the planetary orbits are elliptical, not circular, and the Sun rotates on its axis, for example, but his ideas nonetheless revolutionized astronomical thought.

❖ see GEOCENTRIC p136

Geocentric

Having the Earth for a centre. It was originally believed that the Earth lay at the centre of the Universe. Our modern view of astronomy in which the Earth rotates on its axis and revolves around the Sun evolved in the sixteenth and seventeenth centuries, largely from the works of Copernicus, although it had been postulated much earlier. Geocentric theory appears to have originated with the Greeks or Egyptians prior to 300 BC. It was summarized by Claudius Ptolemy. Astrology relies on a geocentric view of the Universe, although astrologers are perfectly aware that the Earth orbits the Sun.

❖ see HELIOCENTRIC p136

Heliacal

Of, or relating to, the Sun, especially that which rises and sets with the Sun. From the Greek helios, meaning 'Sun'. It refers to the rising of a celestial object late in the morning twilight, just before the rising of the Sun. Venus has its heliacal rising when it is moving retrograde, and in ancient times it was considered to be destructive during this period. The Babylonians were particularly interested in heliacal risings and settings of planets and stars, and gave the dates and positions of these in their ephemerides. In ancient Egypt the seasons were determined not by the solar equinox or solstice, but by the heliacal rising of the star Sirius.

❖ see SUN p62

BELOW: *A heliocentric universe, in which the Earth circles the Sun*

ASTROLOGY TERMS

Astrology is classed as a type of divination that consists of interpreting the influence of the planets and stars on earthly affairs, to predict or affect the destinies of individuals, groups or nations. The terminology associated with astrology relates to the charts that are cast and their interpretation, as well as definitions of types, positions and movements of planets, and what this means for the subject of the horoscope.

Horoscope

The word 'horoscope' is derived from the Greek *horoscopos* meaning 'I watch the rising', which is the ascending point or sign rising over the eastern horizon at the time. As generally used nowadays, it indicates the map of the heavens drawn for a given date, location and time by an astrologer for judging character and making predictions. Also often simply called a 'chart'. It is a diagram that depicts the position of the planets in relation to the Earth. An astrologer interprets the positions of the planets and their relation to the 12 signs of the zodiac. A horoscope can be cast for an event or question, as well as a person.

❖ see RELATIONSHIP CHART p139

Native

The birth chart was, until relatively recent times, known as a nativity – a reflection of the birth moment. The person for whom the chart was cast was therefore known as the native. Curiously, the field of astrology now known as natal was commonly called 'genethliacal' or 'pertaining to birth' when the term 'native' was in common use. There is no single term in general use today.

❖ see HOROSCOPE p138

Birth Moment

A horoscope is calculated for the time, date and place that a person is born, or that an event takes place. In horary astrology the chart is cast for the birth time of a question. For an individual's horoscope the moment of birth is classed as when the child takes its first breath or makes its first cry after being completely out of the mother. Recorded times of birth are often later than this. It has always been a source of controversy, as many believe that conception marks the beginning of life.

❖ see RECTIFICATION p138

Rectification

Rectification is the art of taking an approximate time of birth and refining it through astrological techniques. Many birth times are not recorded accurately – if at all. There are a variety of methods used to rectify the birth chart. Predictive techniques are often used retrospectively. Primary directions were most commonly used in the past but today progressions and transits are most often used. Knowing the astrological patterns that would be expected to coincide with a certain event, the astrologer moves the angles and house cusps in the birth chart until a chart is found which gives the expected prediction for the date of the event. Another method of rectification is the pre-natal epoch. The most condemning objection to its use is the birth of identical twins, which presumably have the same pre-natal epoch, but are nevertheless born at different times.

❖ see PRE-NATAL EPOCH p139

Pre-Natal Epoch

Method of rectifying a chart when the time of birth is unknown; also called the Trutine of Hermes. The theory, which dates back to the time of Ptolemy, states that at the time of conception the Moon should be in conjunction with, or in opposition to, the natal ascendant, and the ascendant in conjunction or opposition with the natal Moon. Pre-natal epoch theory allows for a symbolic chart to be calculated for nine months before birth, based on the relationship between the Sun, Moon and ascendant in the horoscope. Taking this chart forward allows for the birth chart to be fine-tuned, giving an 'accurate' birth time. The astrological moment of conception is approximately nine months before birth, but not necessarily coinciding with the exact time of birth.

❖ see RECTIFICATION p138

Relationship Chart

Although sometimes used to describe a chart cast for the start of a relationship, this usually describes a technique whereby the charts of both people in a relationship are combined. An imaginary birth place, date and time is established, based on the halfway point between both people's place, date and time of birth. This chart is then taken to describe the nature and quality of the relationship between the two people concerned. The relationship chart may be compared with the two birth charts used to see what contributions each makes to the relationship. This technique may be taken further by calculating a new chart for the halfway point between the relationship chart and the chart of each person individually. This shows the relationship of each to the relationship itself. The technique was first described by Ronald Davison in his book *Synastry* in 1977.

❖ see SYNASTRY p141

ABOVE: *Astrologer Jack Adams prepares a horoscope for a woman ('the Queen of Sluts'), whose mother wonders if she is a princess*

Radical

The term refers to the state of the birth chart, also known as the radix. In horary astrology it describes a chart that is fit to be judged. It must be decided if the conditions for judgement have been fulfilled; if the chart has no factors in it included in the considerations then the chart is judged. Astrologers apply the considerations in different ways so there are differences of opinion over whether certain charts are valid. The radical position of any planet or chart point is the birth position of the planets as distinguished from any directed or progressed positions.

❖ see HOROSCOPE p138

Earth Zodiac

In the past, vast tracts of land were laid out so that they might be explored using maps of the constellations; these are known as the terrestrial or Earth zodiacs. So far a total of 13 have been discovered in Britain including the zodiacs at the Lizard, Bodmin Moor, Ffarmers in Wales, Glastonbury, Althorp Park, Kingston-upon-Thames, Cambridge and Hebden Bridge. They have as their centre the stone circle at Arbor Low, Derbyshire.

❖ see JOHN DEE p15

Flat Chart

Chart created when no birth time is available. As birth times are not commonly recorded in the UK many people do not know their birth times. In this case a horoscope is

erected for an arbitrary time, often noon or sunrise, and the chart is described either by the substitute time used or as a flat chart. The angles and houses are ignored on such charts.

❖ see HOROSCOPE p138

Jupiter Return

Jupiter's orbit is 11.86 years and after that time it will return to the same zodiacal position that it held at the time that the chart was cast. This is referred to as the Jupiter return, and a chart is cast for this moment, using the location of the subject at that time. Return charts may be cast for any planet. It is used as a stand-alone chart representing the end of one Jupiter cycle and the beginning of another, as well as in comparison to the birth chart.

❖ see JUPITER p64

Saturn Return

Saturn has a rotational cycle of 29.458 years. A Saturn return chart is constructed for the moment when this planet returns to the zodiacal degree it occupied at the native's birth. Since Saturn is connected with the need to structure one's life and with life's learning processes, this chart provides information as to how the individual will tend to process the lessons of the first 29 years and which life direction will henceforth be chosen.

❖ see SATURN p66

Solar return

In modern astrology, the solar return chart is calculated when the Sun returns to the exact degree and minute of the Sun in the natal chart. This occurs around one's birthday. The effects of a solar return chart last for about one year. Some astrologers claim the chart can take hold a few months prior to the birthday. The location used for the solar return chart is in dispute

LEFT: *The relationship between this woman and her child can be analyzed by comparing their horoscopes*

LEFT: *The title page of Parker's* Ephemeris

calendars are largely limited to the phases of the Moon. Almanacs, astrological calendars and ephemerides often include eclipses, void-of-course Moon, ingresses of the Moon and other planets, retrograde periods and daily aspects of the Moon.

❖ *see* VOID OF COURSE p146

Ephemeris

A set of tables listing the 'ephemeral', or rapidly changing positions, which each Solar-System body will occupy on each day of the year; their longitude, latitude, declination and similar astronomical phenomena. An astrologer's ephemeris lists these positions in relation to the Earth. An ephemeris for the year of birth is essential to calculate a horoscope. Before 1925 the astronomical day began at noon, so positions in older ephemerides were always given for that time.

❖ *see* ASPECTARIAN p141

Diurnal

Refers to a chart when the Sun is in the top half and the individual is born in daylight hours. It can also refer to the motion of a planet. It is often used to describe the motion of any planet from midnight to midnight along the ecliptic.

❖ *see* NOCTURNAL p141

Nocturnal

A way of referring to a chart for someone born during the night with the Sun in the lower half of the chart. In traditional astrology planets are classified as nocturnal or diurnal, no matter where they are located in the chart.

❖ *see* DIURNAL p141

Synastry

The word synastry comes from the Greek prefix *syn* ('bringing together') and *astron* ('star'). It is the comparison of two or more horoscopes to determine compatibility. Any relationship can be analyzed synastrically. This

among astrologers. Some prefer to use the same location for the birth chart. Others calculate the chart using the primary living location for that year. Still others claim that the location where a person has travelled to on the birthday should be used for the chart for the entire year. This method is not accepted generally. The primary living location is a better contestant with the birth location. If you consider the ascendant and the houses as a major factor in the chart, shifts in location can make a huge difference in interpretation.

❖ *see* SATURN RETURN p140

Aspectarian

An aspectarian lists the occurrence of specific astrological phenomena in chronological order and is found in modern ephemerides, calendars or almanacs. Aspectarians in

technique will identify areas of strength and weakness, harmony and disharmony in relationships. The charts of each of the people in the relationship are cast first. Then the astrologer studies the charts, noting connections such as which houses the planets belonging to one person fall into in the second person's chart, and which aspects are formed between the planets in one chart and planets and chart points in the other.

❖ see RELATIONSHIP CHART p139

Mode

The term 'mode' originates from the Latin word *modus* ('way of') and refers to the different modes of operation and temperament that characterize each sign. Confusingly though, astrological language uses it in three different ways. The first meaning refers to the division of the signs by quality, e.g. cardinal, fixed and mutable. These 'modes' or 'qualities' are also known as 'quadruplicities' and categorize the different manners of expression of each element. The second meaning refers to the Aristotelian principles 'hot', 'dry', 'cold', and 'moist' in combination with the astrological elements fire, earth, air and water, respectively. The third meaning of the word 'mode' refers to the division of the signs into 'feminine' and 'masculine'. The signs of the masculine mode are said to be of an active nature, while the signs of the feminine mode are regarded as operating in a re-active way.

❖ see QUADRUPLICITY p143

Quality

In astrological language, the term 'quality' refers to certain characteristics of the signs. It is used in two ways: it either refers to the quadruplicities, a categorization of the signs as cardinal, fixed or mutable; or it pertains to the nature of the signs as implied by the combination of elements and the four classic principles. In the first sense, the term 'cardinal', 'fixed' or 'mutable' quality summarizes the energy flow within the sign in question and characterizes the way in which the sign tends to express the element to which it belongs. The second meaning of the term, quality, plays an important role in medical astrology. By linking each triplicity with combinations of the four classic principles, e.g. fire with heat and dryness, earth with dryness and cold, air with heat and moisture, and water with moisture and cold, each sign ends up with a certain quality, which is also reflected in the physical body.

❖ see ELEMENT p54

Triplicity

In modern astrology, triplicity refers to the breakdown of the signs into the four elemental groups: fire, earth, air and water. However, there is another form of triplicity that refers to day and night triplicity rulers. For example, Aries is ruled by the Sun by day and Jupiter by night. Water signs have Mars as both day and night ruler. Planets in their own triplicity are generally considered lucky. Good things happen not

ABOVE: Modes are a way of classifying the zodiac signs, which appear on this carving from Ancient Gaul, representing the god Mithras.

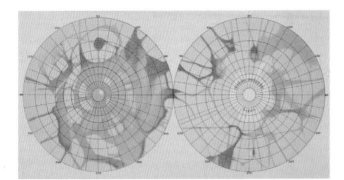

LEFT: *The two hemispheres of Mars, one of the malefics which can be responsible for an impedited planet*

because they are worked at but because you have stumbled on a good result. The triplicities were derived from the sign and exaltation rulerships and in medieval astrology used in preference.

❖ see ELEMENT p54

Quadruplicity

The signs of the zodiac are grouped in three quadruplicities: cardinal, fixed and mutable. The term refers to each category containing four signs, one of each element. The quadruplicities indicate how the elements are being expressed throughout the signs, i.e. how the individual deals with life after perceiving it in the way suggested by the elements. The cardinal quadruplicity consists of Aries, Cancer, Libra and Capricorn, and is ascribed initiating and motivating qualities. The orientation is extrovert; exchange with the environment and adaptation to outer circumstances are of highest importance. The fixed quadruplicity contains Taurus, Leo, Scorpio and Aquarius and is characterized as securing and stabilizing. The orientation is introvert; personal values and motifs have priority over the demands of the environment. Gemini, Virgo, Sagittarius and Pisces belong to the mutable quadruplicity, which is characterized as a mixture of the two others.

❖ see QUALITY p142

Benefic

The planets Venus and Jupiter are classified as benefics, meaning their influence is generally positive. Venus and Jupiter are also often referred to as the 'Lesser Benefic' and the 'Greater Benefic', respectively. The Sun, the Moon and the north node of the Moon (the dragon's head) are also regarded as benefics if they are dignified or well aspected. The term 'benefic' is also applied to aspects. The trine is regarded as positive, because the planets in question operate within signs of the same element, whereas the sextile involves planets in signs of either feminine or masculine disposition.

❖ see MALEFIC p143

Malefic

The term 'malefic' (Latin for 'evil-doer') is applied to certain planets and aspects by traditional astrology. Mars and Saturn are regarded as malefics because their manifestations are often opposed to everything humans regard as constructive, positive and fun. Saturn – also called the 'greater infortune' – symbolizes rigidity and obstruction, while Mars – the 'lesser infortune' – is seen as the creator of quarrel and strife. The aspects classified as malefic are the square and the semi-square, which involve planets operating from conflicting elements or opposing modes. Modern astrology has a slightly different view on the positive potential of the malefics.

❖ see BENEFIC p143

Anareta

Planet showing means of death. From the Greek for 'destroyer', this is the planet in the birth chart which shows how you are likely to die. It is concerned with physical death and there can be only one anareta in the chart. Although there are various methods of calculation, it is usually the planet that makes a difficult aspect to (i.e. has angular relationship with) the hyleg both in the birth chart

LEFT: *The Anareta planet is concerned with physical death*

and Mars in the horoscope and is within orb of an aspect (angular relationship) with both planets. In the past, planets that lay between Venus and Jupiter were said to be fortunately besieged and were considered to be positive in meaning. Today, however, the term is used in its negative sense and restricted to horary astrology.

❖ see HORORY ASTROLOGY p28

Significator

A planet pertaining to a particular issue. A planet may be taken as a significator of a person, an event or of affairs ruled by a house. Its strength by virtue of its sign and house position, and its relationship by aspect, are all consulted when judging a horary chart. In horary astrology the Moon always acts as a secondary significator. In a birth chart the strongest planet is usually taken as the significator of the person for whom the chart is cast.

❖ see RULER p145

Cosignificator

Like the significator, this planet represents a certain person, matter or area of life. Generally, the ruler of an intercepted sign is the cosignificator of the house that contains the interception. It provides additional information, but weighs less in interpretation than the main significator. In horary astrology, certain houses are given signs or planets as cosignificators.

❖ see SIGNIFICATOR p144

Dispositor

The ruler of the sign in which a planet finds itself disposes of or is the dispositor of that planet. The disposing planet has influence over the planet being disposed of. A chart may have a 'final dispositor'; in this case the planet concerned acts almost like a chart ruler. According to other authorities the ruler of the sign on the cusp of a house is the dispositor of a planet that is placed in that house.

❖ see PROMITTOR p145

and by direction. The twenty-ninth degree of a sign is said to be an anaretic degree.

❖ see FORTUNE p145

Besiegement

A trapped planet, bound on either side by an unhelpful planet which limits its scope. A besieged planet is taken to be unfortunate in traditional astrology. Generally, besiegement involves a planet that falls between Saturn

Promittor

The planet to which another planet may be 'directed' or moved by a system in order to form an aspect (angular relationship) between it and the directed planet. The promittor is the planet in the birth chart that other planets are moved towards when predicting. The distance that the moved planet must travel to meet the promittor is called the arc of direction, and this is usually about the rate of one degree for a year and five minutes for a month, although systems vary slightly, giving differing results.

❖ see BIRTH MOMENT p138

Fortune

Name for Jupiter or Venus. The fortunes are the benefic planets; Jupiter is classed as the greater fortune and Venus as the lesser. The Sun and Mercury (or according to some authorities, the Moon and Mercury) are also classed as fortunes when well placed and aspected, especially if by Jupiter or Venus.

❖ see INFORTUNE p145

Infortune

The malefic planets, Mars and Saturn. Saturn is classed as the greater infortune and Mars as the lesser. Other planets may be counted as infortunes if they make difficult aspects to either Saturn or Mars. A traditional term rarely used in modern astrology.

❖ see FORTUNE p145

Impedited

Term used to describe a planet that is badly aspected, particularly by the malefics, Mars and Saturn; also termed 'impeded'. It also describes the Moon when it is moving to a conjunction, square or opposition to the Sun, Mars or Saturn. In modern astrology a planet is also counted as impedited when aspecting Neptune, Uranus and Pluto, although the term is not generally used except in traditional forms of astrology, such as horary.

❖ see MALEFIC p143

Luminary

The Sun and Moon; a term used to indicate their particular importance. The term 'light of the time' refers to the Sun during the day or in a daytime horoscope and to the Moon during the night or in a night-time horoscope.

❖ see SUN p62

Ruler

Firstly, it indicates a planet incorporating and expressing the characteristics of the sign it 'rules'. If situated in this sign, the planet is dignified. Secondly, astrology works with 'rulers' of houses, which should correctly be called 'lords'. The 'natural' lord of a house is the ruler of its corresponding sign. Thirdly, a planet, sign or house may represent or 'rule' certain people or phenomena. Lastly, the 'lord of chart' or 'chart ruler' is believed to be the most influential planet.

❖ see FORTUNE p145

LEFT: The Moon, the secondary significator in horary astrology

Matutine

Term used to describe a planet that rises in the morning in the east before the Sun. This used to refer to Mercury, the Moon and Venus when they appeared in the morning. When a star or planet rises before the Sun, it is called matutine until it reaches its first station or appears to stop moving, before it becomes retrograde (or appears to move backwards).

❖ see VESPERTINE p146

ABOVE: *The Sun and Moon*

Vespertine

Planet that sets in the west after the Sun has set; the reverse of matutine. The name was traditionally given to the planet Venus by the Greeks, as it was noted for its brightness in the evening. (Venus was also occasionally called Herald of the Dawn as it can also rise before the Sun.) It was originally believed that the evening and morning views of Venus represented two separate planets.

❖ see MATUTINE p146

Blue Moon

Second of two full Moons in one month. The expression 'blue Moon' usually refers to this second full Moon. Because the Moon and our calendar are not in sync and all the months except February are longer than the Moon's cycle, a blue Moon occurs about seven times in 19 years. Blue Moons were actually printed in blue in older planetary tables, although it is not known where the term comes from.

❖ see MOON p63

Moiety

Traditional astrology considers every planet to be surrounded by an orb of light which defines its sphere of influence. Half the diameter of this orb is called the moiety of the planet. To determine the orb of aspects between two planets, their orbs are added up and then divided by

two. Al-Biruni made the first recorded list of planetary orbs, which was slightly altered by William Lilly.

❖ see WILLIAM LILLY p17

Posited

The word literally means 'placed' and is used in older texts to describe the position occupied by a body in the heavens or in the signs and houses of a birth chart. It is usually used in reference to planets, but may also be used to describe the position of other chart points.

❖ see CHALDEAN ORDER p146

Chaldean Order

The Chaldean order of planets is Saturn, Jupiter, Mars, Sun, Venus, Mercury, Moon. The first (furthest from the Earth) Chaldean planet, Saturn, is the 'heaviest' or 'slowest', and the seventh or last (closest to the Earth) Chaldean 'planet', the Moon, is the 'lightest' or 'swiftest.' The order is used when calculating planetary hours.

❖ see SATURN p66

Void of Course

A planet is said to be void of course if it makes no complete major aspect before it leaves the sign in which it is placed. Although any planet may be void of course, the term is most frequently applied to the Moon. It is a technique used in horary astrology and one of the considerations before judgement, as it means that there is nothing that can be done about the matter under question. The Moon is void of course every few days for a length of time ranging from a few minutes to a day or more.

❖ *see* HORARY ASTROLOGY p28

Ascending

A planet is rising if it falls close to the ascendant, generally taken to be up to five degrees either side of the ascendant. A planet in this position is particularly strong and has a close relationship with the ascendant, and how the person presents themselves to the world. In older texts the term may refer to any planet on the left-hand side of the chart or a planet in the first house.

❖ *see* FIRST HOUSE p84

Combust

A planet is combust if it lies in the same sign as the Sun and is within eight-and-a-half degrees of its position. It is a form of debility and damages the planet concerned, as it is believed to be burned by the Sun and its power thereby

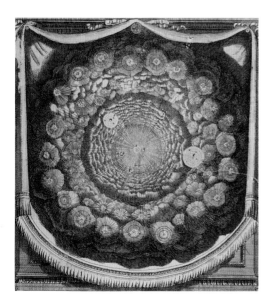

reduced. Traditionally, the Moon is especially debilitated when combust. A combust Moon is a new Moon. It can indicate fear or being overpowered by another person in a horary chart. Combust is a traditional description, rarely used today except in horary astrology.

❖ *see* CAZIMI p147

Cazimi

An Arabic term meaning 'in the heart of the Sun', cazimi describes a position up to 17 minutes either side of the Sun. Traditionally, a planet in this position is strengthened. The specific qualities it imparts vary depending on the planet involved. It may indicate a particularly close relationship in a horary chart. Because of the closeness of the path of Mercury's orbit to that of the Sun, Mercury is the planet most commonly cazimi.

❖ *see* COMBUST p147

Under Sunbeams

A planet is said to be under sunbeams if it is between 8 1/2 and 17 degrees away from the Sun. It is slightly weakened in its effect, less so if it is not in the same sign as the Sun. Mars, however, is strengthened in this position as it is of the same hot and dry nature as the Sun.

❖ *see* CAZIMI p147

Mixed Reception

This occurs when two planets are in dignities assigned to the other, but the nature of the dignities are different. For example, Mars is in Cancer, ruled by the Moon, and the Moon is in Capricorn where Mars is exalted. It is stronger if the two planets concerned are also making an aspect to each other. It gives a bond between the two planets and they can be read as if they had changed places in the chart. Only rulership and exaltation tend to be used, although technically any of the five dignities may be applied.

❖ *see* EXALTATION p157

LEFT: *A posited can refer to the placement of a planet in the heavens*

Mutual Reception

This occurs when two planets are in each other's dignity. For example, Mars in Gemini and Mercury in Aries are in mutual reception because Mars rules Aries and Mercury rules Gemini. Mutual reception by ruling sign is the strongest. In order of strength, there can be reception by sign, exaltation, triplicity, term or face. Only rulership and exaltation tend to be used, although technically any of the five dignities may be applied.

❖ see MIXED RECEPTION p147

Reception

Reception may take two forms. Mutual reception occurs when two planets are in each other's dignity. For example, Mars in Gemini and Mercury in Aries are in mutual reception because Mars rules Aries and Mercury rules Gemini. Mutual reception by ruling sign is the strongest. Mixed reception occurs when two planets are in dignities assigned to the other, but the nature of the dignities are different. It is stronger if the two planets concerned are also making an aspect to one another.

❖ see MIXED RECEPTION p147

Quotidian

The quotidian is the name given to the rate of movement when secondary progressions are used for predictive work. The most commonly used rate is called Q2 and it is based on the ratio of one tropical day for a year (1: 365.24219879). An alternative rate is called Q1 or Bija correction and this is based on the ratio of one sidereal day for a year (1: 366.2563992).

❖ see TROPICAL YEAR p121

Separation

This indicates the movement of one planet away from another planet, house cusp or sensitive point, after the formation of an aspect or angular relationship. The two are

LEFT: *The signs of the zodiac*

moving away from each other and so the effect is becoming weaker. A separating aspect is weaker than an applying one.

❖ see RECEPTION p149

Application

The movement of one planet towards another planet, house cusp or sensitive point approaching the formation of an aspect. The term 'mutual application' is used when a planet travelling direct is moving towards one that is retrograde and each of them is heading towards the other. The faster-moving planet 'casts its rays' to aspect the slower one. Although two planets need not be in aspect to apply to each other, the term is generally used when they are already in aspect and it is becoming exact.

❖ see RETROGRADE p150

Increasing in Motion

The term relates to the daily movement of a planet, which increases when the planet is in its apogee (closest to Earth); at the end of a period of retrograde motion, having passed through the stationary period, a planet picks up speed, i.e. increases in motion.

❖ see STATION p150

Increasing in Light

Due to the visibility of the Sun by day, a planet in conjunction with the Sun is invisible in the sky. It is said to increase in light as it becomes visible, after the conjunction has been completed. For example, after the new Moon, the waxing Moon increases in light.

❖ see LUMINARY p145

Decreasing in Light

During the period that the Moon is going from full to new, it is said to be decreasing in light. Although generally applied to the Moon, the term is also applicable to any planet passing from an opposition to conjunction with the Sun.

❖ see INCREASING IN LIGHT p149

Slow in Course

A planet is said to be slow in course when its travel in a 24-hour period is less than its mean motion. The average daily motions of the planets are: Moon 13 degrees 10 minutes 36 seconds, Sun 0 59 08, Mercury and Venus 0 59 08 (same as the Sun), Mars 0 31 27, Jupiter 0 4 59, Saturn 0 2 1.

❖ see INCREASING IN MOTION p149

Lunation

Complete cycle between two new Moons; also known as a synodic month and a syzygy. Lunations average 29 days, 12 hours and 44 minutes. The new Moon falling on sensitive points in the chart is significant of coming events in the next month. The term is often used interchangeably with new Moon. New Moons fall in the same degree and sign only once every 19 years. A sidereal lunation is the period between two passages of the Moon over the same degree. An embolismic lunation is an intercalary month.

❖ see NEW MOON p128

BELOW: *The Sun and the Moon*

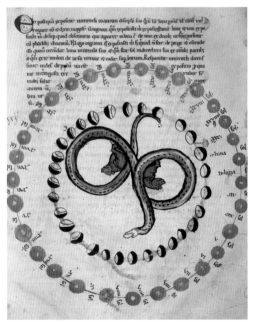

Retrograde

The term 'retrograde' is applied to an apparent backward motion in the zodiac of certain planets when decreasing in longitude as viewed from the Earth. After a time, the planet then appears to stop once again and reverse its movement through the sky. The planet then goes 'direct' and is back on its normal cyclic path through the sky. This traditional concept arises in the illusory planetary motion created by the orbital rotation of the Earth, with relation to other planets in our Solar System. Planets are never actually retrograde or stationary, they just seem that way. Except for the Sun and Moon, all planets may be retrograde, but Mercury spends the longest period retrograde, about 20 per cent of the time. A retrograde period is seen as a cycle, beginning when the planet begins to slow to a halt before travelling backwards through the zodiac and ending when the planet returns to the point where it first paused.

❖ see STATION p150

Revolution

Loosely applied to anything that pursues an orbit. Also used in connection with directions involving the return of the Sun, Moon or any other planet to the place it was in the original chart. These charts are often referred to as return charts in modern astrology. The chart is cast for the time of return and judged as a separate chart as well as in comparison with the original chart for the purpose of making predictions relating to the planet.

❖ see SATURN RETURN p140

Station

A planet makes a station when it appears motionless before reversing direction in its orbit, as viewed from Earth. Thus, a planet can make a station when going from retrograde to direct, or from direct to retrograde. Stationary planets are considered to be quite influential. When turning retrograde, they symbolize a reversal or delay. When turning direct, they indicate a renewal or

LEFT: *Consulting an astrologer*

revitalization. Mercury is the planet most frequently retrograde, and therefore makes the most stations. The Sun and Moon are never stationary and never retrograde.

❖ see RETROGRADE p150

Translation of Light

Planetary combination. Translation occurs when a swifter planet leaves a heavier one and then catches up with another heavier planet. The swift one then translates, or passes on, the light from one to the other. The two heavier planets can be separating from an aspect, or approaching an aspect. Ideally, the translating planet should share a dignity with the first heavier planet, showing sympathy. It indicates help that may be given by another party in a horary question. It can also indicate contact being made between the people indicated by the planets.

❖ see PROHIBITION p151

Collection of Light

Collection occurs when a slower planet receives aspects from two faster planets that are not themselves in aspect, or forming an angular relationship to one another. In horary astrology the slower planet is said to collect the light of the faster planets and symbolizes that the matter in question may occur, or be brought about, through an intermediary described by the slow third planet.

❖ see REFRANATION p151

Refranation

Refranation occurs when one planet is travelling towards another, but before it reaches it and the aspect becomes exact, it goes retrograde and so the aspect does not occur. Alternatively, the planet it is moving towards moves into the next sign before it reaches it. This is taken as an indicator in horary astrology that the matter under negotiation will not be brought to a successful, or the desired, conclusion. Refranation is another form of prohibition, preventing the results shown on a cursory look at a chart.

❖ see RETROGRADE p150

Prohibition

If two planets are travelling towards and forming an angular relationship with one another, but before the aspect becomes exact another faster planet makes an aspect with one of them, this is a form of prohibition. In a horary chart it prevents the matter being questioned about occurring. If the question was, 'Will I get a job interview?' it would show that an outside factor prevents it from happening. If prohibition occurs by conjunction, it is referred to as 'bodily prohibition'. If Venus is at five degrees of Cancer and moving towards Jupiter at 10 degrees of Cancer but before it gets there Mercury, which was at four degrees, passes Venus and reaches Jupiter first, there is prohibition.

❖ see FRUSTRATION p152

Frustration

Frustration means that a faster planet is travelling towards a slower one, but before they join in a conjunction the slow one joins up with a different planet. The first two planets are held to signify an event in horary or electional astrology. The third planet produces an abscission of light that frustrates the promised effect of the slower-moving aspect; meaning that what is promised cannot take place. At the least the matter will be delayed in a way that is related to the house of which the planet that frustrates is the ruler.

❖ *see* ABSCISSION OF LIGHT p152

Abscission of Light

Derived from the Latin *abscissio* (from *abscindere* – 'to cut off'), this is synonymous with frustration and describes a configuration that prevents something from happening. It is only used in horary, nowadays. When the planet that signifies the issue being considered makes an aspect to a planet that moves more slowly, or when two planets that signify the issue are about to reach an aspect but a faster-moving planet makes an aspect with one of them before

that can become exact, abscission occurs. In each case the light of the approaching significator is cut off by the rays of the third planet. It interferes with whatever is promised by the aspect between the two significators.

❖ *see* FRUSTRATION p152

Stellium

A stellium, also known as satellitium, is a gathering of three or more planets, grouped together in the same sign or house, preferably within less than 30 degrees of arc. The planets involved are connected by conjunction, even if the orb between the first and the last planet of the stellium is wider than usually accepted. A conjunction describes the combined forces of the planets involved; therefore, the stellium indicates a massive concentration of energies in the sign and house in question. In mundane astrology a stellium, often called planetary line-up, indicates a quick succession of events in accordance with the nature of the planets involved and the zodiacal area they occupy. Natally, the characteristics of the sign will be clearly recognizable in the individual's character.

❖ *see* MUNDANE ASTROLOGY p28

BELOW: The rules of antipathy do not allow for the traditional friendliness between Mars and Venus, as depicted in Sandro Botticelli's painting

Antipathy

The term 'antipathy' is used in various ways, but it always indicates that the planets involved are incompatible or 'unfriendly', meaning that one planet weakens the other or obstructs its manifestation. Some planets have a natural antipathy according to their conflicting natures, such as the Moon to Mars and Saturn or Jupiter to Mars. The rulers of opposing signs are also said to be in antipathy towards one another, although this contradicts the traditional rule that Mars is friendly towards Venus.

❖ see SYNASTRY p141

Colours

To identify planetary influences in objects of daily life, which is of special importance in horary astrology, the astrologer looks for correspondences with the nature of the planet. This can be the material, the use, the shape or the colour of the object. Since there are about as many lists of colour correspondences as there are astrological works, the following can but provide general indications: Moon – white, silver, pale green; Mercury - yellow, azure, spotted or striped mixtures; Venus – pastels, light blues and greens, indigo; Sun – gold, orange, yellow; Mars – deep red, magenta, deep orange; Jupiter – purple, violet, all sky blues; Saturn – black, brown, green, all dark colours; Uranus – all electric or metallic shades; Neptune – greyish pastels, sea colours, changeants; Pluto – black, blood red.

❖ see BIRTHSTONE p165

Affliction

Traditional astrology knows several forms of affliction, which weaken a planet or cause it to express its energies in a negative way. A planet can be afflicted by receiving a 'malefic' aspect from another planet. Instead of combining their forces, the planets involved are then at cross-purposes, especially when they are considered to be 'unfriendly' towards each other. Another affliction occurs

when a planet is 'besieged', meaning that it is positioned between two other planets, thus obstructing its expression.

❖ see BESIEGEMENT p144

Planetary Period

In traditional astrology, the planetary periods, also known as 'alfridaria' or 'firdar', constitute a system of long-term prediction very similar to the dasas and bhuktis in Vedic astrology. All planets and the nodes are assigned rulership over a certain number of years corresponding to a person's age. Each of these planetary periods is divided into seven equal parts, which are assigned to planetary sub-rulers following the Chaldean order. These give further detailed information about the nature of events that can be expected. There are several such systems documented in Greek, Persian and Arabic literature.

❖ see YEAR p119

Alfridaria

System of planetary periods. Derived from a Latin translation of the Arabic term 'firdar', this is a system of planetary periods that appears to be of Persian origin. The planets are assigned rulerships over periods of time in life, according to a specific scheme. There are two or more planets holding rulership over any particular time. The major ruler has a long period and is divided into sub-periods which are assigned minor rulers. The issues over which the planets have rulership are heightened and brought to the fore during this time.

❖❖ see RULER p145

Behold

When two planets are within orb of an aspect, they are said to behold one another. Signs that have the same declination, or are at equal distances from the tropics, i.e. Aries/Virgo, Taurus/Leo, Gemini/Cancer, Libra/Pisces, Scorpio/Aquarius, Sagittarius/Capricorn, are also said to behold each other. Zodiac signs can behold one another in one of three ways: by major aspect (conjunction, sextile, square, trine, opposition), by antiscion, or by contra-antiscion.

❖❖ see TAURUS p38

Partile

The term, originating from the Greek reference to the degrees as 'parts', is applied to aspects formed by two or more planets from the same degree of their respective signs. Some astrologers use it only when the bodies are also forming an exact parallel. In horary astrology some practitioners work with the assumption that partiles with the nodes signal an intervention of fate according to the nature of the aspect in question.

❖❖ see PLACTIC p157

Dissociate

A dissociate is an aspect in which the planets involved are not in the expected signs. For example, when in opposition they are not actually in opposite signs. In older texts this term was used as an alternative name for the quincunx aspect, as this always involves incompatible signs. Whatever the aspect, the term describes an uncomfortable combination.

❖❖ see MAJOR ASPECTS p72

Parallel

In the tables of the ephemeris, the planetary positions are given in longitude (horizontal) and latitude (vertical) relative to the ecliptic. The longitude determines a planet's zodiacal position. Its latitude describes how far the planet in question is above or below, i.e. north or south of, the ecliptic. The angular relationships (aspects) between planets are usually measured by their position in the zodiac, i.e. their longitude. But if two planets are at the same vertical distance from the ecliptic and thus share the same degree of latitude, they are said to form a parallel or to be in parallel aspect. If these parallel planets are in an angular relationship in the horoscope as well, this will be re-inforced by the parallel. But even if they are not forming a vertical aspect in the chart, the planets are considered to cooperate. The parallel planets are either on the same side, i.e. north or south, of the ecliptic (parallel) or one of them has a northern and the other a southern latitude (contra-parallel).

❖❖ see CONTRA-PARALLEL p154

Contra-Parallel

Two planets with the same degree of declination are said to be 'in parallel'. While traditional astrology ignores the northern or southern position of the planets, modern astrology calls a parallel between a planet of northern and another of southern declination contra-parallel. It is said to have the same connotations as an opposition. Many astrologers only consider parallel aspects if the planets are also connected by another aspect in the chart.

❖❖ see PARALLEL p154

Ptolemaic Aspects

The Ptolemaic aspects are those mentioned in Ptolemy's *Tetrabiblos*, a standard text for astrologers, which has been in common use since translations were made in the sixteenth century. The aspects are the opposition, trine, square and sextile. The conjunction is often included in this list, and it is certainly used in Ptolemy's work, but it is more correctly termed a position as the word 'aspect' means 'to look at one another' and two planets in conjunction are placed side by side. Numerous other aspects have been added but these remain the primary ones.

❖ see MAJOR ASPECTS p72

Sinister

Sinister means 'on the left-hand side'. A sinister aspect is one in which the faster planet is waning, or decreasing in light, with respect to the slower one. The faster planet is casting its rays to the left .

❖ see DEXTER p155

Dexter

Dexter means 'on the right-hand side' and is a direction of an aspect. A dexter aspect is one in which the faster planet is waxing, or increasing in light with respect to the slower one. The faster planet is casting its rays to the right because the slower planet is on the right side of the applying planet when viewed from the Earth. It goes against the direction of the signs. A dexter aspect is more potent than than a sinister aspect (one that falls to the left).

❖ see SINISTER p155

BELOW: *Perhaps the best-known reference to astrology in the Bible is the Three Wise Men following the star to Bethlehem.*

Perfection

The term 'perfection' is used in two different ways. When an aspect becomes exact (two planets that are square to one another are precisely 90 degrees apart) the aspect concerned can be said to have perfected. In horary astrology, the term refers to a planetary combination that gives a positive answer to the question asked, and no other planet is involved in the configuration to interfere. An aspect that has not yet become exact but is approaching exactitude will give a positive answer, and the number of degrees the planets are apart from an exact aspect can indicate when it will happen. For example, if there are three degrees between Venus and Jupiter in the chart and no other planet interferes, the event in question may occur within three days. Other factors, such as reception and dignity also need to be considered when deciding if a matter will come to perfection.

❖ see HORARY ASTROLOGY p28

Plactic

The term 'plactic' or 'platick' has two meanings. In Greek astrology, it referred to aspects by sign. For example, a planet in Libra would be in plactic trine with any planet in Gemini, regardless of the occupied degrees. In traditional astrology, a plactic is an inexact aspect within the allowed planetary orb. For example, an exact square has 90 degrees; an aspect of 89 or 92 degrees is a plactic square.

❖ see LIBRA p45

Exaltation

A planet in its own exaltation acts as if it were a welcomed guest, having things done for it but not having complete control over the situation. The strength of the planet is augmented and its virtues are magnified. It is only slightly less favourably placed than when it is in its own sign. The opposite sign to the sign of exaltation is that of

fall, taking the opposite meaning. Exaltation is a traditional technique that may be used in any form of astrology but is primarily used in electional and horary. The Sun is exalted in Aries, especially at 19 degrees; the Moon in Taurus, especially at three degrees; Mercury in Virgo, especially at 15 degrees; Venus in Pisces, especially at 27 degrees; Mars in Capricorn, especially at 28 degrees; Jupiter in Cancer, especially at 15 degrees and Saturn in Libra, especially at 21 degrees. The modern planets, Uranus, Neptune and Pluto, are not included in the scheme as they were undiscovered when the system was devised.

❖ see ELECTIONAL ASTROLOGY p29

Face

A planet in its own face is slightly fortunate. Face is little used in modern astrology, although with the re-establishment of horary astrology it has become more popular in recent years. The division of the 360-degree circle into units of 10 degrees was developed by the Egyptians and then adopted by other civilizations. Beginning with zero degrees of Aries, the first 10 degrees are assigned to Mars, its ruler. From there each face ruler in sequence is in Chaldean order: Mars, Sun, Venus, Mercury, Moon, Saturn, Jupiter. Thus, up to 10 degrees of Aries is ruled by Mars, from 10 to 20 by the Sun, from 20 to 30 by Venus; the first 10 degrees of Taurus by Mercury and so on. In the past, faces were used extensively in weather forecasting. The faces represent worry or concern about matters related to the planet in question. Some authorities have assigned fear to the faces.

❖ see MARS p64

Term

The word means 'boundary', or 'termini of signs'. There are two sets of terms, the Egyptian and Ptolemaic, now known as Chaldean. The basis for assigning terms is to reward those planets with greater numbers of essential dignities in a sign, and to assign the benefics, Jupiter and Venus, more degrees than the malefics, Mars and Saturn. The planet that

LEFT: *Rudolf II's astrologer, shown here with the emperor at his court in Prague, would speak of perfection when he had reached an affirmative answer*

ABOVE: *Aldebaran one of the four Guardians of Heaven*

rules the sign being considered as that sign's ruler, or by being its own exaltation or triplicity, tends to be granted the first position most frequently. The last few degrees of a sign are always ruled by Mars or Saturn. This appears to be the origin of the idea that the final degrees of a sign have bad qualities. Planets in their own terms denote participation of matters in the business of that planet, but not from a position of power. In horary astrology they are used to describe the person in question.

❖ see MALEFIC p143

Fall

A planet in fall is opposite the sign of its exaltation. It is believed to be severely weakened because the sign's characteristics are inimical to the natural expression of the planetary energy. It refers to a situation where the planet concerned drops out of sight, not allowing the issue to be perceived properly. In an horary chart a significator (a planet that symbolizes the matter or person in question) in its fall may indicate an unfortunate, helpless, insolvent or cruel person. It may refer to a person who has fallen, been disgraced or suffered some kind of limitation. In charts about a missing object, it may have fallen down from where it was originally.

❖ see EXHALTATION p157

Guardians of Heaven

The Guardians of Heaven, also known as The Four Watchers or the Royal Stars, are four fixed stars individually named Aldebaran, Regulus, Antares and Fomalhaut. Their astronomical positions in the constellations of Taurus, Leo, Scorpio and Pisces form a cross; therefore one of them appears above the horizon every six hours approximately. Persian astrologers used them, instead of cardinal points, to mark the four quarters of the heavens as early as 3000 BC.

❖ see CARDINAL POINTS p90

Aldebaran

Its name comes from the Arabic Al Dabaran meaning 'follower'. Aldebaran presently lies at almost 10 degrees of Gemini. It is a pale rose star marking the left eye of the Bull, Taurus. It is one of the four Guardians of Heaven – sentinels watching over other stars. It formed one of the four royal stars of Persia as Watcher of the East. Aldebaran is said to confer honour or power.

❖ see FIXED STARS p127

Royal Stars

There are four royal stars: Aldebaran, Regulus, Antares and Fomalhaut. Regulus is usually considered the 'most' royal, although Aldebaran also has proponents. When a chart point or planet is near one of these stars (within one degree), it promises great success so long as certain conditions are fulfilled. These stars are also known as the 'watchers of the heavens'. Each one of these stars rules over one of the four cardinal points.

❖ see ALDEBARAN p158

Primum Mobile

The term 'primum mobile' means 'first mover'. The theory was expostulated by Aristotle to explain a pattern of westward flow in the oceans. The first mover, a theological being, was unmoved but acted on the circumference of the Universe, causing it to move. The shape of heaven is spherical and encloses successively smaller spheres down to the centre, i.e. Earth, with the motion of the outermost sphere being uniform and that of the inner spheres increasingly irregular as the centre is approached. Since the Sun and stars appeared to move west in an outer sphere, the first mover must be moving things in that direction.

❖ *see* ARISTOTLE p10

Karma

Derived from Sanskrit, the word is used in Buddhism and Hinduism; it refers to the total effect of a person's actions and conduct during the successive phases of existence, and is regarded as determining destiny in the next incarnation.

Reincarnation is implicit in karma. Often it is used interchangeably with fate or destiny, although correctly it implies a person's responsibility for their own actions. Within astrology the term is used when discussing past lives as shown by the chart, or when referring to a person's spiritual path. In this context the Moon's nodes and the planet Saturn are the most important chart points to consider.

❖ *see* MOON p63

Free Will

Free will refers to the ability or discretion of human beings to make a free choice and the power of making free choices that are unconstrained by external circumstances or by an agency such as fate or divine will. It implies that there is no coercion or restraint on taking action borne of necessity or of a physical nature. The concept of predestination clashed with that of free will in ancient Greek culture as much as in Christian theology. Caught up between the idea of blind and merciless fate and the belief that humanity was responsible for its own actions meant that the Greeks threw the burden back on to the shoulders of the Fates. One astrologer to grapple with the problem of free will was Abumassar, who made a distinction between the influence of the planets and of the fixed stars; the former controlled – or could control – the details of everyday life and the latter affected only the grand design of the Universe in a way that was so slow it was scarcely visible to the human eye.

❖ *see* ABUMASSAR p12

Fate

Fate is the supposed force, principle or power that predetermines incidents and the inevitable events predestined by this force. It describes, therefore, a final result or consequence – an outcome. Fate is seen as something ordained by the gods, our destiny. It describes circumstances against which it is useless to struggle and it

LEFT: *Cosmic fatality*

LEFT: *The music of the spheres*

the planets depended upon the ratios of their orbits. Kepler found that the angular velocities of all the planets closely correspond to musical intervals. When he compared the extremes for combined pairs of planets, they yielded the intervals of a complete scale.

❖ see JOHANNES KEPLER p16

Body, Parts of

The tradition of assigning signs and planets to the parts of the body has often been illustrated by pictures of the 'Melothesic Man', a figure with the zodiac symbols arranged along the body. The traditional correspondences are:

Aries	head
Taurus	neck, throat
Gemini	shoulders, arms, lungs
Cancer	breasts, ribcage
Leo	heart
Virgo	stomach, bowels, womb
Libra	kidneys, lower back
Scorpio	sexual organs
Sagittarius	hips, thighs, liver
Capricorn	bones, joints, skin
Aquarius	shins, ankles, circulatory system
Pisces	feet

❖ see MEDICAL ASTROLOGY p28

has been common to talk of fate as if it were a power superior even to the gods. Christian theology places God above the laws of nature, ordaining things to His will. To accept a fatalistic view of the Universe, therefore, is in direct opposition to Christian — and indeed many other — belief systems. Astrology has long struggled with this issue and answers the conflict of whether or not it is fatalistic by the statement that the stars impel, not compel. Therefore, an element of choice remains and all is not ordained.

❖ see FREE WILL p159

Music of the Spheres

Pythagoras discovered that the pitch of a musical note depends on the length of the string that produces it. He was able then to correlate the intervals of the musical scale with simple numerical ratios. The Pythagoreans thought that earthly music was no more than an echo of the 'harmony of the spheres'. Each sphere corresponded to a different note of a musical scale. The tones emitted by

Fortitude

A quality or strength possessed by a planet when it is in its own sign or in the sign of its exaltation. It is often used to describe how dignified or debilitated a planet is. A high degree of fortitude means that the planet concerned is heavily dignified. The term is generally applied to essential dignity only, not accidental dignity.

❖ see FREE WILL p159

RIGHT: **Fortitude**, *from Ambrogio Lorenzetti's* **Allegory of Good Government**

ABOVE: *An Italian astrolabe*

Moisture

One of the four principles formulated by Aristotle and regarded as underlying all phenomena. Ptolemy's classification of the signs and planets to describe their essential characteristics is also used by traditional astrology. The air signs, Gemini, Libra and Aquarius are regarded as hot and moist, while the water signs, Cancer, Scorpio and Pisces are classified as cold and moist. Of the planets, Venus and the Moon are regarded as cold and moist, while Jupiter combines moisture with heat. These descriptions are quite important in the horary judgement of illnesses and can also literally apply to locations.

❖ see DRYNESS p162

Joy

Term used in older texts to describe an affinity between certain planets and signs, not necessarily of the nature of dignities. A planet is said to be 'in joy' when, although in debility, another planet with which it shares some similarity is placed in one of its dignities. At a later date the idea of planets having joy in certain houses developed. Saturn is considered to have joy in the twelfth, Jupiter the eleventh, Mars the sixth, Venus the fifth, Mercury the first, the Sun in the tenth and the Moon in the third.

❖ see HOUSE SYSTEMS p80

Ray

A ray is a force or energy with the emphasis on the quality that force exhibits rather than the form it creates. The astrologer Al-kindi (AD 800–873) attempted a rational explanation of astrological effects in terms of rays in his book *On the Stellar Rays*. The book also invokes terrestrial rays as an explanation for the efficacy of amulets, incantations, curses and sacrifice. He explained how the stellar rays interacted with various elements as they passed through space and came into contact with an individual. This work was influential in creating a belief in astrological magic. Medieval astrologers took hold of the idea of a physical cause for astrological influence. For years planets were held to emit rays that carried the nature of that planet – what might now be called its characteristics. From 1936 the theosophist Alice A. Bailey wrote a series of books entitled *Esoteric Astrology*. She took various traditional views and presented them in a more elaborated form. Central to her theories was the idea of the Seven Rays – one for each of the planets.

❖ see ESOTERIC ASTROLOGY p30

Dryness

Aristotelian principle. Dryness is one of the four principles formulated by Aristotle and regarded as underlying all phenomena. Ptolemy's classification of signs and planets is also used in traditional astrology to describe their essential nature. The fire signs – Aries, Leo and Sagittarius – are hot and dry; the earth signs – Taurus, Virgo and Capricorn – are considered to be cold and dry. Of the planets, the Sun and Mars are classified as hot and dry, while Mercury and Saturn are regarded as cold and dry. These descriptions are used in medical astrology and are also taken quite literally when pertaining to locations.

❖ see MOISTURE p162

Synchronicity

Synchronicity is a term coined by the psychologist Carl Jung to describe a connectedness of events that cannot be related causally. Jung quotes astrology as an excellent example of manifest synchronicity, and this theory is at the basis of modern psychological astrology. Jung described astrology as representing 'the summation of all the psychological knowledge of antiquity'. The origin of the principle of synchronicity is linked with Jung's acquaintance with the I Ching, although the Chinese regard the working of this oracle in terms of the operation of spirits – in other words, an animistic causality.

❖ see CARL JUNG p20

Speculum

The term 'speculum', from the Latin *specere*, meaning 'to look at', has been used to describe a number of tools. \In astrology it is primarily a table of data used as an aid in calculating directions. A speculum of aspects is a table of every degree in the horoscope that may be in aspect with the planets. A speculum may include information such as declination, right ascension or latitude. Any drawing or table that gives information showing the relative positions of the planets may be called a speculum. An instrument used to ascertain the true horizon is also called a speculum.

❖ see ASTROLABE p163

Cosmogram

The cosmogram is a tool used in cosmobiology. It is a 90-degree dial on which one degree represents one degree of the zodiac. The numbering begins at the top of the dial and moves in an anticlockwise direction. The first 30 degrees represent the cardinal signs (Aries, Cancer, Libra, Capricorn), the next 30 the fixed signs (Taurus, Leo, Scorpio, Aquarius) and the last 30 the mutable signs (Gemini, Virgo, Sagittarius, Pisces). When all the planets are placed around the dial the conjunctions, squares and oppositions can be seen easily. The instrument was designed to reveal these aspects or angular relationships.

❖ see COSMOBIOLOGY p31

Astrolabe

The astrolabe had become highly developed by AD 800 and was introduced to Europe from Spain in the early twelfth century. The astrolabe is an instrument for computing problems relating to time and the position of the Sun in the sky. In its heyday, the most popular version of the instrument was the planispheric astrolabe, on which the celestial sphere was projected on to the plane of the equator. A typical astrolabe was made of brass and about 15 cm (6 in) in diameter. An astrolabe shows how the sky looks at a specific place at a given time. This is done by drawing on the face of the astrolabe and marking it so that positions in the sky are easy to find. To use it you adjust the moveable components. Once set, the whole sky is represented on the face of the instrument.

❖ see ARMILLARY SPHERE p163

Armillary Sphere

Astrological tool. A representation of the celestial sphere used by the Greeks from the third century BC. Its name

BELOW: *A wooden Ptolemaic armillary sphere*

LEFT: *The Sun-signs, whose characteristics may be overridden by those of the stellium, or planetary line-up, in mundane astrology*

comes from the Latin *armilla*, meaning 'circle' or 'bracelet'. Armillary spheres were used well into the seventeenth century to teach the concepts and coordinate systems of spherical astronomy. The Earth is at the centre of the device and rings represent the horizon, equator, tropics and ecliptic. The cage as a whole revolves around the axis of the celestial poles. Armillary spheres sometimes incorporate models showing the motion of the Sun, Moon and other planets.

❖ see ASTROLABE p163

Glyph

The symbols used to represent the planets, signs and aspects in astrology are designated glyphs. They are of ancient origin and have meanings derived from the combination of circles, crescents, crosses and straight lines. The glyphs that represent signs are representative of the images used for the signs.

❖ see GLYPHS p166

Birthstone

Astrological talisman. Astrology associates a variety of gems and precious stones with certain signs or planets. To wear a stone associated with one's Sun-sign or the ruler thereof is believed to offer protection and to promote the wearer's health and success in life by filtering and focusing cosmic energies. Such a stone is referred to as the birthstone. This ancient tradition is still much used in Vedic astrology, whereas in the West birthstones are often only commercially exploited. Unfortunately, there is no conclusive answer as to which stone belongs to which sign or planet; the following list can therefore only give an indication:

Sun	diamond, ruby
Mercury	yellow topaz, citrine
Venus	jade, emerald

ABOVE: *The birthstone turquoise, shown here in a Tibetan pendant, is associated with the planet Uranus*

Mars	carnelian, jasper
Jupiter	lapis lazuli, amethyst
Saturn	falcon's eye, black star
Uranus	turquoise
Neptune	labradorite
Pluto	granite

The colour of the stone may be seen as a general indicator of its planetary connection. It is advisable to consider that a birthstone may enhance not only one's strength and fortune, but also the negative qualities of the planet by which it is ruled.

❖ see COLOURS p153

Astrologers use a number of symbols, known as glyphs, to represent the planets, signs and aspects. These are used as a type of shorthand amongst astrologers and on the horoscope itself. As well as the symbols there is an internationally accepted convention of abbreviations astrologers use when writing. These abbreviations are also listed here.

The glyphs have evolved over centuries of use. Those used to represent the signs are derived from the images that are associated with the signs. For example, the symbol for Aries is a stylized representation of the horns of the ram. The glyphs that represent the planets are related to the planets, meanings and are combinations of the circle, crescent, cross and line. The glyphs for the aspects are simple representations of the shape formed by the aspect if lines are drawn between the two planets concerned.

ABOVE: *Nostradamus*

SIGNS

Aries ♈ AR

The glyph for Aries represents the horns of the ram.

Taurus ♉ TA

The glyph for Taurus represents the head and horns of the bull.

Gemini ♊ GE

The glyph for Gemini represents twins and duality.

Cancer ♋ CA

The glyph for Cancer represents breasts and relates to the association of the sign with the mother figure and sustenance.

Leo ♌ LE

The glyph for Leo represents the mane of the lion.

Virgo ♍ VI

The glyph for Virgo represents an ear of corn and the harvest that takes place during the time that the Sun is in Virgo.

Libra ♎ LI

The glyph for Libra represents a set of scales.

Scorpio ♏ SC

The glyph for Scorpio represents the sting of the scorpion.

Sagittarius ♐ SAG

The glyph for Sagittarius represents the arrow fired by the centaur.

Capricorn ♑ or less commonly ♑ CAP

The glyph for Capricorn represents the horns of the goat.

Aquarius ♒ AQ

The glyph for Aquarius represents the water flowing into the jug of the water carrier and therefore the flow of ideas.

Pisces ♓ PIS

The glyph for Pisces represents two fish swimming in opposing directions.

PLANETS

Sun ☉ SO
Moon ☽ MO
Mercury ☿ ME
Venus ♀ VE
Mars ♂ MA
Jupiter ♃ JU
Saturn ♄ SA
Uranus ♅ UR
Neptune ♆ NE
Pluto ♇ or ♇ PL

MAJOR ASPECTS

Conjunction (0 degrees) ☌ CNJ
Square (90) □ SQ
Trine (120) △ TR
Opposition (180) ☍ OPP
Sextile (60) ✳ SEX

COMMON MINOR ASPECTS

Quincunx (150) ⚻ QCX
Semi-square (45) ∠ SSX
Semi-sextile (30) ⊻ SSQ
Sesquiquadrate (135) ⊡ SQQ

LESS COMMON ASPECTS

Quintile (72) **Q** Q
Septile (51°26') ⑦ s
Novile (40) ⑨ n
Biquintile (144) **Bq** Bq
Parallel ‖ P
Contra-Parallel ‖ Cp

OTHER ASTROLOGICAL GLYPHS

☊ North Node of Moon   NN
☋ South Node of Moon   SN
⚷ Chiron   CH
⊕ Earth   EA
⊗ Part of Fortune   PF

COMMONLY USED ABBREVIATIONS

Asc Ascendant or Rising Sign
Dsc Descendant or Seventh House Cusp
Mc Midheaven or Tenth House Cusp
Ic Immum Coeli or Fourth House Cusp
Rx Retrograde
St Stationary
Dt Direct
Tr Transiting Planet
Pr Progressed Planet or House Cusp
Ntl Natal Chart
Vx Vertex

MINOR PLANETS

Ceres   ⚳
Pallas   ⚴
Juno   ⚵
Vesta   ⚶
Transpluto   ⟠

URANIANS

Cupido   ⚴
Apollon   ♃
Hades   ♇
Vulcanus   ⚴
Zeus   ⚴
Cronos   ♈
Poseidon   ✳

THE HOROSCOPE

There is now a wealth of computer software available to calculate horoscopes and free programs are available through the Internet. Most astrologers, however, learn to calculate horoscopes by hand using sets of tables.

To calculate a horoscope by hand you need the relevant sets of tables. Firstly, you need an ephemeris for the year the chart is to be calculated for. This gives the positions of the planets for each day of the year at midnight or noon. These positions are adjusted according to the time of day that you were born. Ephemerides are available for individual years or for a number of years at a time.

To calculate house cusps you need a set of tables of houses. These enable you to calculate the rising sign and midheaven of the chart. If you use Equal or Porphyry house systems the intermediate house cusps are derived from the ascendant. For other house systems the intermediate house cusps are listed in the tables.

The most easily available tables are for the Placidus house system. Annual ephemerides often carry tables of houses for common locations. House cusps vary with latitude so tables give cusps for a variety of latitudes. If you are calculating a chart for a place between the latitudes given you need to work out the position of the cusps by using the tables for the two closest locations.

Ephemerides and tables of houses may be bought through major booksellers such as Amazon.com or from specialist New Age bookshops. Major booksellers sometimes stock them, or can order them for you on request. Raphael's annual ephemeris is the most popular and is easily available. Many ephemerides include a selection of tables of houses, and a selection of tables published by the American Federation of Astrologers, amongst others available from the Astrology Center of America and specialist bookshops. The log tables referred to here are reproduced in Raphael's annual ephemeris as well as in tables of houses and many astrology textbooks.

Calculating a horoscope

Before beginning calculation you need to ensure that you have the correct information. The first thing you need is the time that the chart is being calculated for. In the UK birth times are not recorded on birth certificates (unless you are one of a set of twins). The exception to this is for people born in Scotland. Apart from asking family members if they remember your time of birth, it may be recorded in a baby book or in medical records. If you were born in hospital it may be possible to find out from there, but if there is no way of finding out an accurate time of birth, it is best to work with the closest time you have. If you do not know your birth time, the chart is drawn up with Aries being placed on the middle of the left side and

Summer Time in the UK

1950 16 Apr–22 Oct	1960 10 Apr–2 Oct	1973 18 Mar–28 Oct	1983 27 Mar–23 Oct
1951 15 Apr–21 Oct	1961 26 Mar–29 Oct	1974 17 Mar–27 Oct	1984 25 Mar–28 Oct
1952 20 Apr–26 Oct	1962 25 Mar–28 Oct	1975 16 Mar–26 Oct	1985 31 Mar–27 Oct
1953 19 Apr–4 Oct	1963 31 Mar–27 Oct	1976 21 Mar–24 Oct	1986 30 Mar–26 Oct
1954 11 Apr–3 Oct	1964 22 Mar–25 Oct	1977 20 Mar–23 Oct	1987 29 Mar–25 Oct
1955 17 Apr–2 Oct	1965 21 Mar–24 Oct	1978 19 Mar–29 Oct	1988 27 Mar–23 Oct
1956 22 Apr–7 Oct	1966 20 Mar–24 Oct	1979 18 Mar–28 Oct	1989 26 Mar–29 Oct
1957 17 Apr–6 Oct	1967 19 Mar–29 Oct	1980 16 Mar–26 Oct	1990 25 Mar–28 Oct
1958 20 Apr–5 Oct	1968 18 Feb–31 Oct 1971	1981 29 Mar–25 Oct	1991 31 Mar–27 Oct
1959 19 Apr–4 Oct	1972 19 Mar–29 Oct	1982 28 Mar–24 Oct	1992 29 Mar–25 Oct

the planets drawn in with no houses marked. There will still be enough information to partially interpret the chart.

Assuming that you have a time to work with, the next step is to convert that time to Greenwich Mean Time. You should always work in the 24-hour clock system to avoid error. Greenwich Mean Time operates in the UK between late October and early March. If you were born in the UK between late March and late October when British Summer Time was in operation, you need to begin by taking one hour off. The exact dates the clocks change vary each year, but it is usually the third Sunday in March and the fourth Sunday in October. From 25 February 1940 to 7 October 1945 Summer Time remained throughout and an additional hour was deducted for Double Summer Time during the summer months. If you were born between 18 February 1968 and 31 October 1971 British Summer Time was in operation throughout this period, so you need to deduct one hour for GMT whatever date you were born on. Ireland uses the same time as Great Britain. Before 1981 the

times changed at 2 a.m. on the dates given above. From 1981 onwards the times changed at 1 a.m.

If you were born overseas, then you need to find out the time difference between your place of birth and Greenwich Mean Time. If you were born around midnight this could mean that the date changes. For example, if you were born at 11 p.m. in New York on 11 April, which is five hours earlier, you would add five hours for GMT. This would give you the time of 4 a.m. on 12 April, five hours later. You also need to check if your country was keeping summer time when you were born. In the case of New York, in summer months the time difference would be four hours, rather than five.

The next step is to find the latitude and longitude of the place where you were born. A good atlas will give the longitude and latitude of most places. But most astrologers use *The International Atlas* or *The American Atlas* by Thomas Shanks published by ACS, which also gives time zones and time changes.

SIDEREAL TIME

Having found Greenwich Mean Time the next step is to convert this to sidereal, or star, time. Looking in the ephemeris for your date of birth you will find that the sidereal time at noon or midnight of that date is given. You now need to calculate the difference between then and the time you were born to give the precise sidereal time for the time of your birth. The interval between the given time and noon is subtracted if it is earlier and added if later.

As a solar day is shorter than a sidereal day (about 10 seconds per hour) we need to make an adjustment. So, if we were looking at a set of tables for noon for each hour after noon you add 10 seconds for each hour. If before noon, you subtract 10 seconds. For each part of an hour you add, or subtract, the correct portion of ten seconds, with one second being equivalent to every six minutes. For example, fifteen minutes = 2.5 seconds.

This gives the sidereal time for your time of birth if you are born on the Greenwich meridian: at 0 degrees of longitude. A correction needs to be made for longitude if you are born elsewhere. Each degree of longitude is equivalent to four minutes of time, or 15 degrees of longitude is equivalent to one hour. Therefore the longitude of your place of birth needs to be divided by 15 and added, if you are born east of Greenwich, or subtracted, if you are born west of Greenwich.

Example one

Katie is born at 10:20h on 3 July 1976 in London. As this is during summer time we need to begin by deducting one hour to convert this time to GMT. Katie's birth time is, therefore, 9:20 GMT. Looking at a set of accurate tables for the sidereal time at noon on her date of birth we find that it is 6:46:33. As she is born two hours and forty minutes before noon, we need to subtract that

figure. Remembering that there are 60 seconds in a minute and 60 minutes to the degree that gives us:

```
6    46    33 -
2    40    00
_____
4    06    33
```

We now need to subtract 10 seconds per hour which in this case is 20 seconds for the two hours and 6.66 seconds (rounded up to seven seconds) for the 40 minutes.

```
4    06    33 -
           27
_____
4    06    06
```

Example two

Nathan is born at 17:35h on 2 October 1978 in New York. The sidereal time at noon on this date is 12:43:24. New York keeps Eastern Standard Time. A check reveals that Summer Time was in operation then so the difference is four hours. Therefore four hours need to be added giving 21:35 GMT. This is nine hours and 35 minutes after noon and so this figure needs to be added to the sidereal time.

```
12    43    24 +
09    35    00
_____
22    18    24
```

We then add 50 seconds for the five hours and six seconds for the 35 minutes giving a total of 56 seconds to be added. This gives us a sidereal time of 22:19:20. New York is 73 degrees 57 minutes west of Greenwich. Divided by 15 this gives four hours, 55 minutes and 48 seconds.

```
22    19    20 -
04    55    48
_____
17    23    32
```

This is the sidereal time for Nathan.

LONGITUDE AND LATITUDE OF MAJOR TOWNS AND CITIES IN THE UK AND IRELAND

ENGLAND

Barnsley 51N33 1W30
Basingstoke 51N16 1W07
Bath 51N22 2W23
Bedford 52N08 0W29
Berkshire 51N30 1W20
Birmingham 52N30 1W50
Blackpool 53N50 3W03
Bletchley 52N00 0W46
Bognor Regis 50N47 0W41
Bolton 53N35 2W26
Bournemouth 50N43 1W54
Bradford 53N48 1W45
Brighton 50N50 0W08
Buckinghamshire 51N45 0W48
Bury St Edmunds 52N15 0E43
Cambridgeshire 52N20 0E05
Canterbury 51N17 1E05
Carlisle 54N54 2W55
Cheltenham 51N54 2W04
Chester 53N12 2W54
Cirencester 51N44 1W59
Cornwall 50N30 4W40
Coventry 52N25 1W30
Crewe 53N05 2W27
Cumbria 54N30 3W00
Darlington 54N3331 1W34
Derby 53N55 1W29
Derbyshire 53N00 1W33
Devon 50N45 3W50
Doncaster 53N32 1W07
Dover 51N08 1E19
Essex 51N49 0E40
Exeter 50N43 3W31
Frome 51N14 2W20
Gateshead 54N58 1W37
Glastonbury 51N06 2W30
Gloucester 51N53 2W14
Great Yarmouth 52N37 1E44
Grimsby 53N35 0W05
Guildford 51N14 0W35
Halifax 53N44 1W52
Hampshire 51N05 1W15
Hove 50N49 0W10
Huddersfield 53N39 1W47
Ipswich 52N04 1E10

Kent 51N15 0E40
Lancashire 53N03 2W30
Lancaster 54N03 2W48
Leeds 53N50 1W35
Leicester 52N38 1W05
Leicestershire 52N46 0W53
Liverpool 53N25 2W55
London 51N30 0W53
Macclesfield 53N16 2W07
Manchester 53N30 2W15
Margate 51N24 1E24
Middlesex 51N29 0W22
Newcastle 52N26 3W06
Newcastle under Lyme
    53N00 2W14
Newcastle upon Tyne
    54N59 1W35
Northamptonshire
    52N20 0W50
Norwich 52N38 1E18
Nottingham 52N58 1W10
Nottinghamshire
    53N00 1W00
Oldham 53N33 2W007
Oxford 51N46 1W15
Oxfordshire 51N39 1W10
Peak Forest 53N13 1W50
Penzance 50N07 5W33
Plymouth 50N23 4W10
Portsmouth 50N48 1W05
Preston 53N46 0W12
Rotherham 53N26 1W20
Rugby 52N23 1W15
Salisbury 53N47 1W48
Scunthorpe 53N36 0W38
Sheffield 53N23 1W30
Shrewsbury 52N43 2W45
Shropshire 52N40 2W00
Skegness 53N10 0E21
Slough 51N31 0W36
Somerset 51N08 3W00
Southport 53N39 3W01
Stafford 52N48 2W07
Staffordshire 52N50 2W00
Stockport 53N25 2W10
Stoke 51N27 0E37

Stratford upon Avon
    52N12 1W41
Suffolk 52N15 0E43
Surrey 51N10 0W20
Sussex 50N55 0E15
Taunton 51N01 3W06
Torquay 50N28 3W30
Warwick 52N17 1W34
Warwickshire 52N13 1W34
Weymouth 50N36 2W28
Wiltshire 51N15 1W50
Winchester 51N04 1W19
Woking 51N20 0W34
Wolverhampton 52N36 2W08
York 53N58 1W05
Yorkshire South 53N30 1W15
Yorkshire W 53N45 1W40

SCOTLAND

Aberdeen 57N10
Ayr 57N28 4W38
Balmoral 57N02 3W13
Dalkeith 55N54 0W04
Dumfries 55N04 3W27
Dundee 56N28 3W00
East Kilbride 55N46 4W10
Edinburgh 55N57 3W13
Falkirk 56N00 3W48
Fort William 56N49 5W07
Glasgow 55N53 4W15
Gretna Green 554N59 3W04
Inverness 57N27 4W15
Kilbride 57N05 7W27
Leith 55N59 3W10
Motherwell 55N48 4W00
Oban 56N25 5W29
Paisley 55N50 4W26
Peebles 55N39 3W12
Perth 56N24 3W28
Selkirk 55N33 2W50

WALES

Abergavenny 51N50 3W00
Aberystwyth 52N25 4W05
Bangor 53N13 4W08
Barry 51N24 3W15

Caernarfon 53N08 4W16
Caerphilly 51N35 3W14
Cardiff 51N29 3W13
Cardigan 52N06 4W40
Harlech 53N52 4W0007
Hay on Wye 52N04 3W07
Holyhead 53N19 4W38
Llandudno 53N19 3W49
Merthyr Tydfil 51N46 3W23
Monmouth 51N50 2W43
Pembroke 51N41
Pontypool 51N43 3W02
Rhyl 53N19 3W29
Swansea 51N38 3W57
Tenby 51N41 4W43
Wrexham 52N03 3W00

NORTHERN IRELAND

Antrim 54N43 6W13
Armagh 54N21 5W36
Belfast 54N35 5W55
Derry 55N00 7W19
Omagh 54N36 7W18

EIRE

Adare 52N34 8W48
Carlow 52N50 6W55
Cavan 54N00 7W21
Ennis 52N50 8W29
Shannon 52N41 8W55
Cork 51N54 8W28
Donegal 54N39 9W07
Dublin 52N30 6W15
Galway 53N16 9W03
Dundalk 54N01 6W25
Kildare 53N10 6W55
Kilkenny 52N39 7W15
Leitrim 54N00 8W04
Limerick 52N40 8W38
Longford 53N44 7W47
Louth 53N37 6W53
Roscommon 53N38 8W11
Sligo 54N17 8W28
Tipperary 52N39 8W10
Wicklow 52N59 6W0

ASCENDANTS

When you have worked out the sidereal time all you need to do is look up the time in a set of tables and read across to see what the Ascendant is. Looking at a table of houses for London we take Katie's time of 4:06:33. The closest listed to this time is 4:03:48 and 4:08:00. The tables list the following figures:

Sidereal time	10	11	12	Asc	2	3
	Gemini	Cancer	Leo	Virgo	Libra	Libra
4:03:48	3	10	13	9 33	1	28
4:08:00	4	11	14	10 17	2	29

The column headed 10 gives the position of the midheaven and the other columns give the house cusps as numbered. The time we want lies approximately halfway between the sidereal times given. The first time given is 1:12 earlier than the time we want and the second is 2:27 later. Unless there is a sign change, using the first figure in this type of case would normally be sufficiently accurate. However, as the Ascendant is given more accurately we can interpolate to find a more accurate Ascendant. The difference between the later figure and the one we want is about twice as much as that between the earlier figure and the one we want. Therefore if we calculate the difference between the first and second Ascendant position given, halve that and add it to the earlier figure we will have a more accurate Ascendant.

10 17 − 9 33 = 44
44 / 2 = 22
9 33 + 22 = 9 55 Our Ascendant is therefore 9 55 Virgo.

If the chart was to be set using Placidus house cusps at this stage we would simply take note of the figures given for the relevant cusps as listed. The signs are now drawn on the chart wheel with the Ascendant sign on the left. The positions we have calculated are marked where they fall in the signs. If lines are drawn from these points straight across the wheel we then have the remaining house cusps.

If the chart was to be set using Equal houses we simply mark the Ascendant on the wheel. Each sign following is then marked at the same degree as the Ascendant. Drawing lines across the chart we then have the house cusps. The midheaven is marked with an arrow pointing upwards where it falls.

If the chart was to be set using Porphyry houses the midheaven is marked on the top of the chart. Each sign is marked at the same degree, in a similar fashion to the Equal house system. The Ascendant is then marked by an arrow on the left of the chart.

For other house systems, tables for that particular system are required.

Southern hemisphere charts

The tables of houses are calculated for the northern hemisphere and so an adjustment must be made when calculating charts for the southern hemisphere. When looking up the Ascendant and house cusps, the OPPOSITE sign to the one given is the correct one to use. For example, if the tables show that the Ascendant is in Capricorn, for a southern hemisphere chart it will be in Cancer.

The positions of the planets are given in the ephemeris for noon (or midnight) for the date being considered. To calculate the correct positions for the horoscope we therefore need to amend the positions as given for the time of birth. In the case of Katie the positions given would be:

Sun	Moon	Mercury	Venus	Mars
Cancer	Virgo	Gemini	Cancer	Leo
11 40 10	25 34 49	27 51.5	15 52.8	27 54.3

Jupiter	Saturn	Uranus	Neptune	Pluto
Taurus	Leo	Scorpio	Sagittarius	Libra
22 34.8	3 14.3	3 3.6	11 49.4	8 59.1

We would note at this stage that Uranus and Neptune are marked with an R in the ephemeris, showing that they are retrograde on this date.

Firstly we need to note the difference between noon and the birth time we are using. Katie was born at 10:20h: one hour and 40 minutes before noon. The easiest way to calculate the difference in the planetary positions between our birth time and noon is by using log tables. The log tables used are proportional logarithms using 24 hours as their base and are specifically designed for this type of calculation. They are often included in ephemerides and tables of houses.

To find the figure we need, we simply look along the top of the table for hours, in this case 10, and look down the table to the horizontal column for the minutes, in this case 20. That would give us the number 3695.

Next we take note of how fast the planet we are looking at is moving. In annual ephemerides the motion of the planets is given so no calculation is needed. If it is not given you simply calculate the difference between the planet's position on the date you want and the previous or following day, depending on whether you are looking at a chart for before or after noon. For example, on Katie's date of birth the Sun is at 11 40 10 Cancer. As she was born in the morning we note that on the previous day it was at 10 42 57 Cancer. By subtracting the second number from the first we find that in one day it has moved 57 minutes and 13 seconds.

Using the log tables we look up the log for 57 minutes, discarding the seconds. That gives us 1.4025. The two logs are added together; they should always be added irrespective of whether the birth time is before or after noon.

3695 + 1.4025 = 1.7720

We then look within the log tables to find the closest number to this and read what is given as degrees and minutes. In this case the closest number is 1.7781 and shows a difference of 24 minutes. As we are looking at a morning birth we then deduct 24 minutes from the position given for noon 11 40 10 – 00 24 00 = 11 16 10 of Cancer. This is the position of the Sun in Katie's horoscope. If the result of this calculation is over 30 degrees that simply means that the planet has moved into the next sign and you deduct 30 from your answer while noting the sign change. Similarly, if the answer is less than zero that means that the planet has moved into the preceding sign, which may happen if the planet is retrograde. If this is the case, simply add 30 degrees to your answer.

The same process is undertaken for all of the planets. As Uranus, Neptune and Pluto move so slowly, it is often sufficient to take the noon position with no further adjustment. Once the positions of the planets are calculated they are drawn on the chart in their correct places.

ASPECTS

ASPECTS

Whether you have calculated a chart by hand or on the computer you may need to calculate aspects. No actual calculation is needed for many of the aspects as with practice they can be seen by eye. However, minor aspects are not so easily recognized and some simple calculation is needed. Firstly, you decide which type of aspect you are looking for. Normally we begin by making a search for the major aspects, starting with the conjunction. A decision needs to be made from the outset which orbs you are allowing for the aspects. Although an exact number is given for each aspect, the orb is the 'give and take'. In modern astrology the aspects themselves are given an orb, whereas in traditional astrology it is the planets that give the orb of influence. The orbs will become clear in the examples that follow.

The orbs accepted by most modern astrologers are: conjunction, square, trine, opposition; and square: eight degrees, sextile: four degrees, quincunx: two degrees and all minor aspects: one degree. Some astrologers allow a greater orb when the Sun or Moon is involved.

The orbs used by most traditional astrologers are referred to as moieties. This gives the range either side of the planet that may be considered. An orb, as it is used in modern astrology, is half of the moiety of a planet. The moieties of the planets are as follows: Sun 17, Moon 12, Mercury 7, Venus 8, Mars 7 30, Jupiter 12, Saturn 10. There is no consensus on the moieties of Uranus, Neptune and Pluto, but they are often treated in the same way as Saturn, or given a moiety of eight degrees.

The moieties of each of the planets being considered are added together and this total is halved to give the orb of an aspect between those two planets. For example, for the Sun and Venus 17 + 8 = 25 25 /2 = 12 30. This is the orb for any aspect.

Conjunction

The conjunction is an aspect of 0 degrees. Two planets next to each other in the chart will be in conjunction. As an orb of 8 degrees is used by modern astrologers they may be up to 8 degrees apart. They need not be in the same sign; if they are in different signs this is a dissociate conjunction. For example, if the Sun is at 26 degrees of Cancer, and Venus at one degree of Leo, these two planets are conjunct.

Opposition

This is an aspect of 180 degrees, so the planets are directly opposite on the chart. (They may not be in opposite signs.) If the Sun is at 26 degrees of Cancer and the Moon at 20 degrees of Capricorn they are in opposition.

Square

This is an aspect of 90 degrees, or three signs apart. Occasionally two planets will be in square separated by four signs. The easiest way to spot a square is to count three signs along in either direction from the planet you are looking at and see if there is another planet there. If the Sun is at 26 degrees of Cancer and Jupiter at 29 Libra they are in square.

Trine

This is an aspect of 120 degrees, or about four signs apart, and is worked out in the same way as the square.

Sextile

This is an aspect of 60 degrees, or two signs apart, and worked out as above.

Quincunx

This is an aspect of 150 degrees or five signs apart.

Minor aspects

Although, with experience, it is possible to see minor aspects by eye many of them need to be calculated, especially in the early stages of learning astrology. The position of each planet is converted to absolute longitude. Remembering that each sign is 30 degrees long, the degree within the sign is added to the longitude degree at the start of that sign.

Aries begins at 0 degrees, Taurus 30, Gemini 60, Cancer 90, Leo 120, Virgo 150, Libra 180, Scorpio 210, Sagittarius 240, Capricorn 270, Aquarius 300 and Pisces 330. A planet at 22 Libra is therefore at 202 (180 + 22) degrees of the circle.

After noting the absolute longitude of each planet, and chart point if you are calculating aspects to them, take note of the angular distance of each aspect you are searching for so that you can see if any combination is in their range. The most commonly used minor aspects are: semi-sextile 30, semi-square 45, sesquiquadrate 135, quincunx 150.

Rarely used minor aspects are: decile or semi-quintile 36, novile 40, septile 51 25, quintile 72, sesquiquintile 108, bi-quintile 144.

Beginning with the Sun each planet is considered in relation to the Sun's position. If the Sun is at 26 Cancer, it is at 116 degrees of the circle. If Venus is at 10 Virgo, it is at 160 degrees of the circle. Taking the lower number from the higher (160 –116) we get 44. As the semi-square is an aspect of 45 degrees and has a one degree orb these two planets are in semi-square. Many astrologers use only major aspects unless the commonly used minor aspects are exact, in which case they may be considered.

When the aspects have been calculated they are listed and a note is made as to whether they are applying: the two planets are approaching each other – or separating: the aspect has already been exact. For example, if the Sun is at 4 degrees of Scorpio and Mercury at 8 degrees of Scorpio they are in conjunction. The Sun is the faster planet and is moving towards Mercury, therefore in a few days' time they will be at the same degree. This is an applying aspect. If the Sun was at 10 degrees of Scorpio it would be separating from Mercury. Applying aspects are generally thought of as being stronger.

PLANETARY STRENGTH

In traditional astrology the dignities and debilities of the planets are considered in interpretation. Modern astrologers generally only take note of rulership. The dignities and debilities of the planets are set out in the table below. To read the table you look at the sign the planet is in and read across the columns. For example, if considering 15 degrees of Aries we would note the following:

- It is ruled by Mars (by day).
- The Sun is exalted (especially at 19 degrees).
- It is the Sun's triplicity in the day and Jupiter's at night.
- As it is over 14 degrees and under 21, it is in Mercury's term.
- It is in the Sun's face.
- Venus is in detriment there and Saturn in fall.

If Venus was at this degree it would be in a difficult and weak position, being in detriment.

SIGN		EX	TRIP D/N		TERMS					FACES			DET	FALL
♈	♂ D	☉ 19	☉	♃	♃ 6	♀ 14	☿ 21	♂ 26	♄ 30	♂ 10	☉ 20	♀ 30	♀	♄
♉	♀ N	☽ 3	♀	☽	♀ 8	☿ 15	♃ 22	♄ 26	♂ 30	☿ 10	☽ 20	♄ 30	♂	
♊	☿ D	☊ 3	♄	☿	☿ 7	♃ 14	♀ 21	♄ 25	♂ 30	♃ 10	♂ 20	☉ 30	♃	
♋	☽ D N	♃ 15	♂	♂	♂ 6	♃ 13	☿ 20	♀ 27	♄ 30	♀ 10	☿ 20	☽ 30	♄	♂
♌	☉ D N		☉	♃	♄ 6	☿ 13	♀ 19	♃ 25	♂ 30	♄ 10	♃ 20	♂ 30	♄	
♍	☿ N	☿ 15	☿	☽	☿ 7	♀ 13	♃ 18	♄ 24	♂ 30	☉ 10	♀ 20	☿ 30	♃	♀
♎	♀ D	♄ 21	♄	☿	♄ 6	♀ 11	♃ 19	☿ 24	♂ 30	☽ 10	♄ 20	♃ 30	♂	☉
♏	♂ N		♂	♂	♂ 6	♃ 14	♀ 21	☿ 27	♄ 30	♂ 10	☉ 20	♀ 30	♀	☽
♐	♃ D	☋ 3	☉	♃	♃ 8	♀ 14	☿ 19	♄ 25	♂ 30	☿ 10	☽ 20	♄ 30	☿	
♑	♄ N	♂ 28	♀	☽	♀ 6	☿ 12	♃ 19	♂ 25	♄ 30	♃ 10	♂ 20	☉ 30	☽	♃
♒	♄ D		♄	☿	♄ 6	☿ 12	♀ 20	♃ 25	♂ 30	♀ 10	☿ 20	☽ 30	☉	
♓	♃ N	♀ 27	♂	♂	♀ 8	♃ 14	☿ 20	♂ 26	♄ 30	♄ 10	♃ 20	♂ 30	☿	☿

The planets are given points according to their position in this scheme. A commonly used system is that outlined in the table below.

ESSENTIAL DIGNITY	SCORE	ESSENTIAL DEBILITY	SCORE
Planet in Own Sign	5	Planet in Detriment	-5
Planet in Mutual Reception	5	Planet in Fall	-4
Planet in Exaltation	4	Peregrine	-5
Reception by Exaltation	4	In Own Triplicity	3
In Own Terms	2	In Own Face	1

ACCIDENTAL DIGNITY	SCORE	ACCIDENTAL DEBILITY	SCORE
On MC or Ascendant	5	In 12th House	-5
In 7th, 4th, or 11th house	4	In 8th or 6th house	-4
In 2nd or 5th house	3	Retrograde	-5
In 9th house	2	Slow in Motion	-2
In 3rd house	1	♄ ♃ ♂ Occidental	-2
Direct	4	☿ ♀ Oriental	-2
Swift in Motion	2	☽ Decreasing in Light	-2
♄ ♃ ♂ Oriental	2	Combust	-5
☿ ♀ Occidental	2	Under Sunbeams	-4
☽ Increasing in Light	2	Partile ☌ with ♄ or ♂	-5
Not Combust, nor Under Beams	5	Partile ☌ with ☋	-4
Cazimi	5	Partile ☍ with ♄ or ♂	-4
Partile ☌ with ♃ or ♀	5	Besieged by ♄ or ♂	-5
Partile ☌ with ☊	5	Partile □ with ♄ or ♂	-3
Partile △ with ♃ or ♀	4	Conjunct Algol, or within 5°	-5
Partile ✳ with ♃ or ♀	3		
Partile ☌ with Cor Leonis	6		
Partile ☌	5		

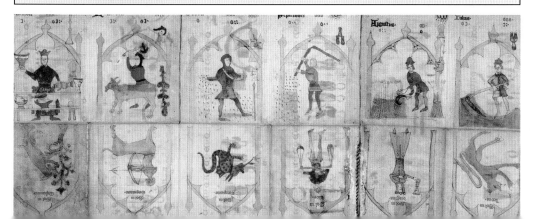

RELATIONSHIPS

Calculating a composite chart

A composite chart is a chart that combines the charts of two people in a relationship and represents the relationship itself, and the shared energies of the people involved. It is formed by determining the midpoints between pairs of planets, angles and the focal points of the two horoscopes concerned. The midpoint is the halfway point between two planets.

Firstly, the birth charts of the two people concerned need to be calculated. The positions of the planets and angles are then listed in terms of absolute longitude, or where they lie on the circle. Remembering that each sign contains 30 degrees, the degree within the sign is added to the longitude degree at the start of that sign. Aries begins at 0 degrees, Taurus 30, Gemini 60, Cancer 90, Leo 120, Virgo 150, Libra 180, Scorpio 210, Sagittarius 240, Capricorn 270, Aquarius 300 and Pisces 330.

The position of the planet in its sign is added to the 0 degree equivalent of that sign. For example, if Jane's Moon is at 21 34 Cancer we add 90 to this position giving an answer of 111 34. If her boyfriend Paul's Moon is at 16 12 Aquarius we add 300 to this position giving an answer of 316 12.

To find the position of their composite Moon these figures are added together and divided by two.

111 34 +
316 12
———————
427 46

Divide this total by two and you get 213 53 (remembering that sixty minutes equal one degree when carrying over numbers).

The nearest beginning of a sign to this figure is Scorpio at 210. As Scorpio is 13 degrees 53 minutes later, the position of the composite Moon is therefore 13 53 Scorpio. The same procedure is applied to each of the planets, the midheavens, Ascendants, Moon's nodes and, if a quadrant house system is used, house cusps. There is no need to refer to a table of houses when calculating the new cusps.

(A slightly different technique involves calculating the midpoints of the latitudes and longitudes of each chart and using the composite midheaven in the relevant set of tables to find the Ascendant and house cusps.)

Each of the new positions are drawn on the circle as a new chart and the resultant aspects calculated. This chart can then be interpreted in a similar way to a birth chart. Transits can be applied to the composite chart to judge the outcome of the relationship. The composite chart cannot be progressed, although if the progressed charts of the two people concerned are calculated, a composite chart can be made from these progressed charts. It is also possible to derive a composite chart for more than two people. If, for example, four people are involved in a relationship, all four positions are added together and then divided by four to find the positions in the composite chart representing that relationship.

The Relationship Chart

An alternative method of deriving a chart for a relationship between two people is to cast a new chart for a birth date, time and place that lies halfway between those of the two people concerned. Whereas the composite chart is a mathematical abstraction, based on the theory of midpoints, the relationship chart is a real chart existing in time and space.

Inter aspects and the synastry grid

The most common way to compare two people's charts in detail is to examine the aspects made from a

	Sun	Moon	Merc	Ven	Mars	Jup	Sat	Ur	Nep	Pl	Asc	mc	Nn
Sun													
Moon													
Merc													
Ven													
Mars													
Jup													
Sat													
Ur													
Ne													
Pl													
Asc													
mc													
Nn													

planet in one chart to a planet in the other. For example, if Jane's Sun is at 22 34 Cancer, and Paul's Venus is at 24 12 Capricorn, these two planets will be in opposition. The orbs for the aspects used in synastry are smaller than those used in judging birth charts. Generally, five degrees are used for the conjunction, four for the opposition, square and trine, three for the sextile and one for all other aspects. There is no accepted consensus on the exact orbs to be used although it is agreed that the closer to exactitude the aspect, the more important it is for the relationship. To make it easier to gain an overview of the inter aspects a grid is drawn up with one person's planets along the top and the other person's down the side as shown above.

The aspects between each pair are then marked in the grid. Stressful aspects may be drawn in red, harmonious aspects in blue and neutral aspects in green. This enables you to see at a glance how problematic the relationship is likely to be.

PREDICTIONS

Transits

Transits are the simplest prediction method available to the astrologer. A transit occurs when a planet, moving in its orbit, forms an aspect to any planet or point in the birth chart. Once the birth chart has been calculated it is possible to look in an ephemeris, or check with a computer program where the planets are on a chosen date. The transiting planets are drawn around the outside of the chart. Any aspects that are formed between the transiting planet and points on the birth chart should be noted. These are then interpreted according to the nature of the planets involved and the particular aspect formed.

Although transits can be calculated using any of the planets, normally only the planets from Mars outwards are used. This is due to the fact that the inner planets move too quickly for practical use. Inner planet transits are only used in very detailed predictive work. There is no general consensus for which of the orbs of the aspects should be used, although they should be smaller than those used in interpreting the birth chart. Many astrologers will only use an orb of one degree, whatever the aspect. Although technically any aspect may be used, only the major aspects are generally considered when interpreting transits.

An awareness of the speed of orbit of the planets means that estimates can be made of upcoming transits. Although their speeds differ, owing to retrograde motion the Sun, Mercury and Venus take about one year to travel through the whole chart, spending about one month in each sign. Mars takes about two years to go around the chart and spends about two months in each sign. Jupiter takes 11.86 years to go around the chart and spends about a year in each sign. Saturn takes about 28 years to go around the chart and spends about two-and-a-half years in each sign. Uranus takes 84 years to go around the chart and spends about seven years in each sign. Neptune takes about 165 years to go around the chart and spends about 14 years in each sign. Pluto takes about 249 years to go around the chart and spends between 12 and 31 years in each sign, owing to its eccentric orbit.

Age	Saturn	Uranus	Neptune	Pluto
7	Square	Semi-sextile		
14	Opposition	Sextile	Semi-sextile	
21	Square	Square		Semi-sextile
28	Conjunction	Trine	Sextile	
35	Square	Quincunx		
42	Opposition	Opposition	Square	Sextile
49	Square	Quincunx		
56	Conjunction	Trine	Trine	
63	Square	Square		Square
70	Opposition	Sextile	Quincunx	
77	Square	Semi-Sextile		
84	Conjunction	Conjunction	Opposition	Trine

Knowing that these types of transits occur at these particular ages means that instead of checking regularly to see if there are any relevant transits upcoming in the birth chart, the astrologer will check the exact date that these transits are likely to take place for the individual concerned. Aspects made to other planets in the birth chart will be considered as well.

ephemeris. (Although the noon ephemeris is described here the methodology remains the same if using a midnight ephemeris – except then we consider the midnight date.) This means that you do not need to calculate the positions of the planets for each year of life in the progressed chart. This date is generally known as the noon date. Someone born in the early part of the day will have a noon date later in the year than the birth date while someone born later in the day will have a noon date earlier than their birth date. The following table gives the equivalent periods of life compared with time in the ephemeris:

Ephemeris	Life
1 day	1 year
12 hours	6 months
6 hours	3 months
2 hours	1 month
1 hour	15 days
30 minutes	About 7-and-a-half days
10 minutes	About 2-and-a-half days
5 minutes	About 1 day

The regular patterns of movement of the planets means that they will transit their position in the birth chart at approximately the same age for each person. The type of aspects made are expressed in the table on the left.

Secondary progression calculation

Secondary progressions are also simple to calculate. Taking the ephemeris for the year of birth you simply count one day forward for each year of birth. Remember that at the age of one you have completed one year of life, so the day AFTER birth represents that year. Again the progressed positions are drawn around the birth chart and aspects made to the planets and points in the birth chart are noted and interpreted.

For greater accuracy than this basic method of calculating progressions some simple arithmetic is required. It is helpful to know the date in the year that corresponds exactly with the noon positions in the

To calculate the noon date you begin by noting the interval to, or from, noon of the birth time. As the ephemeris is calculated using GMT all calculations need to be in GMT.

Example

Laura was born on 6 February 1970.

Her birth time was 10 a.m.

The interval from 10 a.m. to noon is two hours.

As her birth time is before noon her noon date will be later than her birth date.

Two hours = one month (see table above).

Therefore her noon date is 6 January.

Occasionally the noon date may fall into the preceding or following year. An alternative method is to work out what number day in the year the birth date is. 6 February is day number 37 of the year. A birth time of 10 a.m. gives an interval of two hours from noon. This interval converts to one month or approximately 30 days. Subtracting 30 from 37 gives a noon date of 7 January.

Although these methods may yield slightly different results they are adequate for most predictive work. There are more complex arithmetical methods to calculate progressions more accurately, but if greater accuracy is required most astrologers use computer software, which provides exact results.

Having found the noon date the next stage is to find the correct day in the year that corresponds to the year in question. Noon in the ephemeris corresponds to the

6 (or 7) of January prior to Laura's birth. Noon on 6 February corresponds to 6 January in progressed terms.

If we wanted to look at her progressions for age 30 we would begin by adding 30 days to her birth date. 30 days on from 6 February is 8 March. The noon positions for the planets on 8 March would equal the progressed positions for 6 January (the noon date calculated above).

Noon positions 8 March 1970 = progressed positions 6 January 1970

Noon positions 9 March 1970 = progressed positions 6 January 1971

Noon positions 10 March 1970 = progressed positions 6 January 1972

and so on until we reach

Noon positions 7 April 1970 = progressed positions 6 January 2000

Therefore by noting the positions in the ephemeris for 7 April 1970 we have the progressions for 6 January 2000.

If we want to look at a particular month during the year, we need to note the position of the Moon as it moves the fastest. We take the position of the Moon on the date of birth, the position on the following day and subtract one from the other. This gives the motion of the Moon during that day. Dividing this figure by 12 will give the progressed motion in one month. This figure is then added to the position we have for 6 January to give February's progressed Moon position, added again to give the position for March's and so on.

To calculate the progressed Ascendant and midheaven you take the date in the ephemeris that corresponds to the year under investigation. In the above case that would be 8 March 1970. The Ascendant and midheaven are then calculated in the same manner as the birth chart.

A simpler method is to use the solar arc. Subtract the position of the Sun in the birth chart from the position of the progressed Sun. This gives the solar arc. Add this figure to the Midheaven in the birth chart. Using a table of houses for the correct latitude, look up the corresponding ascendant.

It is only worth calculating the progressed midheaven and Ascendant if the birth time is accurate. A few degrees, error in the angles, owing to an incorrect time, will result in a few years, error in timing with progressions.

Converse Progressions

Converse progressions are calculated exactly like secondary progressions except one day before birth is held to equate with one year of life. The noon date, if used, is also different and needs to be calculated in reverse.

Tertiary and Minor progressions

If the basic premise is accepted that a day in the ephemeris can correlate with a year of life, it is a small step to equate it with a month or week. There are two methods of equating a day with a month. The first, using the calendar month, and calculated as above, substituting a month for a year, is known as monthly secondary progressions. Basing the progressions on a lunar month requires special tables to aid in counting forward the days. These are known as tertiary progressions. Minor progressions equate a month in the ephemeris with a year of life.

Solar Arc Directions

To obtain the solar arc subtract the position of the Sun in the birth chart from the position of the progressed Sun. This number is then added to the position of each of the planets (and other chart points) once for each year of life. All the planets move forward at the same rate and the aspects between the planets will always be the same as those in the birth chart.

One degree directions

With this basic method of prediction, one degree is added to each planet or chart point. It varies little from the solar arc method but is much easier to calculate.

FIXED STARS

Although there are about 290 stars and 57 constellations that could be used in astrology, only a small number are regularly used. The fixed stars have an influence when at the Ascendant or angles at birth, or when near the Sun or Moon. Only one degree of orb is allowed and usually only the conjunction is used.

The Arabic Parts are calculated by adding and subtracting the positions of planets and features in a chart. The most common part in use is that of the Part of Fortune. Many parts are calculated by different formulae depending on whether the chart is for a day or night birth. If the Sun is in the upper half of the chart it is of a day birth.

To calculate the Part of Fortune you need to first convert the positions of the Ascendant, Sun and Moon to absolute longitude. Remembering that each sign is 30 degrees long, the degree within the sign is added to the longitude degree at the start of that sign. Aries begins at 0 degrees, Taurus 30, Gemini 60, Cancer 90, Leo 120, Virgo 150, Libra 180, Scorpio 210, Sagittarius 240, Capricorn 270, Aquarius 300 and Pisces 330. A planet at 22 Libra is therefore at 202 (180+22) degrees of the circle. The

formula for a day birth is Ascendant + Moon − Sun = Part of Fortune. The formula for a night birth is Ascendant + Sun − Moon = Part of Fortune.

Example

In John's chart the Ascendant is at 27 21 Cancer, the Sun at 15 42 Leo and the Moon at 2 16 Taurus. Converting these to absolute longitude we get:

Ascendant = 120 + 27 21 = 147 21
Sun = 150 + 15 42 = 165 42
Moon = 60 + 2 16 = 62 16

As this is a night birth (because the Sun lies in the bottom half of the chart) we use the night formula.

Ascendant + Sun − Moon = Part of Fortune

$$
\begin{array}{r}
147\ 21\ + \\
165\ 42 \\
\hline
313\ 03\ - \\
62\ 16 \\
\hline
250\ 47
\end{array}
$$

Star	Position	Meaning
Caput Algol	26 10 Taurus	Failure, difficulties, disaster
Alcyone	00 00 Gemini	Compassion and disappointment
Aldebaran	9 35 Gemini	Violence and victory
Regulus	29 50 Leo	Success and glory
Vindematrix	9 56 Libra	Misfortune, war and widowhood
Spica	23 50 Libra	Success and prosperity
Arcturus	29 14 Libra	Success and prosperity
Antares	9 38 Sagittarius	Conflict and violence
Serpentis	19 Scorpio	Disaster
Vega	15 19 Capricorn	Success in politics or finance
Fomalhaut	3 52 Pisces	Good or bad depending on aspects
Scheat	29 22 Pisces	Failure and difficulties, especially at sea

We then convert this absolute longitude position back to zodiacal longitude. Sagittarius begins at 240 degrees. Therefore John's Part of Fortune lies at 10 47 of Sagittarius. It is then placed in the chart at this position and a note is made of any aspects it may make to the planets in the chart. Only a small orb is generally used (1-2 degrees) and generally only the major aspects are used.

The Arabic Parts, listed, are calculated in the same way. Those that are marked with an asterisk are calculated differently for day and night births. The day formula is given. If a night birth is being used you simply place the plus sign where the minus sign is and vice versa for a night birth.

*Daemon, religion and spirit	Ascendant + Moon – Sun
*Friendship and Love	Ascendant + Daemon – Part of Fortune
*Despair and fraud	Ascendant + Part of Fortune – Daemon
*Captivity and escape	Ascendant + Part of Fortune – Saturn
*Property and goods	Ascendant + 2nd house cusp – Ruler of 2nd house cusp
*Debt	Ascendant + Mercury – Saturn
*Parents	Ascendant + Saturn – Sun
*Grandparents	Ascendant + Saturn – 2nd house cusp
*Children	Ascendant + Saturn – Jupiter
Disease	Ascendant + Mars – Mercury
Captivity	Ascendant + Ruler of house Saturn is in – Saturn
Marriage of men	Ascendant + Venus – Saturn
Marriage of women	Ascendant + Mars – Moon or
	Ascendant + Saturn – Venus
Trickery and deception of men and women	Ascendant + Venus – Sun
Misconduct of women	Ascendant + Mars – Moon
*Lawsuits	Ascendant + Jupiter – Mars
Death	Ascendant + 8th house cusp – Moon
*Danger and violence	Ascendant + Mercury – Saturn
Journeys	Ascendant + 9th house cusp – ruler of 9th house
*Glory	Ascendant + Daemon – Part of fortune
*Friendship and enmity	Ascendant + Daemon – Part of fortune
*Success	Ascendant + Venus – Part of Fortune
*Hope	Ascendant + Mercury – Jupiter
Friends	Ascendant + Mercury – Moon
Violence	Ascendant + Mercury – daemon
Bad luck	Ascendant + Part of fortune – daemon
*Trickery and deceit	Ascendant + daemon – Mercury
Realization	Ascendant + Mercury – Part of fortune
*Retribution	Ascendant + Mars – Mercury
Secrets ruler	Ascendant + midheaven – Ascendant
Marriage	Ascendant + Descendant – Venus
*Sickness	Ascendant + Mars – Saturn
*Love	Ascendant + Jupiter – Venus
*Luck	Ascendant + Moon – Jupiter
*Passion	Mars + Ascendant – Sun

Books suitable for a beginner or the less
experienced marked with *

Ancient Classics

Al-Biruni, *Book of Instruction in the Art of Astrology*, Ascella

Bonatus, Guido, *The Astrologer's Guide*, Ascella

Doretheus of Sidon, *Carmen Astrologicum*, AFA

Manilius, *Astronomica,* Loeb Classics

Mathesos Libri VIII, *Firmicus Maternus*, Ascella

Ptolemy, *Tetrabiblos,* Loeb Classics

Angles

Avery, Jeanne, *The Rising Sign, Your Astrological Mask,* Doubleday

Fenton, Sasha, *Rising Signs, Discover the Truth About Your Personality,* Thorsons*

Mason, Sophia, *You and Your Ascendant,* AFA

Aspects

Carter, Charles, *Astrological Aspects,* AFA and Theosophical Society

Marks, Tracy, *Planetary Aspects, From Conflict to Resolution,* CRCS

Pelletier, Robert, *Planets in Aspect,* Whitford *

Sakoian, Francis & Louis S. Acker, *Minor Aspects,* Copple House

Sakoian, Francis & Louis S. Acker, *That Inconjunct, Quincunx, The Not so Minor Aspect,* Copple House

Tompkins, Sue, *Aspects in Astrology,* Element

Tierney, Bill, *Dynamics of Aspect Analysis,* CRCS

General Interpretation

Cunningham, Donna, *An Astrological Guide to Self-Awareness,* CRCS

Goodman, Linda, *Sun Signs,* Bantam Doubleday Dell*

Greene, Liz, *Astrology for Lovers,* Weiser*

Hand, Robert, *Planets in Youth,* Whitford*

Hone, Margaret E., *The Modern Textbook of Astrology,* Fowler*

March, Marion & Joan McEvers, *Only Way to Learn Astrology, Vols 1 to 5,* ACS*

Marks, Tracy, *The Art of Chart Interpretation,* CRCS

Oken, Alan, *Complete Astrology,* Bantam*

Parker, Derek and Julia, *Parkers' Astrology, New Edition,* Dorling Kindersley*

Sakoian, Francis & Louis S. Acker, *The Astrologer's Handbook,* Harper*

Horary

Barclay, Olivia, *Horary Astrology Rediscovered,* Whitford

Goldstein Jacobson, Ivy, *Simplified Horary Astrology,* privately published, available through Astrology Center of America

Lilly, William, *Christian Astrology,* Ascella

Houses

Houlding, Deborah, *The Houses, Temples of the Sky,* Ascella

Pelletier, Robert, *Planets in Houses,* Whitford*

Sasportas, Howard, *The Twelve Houses,* Harper Collins

Planets

Alexander, Skye, *Planets in Signs,* Whitford

Arroyo, Stephen, *Exploring Jupiter, the Astrological Key to Progress, Prosperity & Potential,* CRCS

Cunningham, Donna, *Healing Pluto Problems,* Weiser

Cunningham, Donna, *Moon Signs, Key to Your Inner Life,* Ballantine

Greene & Sasportas, *Inner Planets,* Weiser

Greene, Liz, *Outer Planets & Their Cycles,* CRCS

Greene, Liz, *Saturn, A New Look at an Old Devil,* Weiser

Greene, Liz, *The Astrological Neptune & the Quest for Redemption* Weiser

Greene, Liz & Howard Sasportas, *The Luminaries,* Weiser

Negus, Joan, *Book of Uranus,* ACS

Sakoian & Acker, *Importance of Mercury
in the Horoscope,* CSA

Van Toen, Donna, *Mars Book,* Weiser

Prediction

Brady, Bernadette, *Predictive Astrology:
The Eagle and the Lark,* Weiser

Sullivan, Erin, *Saturn in Transit,* Weiser

Marks, Tracy, *The Astrology of Self-Discovery,* CRCS

Mason, Sophia, *Forecasting with New,
Full & Quarter Moons,* AFA

Pessin, Dietrech J., *Lunar Shadows, The Lost Key to the
Timing of Eclipses,* Galactic Press

Rodden, Lois, *Modern Transits,* AFA*

Relationships

Davison, Ron, *Synastry,* Aurora

Greene, Liz, *Relating,* Weiser*

Hand, Robert, *Planets in Composite,* Whitford

March, Marion & Joan McEvers, *The Astrology of Human
Relationships,* ACS*

Sakoian, Frances & Louis Sacker,
The Astrology of Relationships, Harper*

Sargent, Lois Haines, *How to Handle your
Human Relations* AFA

Townley, John, *Planets in Love,* Whitford

Miscellaneous

Allen, Richard, *Star Names, Their Lore and Meaning,* Dover

Arroyo, Stephen and Robert Zoller, *Fate, Freewill &
Astrology,* Spica and Ascella, *Astrology, Karma &
Transformation,* CRCS

Baigent, Michael, Nicholas Campion & Charles Harvey,
Mundane Astrology, Thorsons

Bailey, Alice, *Esoteric Astrology,* Lucis Trust

Brady, Bernadette, *Brady's Book of Fixed Stars,* Weiser

Cozzi, Steve, *Planets in Locality,* AFA

Curry, Patrick, *A Confusion of Prophets,* Collins and Brown

Davis, Martin, *Astrolocality Astrology, A Guide to What it is
and How to Use it,* Wessex Astrologer

Devlin, Mary, *Astrology and Past Lives,* Whitford

Ebertin, Reinhold, *The Combination of
Stellar Influences,* AFA

Edmund-Jones, Marc, *The Sabian Symbols
in Astrology,* Aurora

Farnell, Kim, *The Astral Tramp, A Biography
of Sepharial,* Ascella

Fenton, Sasha, *Astrology ...On the Move! Where on Earth
Should You Be,* Thorsons

Frawley, John, *The Real Astrology,* Apprentice Books

Hall, Judy, *Patterns of the Past,* Wessex Astrologer

Hamblin, David, *Harmonic Charts,* Aquarian Press

Harding, Mike & Charles Harvey,
Working with Astrology, Consider

Kempton-Smith, Debbie, *Secrets from a Stargazer's
Notebook,* Topquark*

Koestler, Arthur, *The Sleepwalkers,* Viking

Lehman, J. Lee, *Classical Astrology
for Modern Living,* Whitford

Lehman, J. Lee, *The Ultimate Asteroid Book,* Whitford

Lehman, J. Lee, *Essential Dignities,* Whitford

Lehman, J. Lee, *Book of Rulerships,* Whitford

Reinhart, Melanie, *Chiron and the Healing Journey,*
Penguin Arkana

Robson, Vivian, *Electional Astrology,* Ascella

Schwartz, Jacob, *Asteroid Name Encyclopedia,* Llewellyn

Sullivan, Erin, *Retrograde Planets,* Weiser

Sutton, Komilla, *The Essentials of Vedic Astrology,*
Wessex Astrologer

Schulman, Martin, *Karmic Astrology in Four Volumes,* Weiser

Spencer, Neil, *True as the Stars Above, Adventures in Modern
Astrology,* Victor Gollancz

Zoller, Robert, *Tools and Techniques of the Medieval
Astrologers,* Spica Australia

CONTRIBUTORS

Kim Farnell

Kim Farnell has been a professional astrologer since 1990 when she gained her Diploma from the Faculty of Astrological Studies. She was a member of the Council of the Astrological Association of Great Britain for nine years and is now on the National Executive Committee of the British Astrological and Psychic Society. She has written sun sign columns and features for a number of magazines as well as articles for specialist astrological publications all over the world. She has also been the editor of a number of astrological publications. Kim's books have been published in English, Serbo-Croat and Japanese. She has frequently lectured at astrological conferences in the UK and overseas, taught astrology and has appeared on TV and radio. She has conducted research into the history of astrology, primarily in the seventeenth and nineteenth centuries. Kim continues to work directly with clients.

Cat Javor

Cat Javor began her studies in astrology in Australia in 1983, during which time she worked in radio and television broadcasting. Moving to England in 1988, Cat continued to work in the production of television, live music and theatre whilst maintaining her study of astrology. She became a professional consultant astrologer in 1996 and has written on the subject for the *Astrological Journal*, various national and international newspapers, magazines and the Internet. She also scripted the *Love Match Horoscope Lines* and has lectured at the Astrological Lodge of London. Her love of the subject continues to grow with each day.

Helene Schnitzer

German-born Helene Schnitzer studied astrology and Jungian psychology at the Achernar School for Astrology in Amstelveen (Holland), and Astro*Carto*Graphy with Arielle Guttman in Santa Fe, New Mexico. She has been a professional astrologer since 1986 and has translated several astrological works, including *The Twelfth House* by Karen Hamaker-Zondag and *The Secret Language of Birthdays*, to which she contributed as a writer. Helene currently works and teaches in London.

PICTURE CREDITS

The Art Archive
5, 7, 13, 69, 83, 135, 168, 185 Museo Correr Venice 58, 76,
159 National Gallery London 152, 169 Biblioteca Estense
Modena 1, 3, 27, 44, 65, 73, 98, 133 The British Museum
50, Biblioteca Nazionale Marciana Venice 38, 40, 80, 91,
111, 148, 150, Museo Nazionale Romano Rome 10,
Private Collection Paris 163, British Library 29, 97, San
Apollinare Nuovo Ravenna 155, 175, Ethnic Jewellery
Exhibition Milan 5, 165, Bodleian Library Oxford 118, 177,
179, Archaeological Museum Naples 68, Tate Gallery
London 153, 181, Palazzo Farnese Caprarola 122-123,
125, Victoria and Albert Museum London 31, 182
Buonconsiglio Castle Trento 17, Real Biblioteca De Lo
Escorial 6, 145, University Library Prague 146,
Bibliothèque des Arts Décoratifs Paris 55, Palazzo
Pubblico Siena 161, Biblioteca d'Ajuda Lisbon 71, 140,
Bibliothéque Nationale Paris 42, 53, Bodleian Library
Oxford 39, 48, Musée du Louvre Paris 25, 46, Museo della
Romana Rome 8-9, Salamanca University 62, Maison
Natale de Pasteur Dole 120, Scrovegni Chapel Padua 132,
Château de Blois 85, Turkish and Islamic Art Museum
Istanbul 32, Marine Museum Lisbon 109, NASA 19

Mary Evans Picture Library
11, 14, 15, 16 (l), 18, 20, 26, 28, 30, 37, 41, 43, 45, 47, 49,
51, 56, 57, 60-61, 64, 66, 67, 75, 77, 78-79, 81, 82, 86, 88,
89, 90, 93, 96, 100, 102, 103, 105, 106-107, 108, 112, 113,
115, 116, 118 (t), 121, 126, 127, 128, 129, 130, 134, 137,
139, 141, 142, 143, 147, 151, 156, 158, 160, 164, 166, 188,
189 Explorer Archives 23, 24, 72, 183

Topham Picturepoint
12, 16 (r), 34-35, 54, 59, 87, 95, 101, 124, 136, 144, 162

A

abbreviations 167
abscission of light 152
absolute longitude 114
Abumassar *Introductorium in Astronomium* 12, 159
Adams, Evangeline 21, 27
Adams, Jack 139
Addey, John *Harmonics in Astrology* 32
Adelard of Bath 25
affliction 153
air signs 55
Al-Biruni, Abu Rayhan 12–13, 146
  Elements of the Art of Astrology 12
Al-kindi *On the Stellar Rays* 162
Alcabitius house system 79
Alcocoden 128
Aldebaran 158
Alexander the Great 10, 22
alfridaria 153–54
Algol 128
almuten 97, 115
altitude 112
Amazon.com 168
American Federation of Astrologers 168
anareta 143
angles 90
angular houses 89
Antares 127, 158
antipathy 153
antiscion 92
apex planets 70
aphelion 132
apogee 132
apparent motion 130
application 149
Aquarius 51–52, 55, 56, 57, 58, 59
Aquinas, Thomas 10, 13
Arabian astrology 6, 12–13, 25, 28, 83
  planetary periods 153–54
Arabian Parts 32, 92, 184, 185
Aratus 125
archangel stars 127
arcs 112, 114, 183
Aries 36–38, 54, 56, 57, 58, 59
  Aries point 91
Aristarchus of Samos 136
Aristotle 10, 13, 27, 158
  dryness 162
  Primum Mobile 102
armillary spheres 163–65
ascendants 7, 90, 172
ascending planets 147
ascension 110, 117
aspectarians 141
aspects 7, 174–75

aspect patterns 70–71
  glyphs 167
  major aspects 72–73
  minor aspects 74–77, 175
  Ptolemaic aspects 72, 154–55
asteroids 125–26, 131
astro*carto*graphy 26, 33
astrolabes 163
astrology 6–7, 60
  measurements 106, 114–16
  origins 8, 10–25
  terminology 122, 138–65
Astrology Center of America 168
astrometeorology 29
astronomy 60
  measurements 106, 108–13
  terminology 122, 124–37
Augustine, Saint 12 *The City of God* 12
Augustus 10
azimene 116
azimuth 112
Aztec astrology 23, 24

B

Babylonian astrology 6, 22, 117, 125, 135
  heliacal systems 137
Bailey, Alice A. *Esoteric Astrology* 30, 162
barren planets 68
barren signs 58
behold 154
Belcher, Sir Edward 19
benefic planets 143, 157
besiegement 144
bestial signs 58
bi-corporeal signs 58
bi-quintile 77
Bible and astrology 24
birth certificates 168
birth moment 138
birthstones 165
Blavatsky, Helen 30
blue moon 146
body, parts of 160
Boethius *The Consolation of Philosophy* 25
Bonatus, Guido 13
Brahe, Tycho 15–16
British Standard Time 119
bucket 94
Buddhism 159
Byzantium 24–25

C

cadent house 89
Cairo Calendar 22
calendars 118
callipic cycles 117

Callipus 117
Campanus house system 80
Campanus, Johannes 82
Cancer 41–42, 55, 56, 57, 58, 59
Capricorn 49–51, 55, 56, 57, 58, 59
Caput Algol 128
Cardan, Jerome 14–15
cardinal points 90
cardinal signs 56
Carter, Charles
  Political Astrology 28
Caruso, Enrico 21
Cassiopeia 128
Catherine de Medici 15
cazimi 147
celestial equator 110
celestial latitude and longitude 110
celestial sphere 110, 111
Centaur asteroids 126
Cepheus 128
Ceres 126
Chaldean astrology 22
Chaldean order 146, 153
charts 6–7, 96, 140, 141, 172
  casting 78
  chart points 90–93
  chart shape 94
  composite charts 178
  interpretation 94–101
  relationship charts 139, 178
Cheiro 21
children 99
Chiron 68, 126
Christianity 24, 159, 160
circumpolar stars 128
collection of light 151
colours 153
combust 147
comets 126, 127, 131
  Halley's comet 132
commanding signs 57
common signs 58
composite charts 95–96
configuration 96
conjunction 72, 134–35, 174
considerations before judgement 96
constellations 124–25
contra-antiscion 92
contra-parallel 154
converse directions 103
converse progressions 183
coordinates 112
Cope, David 833
Copernicus, Nicolas 13–14, 130, 136
  De Revolutionibus 14
cosignificators 144
cosmic years 136

cosmobiology 21, 31
cosmograms 163
creative astrology 32
crescent Moon 129
critical degree 93
Cross, Robert Thomas 20
culmination 114
Culpeper, Nicholas 17–18, 27–28
cusps 7, 93, 172
cycle 131

D

Dante 13
dark Moon 69
Davison, Robert *Synastry* 139
days 119
death 143
debility 116, 176, 177
decile 74
declination 110
decreasing in light 149
decumbiture 27–28
Dee, John 15
degrees 112
  degree symbols 92
derived houses 96–97
descendant 91
detriment 115
dexter 155
dignity 115–16, 176, 177
directions 7, 102, 103
dispositors 144
dissociate 154
diurnal charts 141
Djabir, ben 82
Draco 128
dryness 162

E

Earth 6, 11, 60, 63, 131, 150
earth signs 55
earth zodiacs 140
east point 92
Ebertin, Reinhold 21, 31
  Combination of Stellar Influences 21, 31
eclipse 134
ecliptic 134
egress 132–34
Egyptian astrology 6, 11–12, 22, 136, 157
  seasons 137
eighth house 87
electional astrology 29
elements 54
elevation 110
eleventh house 88
Elizabeth I 15
elongation 113
enemies 101

ephemerides 141, 168
Ephemeris 21
Equal house system 79, 172
equator 109
equinox 117
    equinoctial points 131
    equinoctial signs 59
esoteric astrology 30, 32
exaltation 157

F
face 157
fall 158
fate 159–60
feminine signs 56
Feng Shui 33
feral signs 58
fifth house 86
financial astrology 27
firdar 153
fire signs 54
first house 84
fixed signs 57
fixed stars 127–28, 184–85
flat charts 140
Fomalhaut 158
fortitude 160
fortunes 145
Four Watchers 158
fourth house 86
free will 159
Freud, Sigmund 20
friends 101
frustration 152
full Moon 129

G
galactic centre 135–36
galaxies 124
Gann, W.D. 27
Gauquelin, Michel 21
Gemini 39–41, 55, 56, 57, 58, 59
geocentric systems 14, 136–37
geodetic equivalents 105
George VI 21
gibbous Moon 129
glyphs 34, 165, 166
grand cross 70
grand trine 70
Gravelaine, Joëlle de 69
Greece, ancient 6, 10, 24, 26,
    136, 157, 163
    comets 126
    constellations 124–25
    free will 159
    planetary periods 153
Greenwich 108, 120–21, 170
Greenwich mean time 119, 169
Gregorian calendar 118, 119
Gregory XIII 118
Guardians of Heaven 158

H
Halley, Edmund 132, 135
Hamburg school 31, 97
harmonics 32–33
heliacal 137
heliocentric systems 14, 136
hemisphere emphasis 96
Henry, Francis 18
herbalism 17, 18, 27
Hermes Trismegistus 22
    Trutine of Hermes 139
Herschel, William 18, 19
Hinduism 159
home life 99
horary astrology 28–29
horizon 109–10
horoscopes 7, 138
    calculating 168–69
    newspaper horoscopes 21, 30
hour angle 113
house systems 78, 79
houses 84–89
human signs 59
hyleg 144
hypothetical planets 21, 68–69

I
I Ching 162
illness 100
immum coeli 91
impedited 145
inconjunct 77
increasing in light 149
increasing in motion 149
inferior conjunction 134–35
inferior planets 68
infortunes 145
ingress 132
International Atlas 169
interpretation 94
Islam 25

J
James I 15
Jones patterns 94, 95
Jones, Marc Edmund 94
joy 162
Julian calendar 119
Julius Caesar 118
Jung, Carl 20, 30, 162–63
Juno 126
Jupiter 19, 64–66, 143, 144, 145,
    157
    Jupiter return 140

K
karma 159
Kelly, Edward 15
Kepler, Johannes 16–17, 74,
    76, 77
    Three Laws of Planetary

Motion 130
kite 71
Koch house system 81
Koch, Dr Walter 83

L
latitude 7, 11, 108, 110
    UK and Ireland 171
leap year 119
Leo 42–43, 54, 56, 57, 58, 59
Leo, Alan 20, 30
Libra 45–47, 55, 56, 57, 58, 59
Lilith 69
Lilly, William 6, 17, 76, 146
    Christian Astrology 17, 19
local mean time 120
local space astrology 33
locomotive 95
logarithms 114
London Meteorological Society
    19, 29
long ascension 117
longitude 11, 108, 110, 114
    UK and Ireland 171
lord of chart 97, 115, 145
love 99–100
Lucretius 10
luminaries 145
lunar mansions 79–80, 93
lunar progression 104
lunation 150

M
magnitude 113
malefic planets 143, 157
Manilius, Marcus 10–11
Mansur, Abu Nasr 12
marriage 100–01
Mars 64, 143, 144, 145, 157, 158
    Mars Effect 21
masculine signs 56
matutines 146
Mayans 24
measurement 106
    astrology 114–16
    astronomy 108–13
    time 118–21
medical astrology 28
medicine 25
medieval astrology 25
Melosethic Man 160
Mercury 19, 62–63, 147,
    150, 151
meridian 109
Mesopotamia 8
Meton 117
metonic cycle 117
midheaven 7, 91
midpoint 97
midpoint tree 97–99
Milky Way 124, 131, 135, 136

minor progressions 104, 183
minutes 119
mixed reception 147, 149
Modern Astrology 20
modes 142
moiety 146
moisture 162
Montefeltro, Guido de 13
Moon 6, 7, 60, 63–64, 143, 150,
    151
    apogee 132
    blue moon 146
    luminary 145
    lunar mansions 80–81, 93
    lunar progression 104
    lunation 150
    nodes 92
    perigee 132
    phases 128–30
    secondary significator 144
    synodic periods 131, 135, 150
    void of course 146–47
Moore, Francis 18–19
Morgan, John Pierpoint 21, 27
Morrison, Richard James
    Grammar of Astrology 19
motion 130
Müller, Johannes 82
mundane astrology 28
music of the spheres 6, 160
mutable signs 57
mute signs 58
mutual reception 149
mystic rectangle 71

N
Nachepso 22
naibod 104–105
Naibod, Valentine 104
Napier, John 114
natal astrology 26
native 138
Naylor, R.H. 21, 30
Neptune 67, 173
new Moon 128
ninth house 87
nocturnal charts 141
nodes 92, 135
nonagesimal 93
north node 92
northern signs 57
Nostradamus 15, 81
novile 74–75

O
obeying signs 57
obliquity 109
occultation 134
occupations 100
Oken, Alan *Spiritual Astrology* 30
Old Moore's Almanac 18–19

one degree directions 183
opposition 73, 174
orbits 131
Orion 81
Ovid 10

P
Page, Anthony 83
Pallas 126
Paracelsus 27
parallel 154
Pars Fortuna (Part of Fortune) 92, 184, 185
partile 154
Pearce, A.J. 19
peregrine planets 69
perfection 157
perigee 132
perihelion 132
Persian astrology 153, 158
personal planets 68
Petosiris 22
Pisces 52–53, 55, 56, 57, 58
Placidus di Tito 82
Placidus house system 80
plactic 157
planetoids 126
planets 6, 7, 62–69, 173
   anareta 143–44
   glyphs 167
   planetary characteristics 60
   planetary periods 153
   planetary returns 105
   planetary strength 176–77
Plato 10
Plotinus 81
Plutino 126
Pluto 32, 67, 173
Pogson, N.R. 113
Polich, Vendel 833
Porphyry 81
Porphyry house system 11, 79, 172
posited 146
pre-natal epoch 139
predictions 7, 180–83
   methods 102–05
press 6, 21
primary directions 102
prime vertical 112–13
primum mobile 158–59
procession 131
profection 105
progression 103–04
prohibition 151
promittors 145
proper motion 131
Prophetic Messenger 20–21
psychological astrology 30, 32
Ptolemy, Claudius 11–12, 14, 22, 32, 97, 113, 139, 162
   The Almagest 12, 125
   Copernicus, Nicolas 130
   geocentric theory 136–37
   mundane astrology 28
   Ptolemaic aspects 72, 154–55
   Tetrabiblos 6, 12, 80, 81, 154
Pythagoras 6, 81, 126, 160

Q
quadruplicities 142, 143
quality 142
quincunx 77, 175
quindecile 74
quintile 75–76
quotidian 149

R
radical 139–40
Raphael 19–20, 168
rays 162
reception 149
rectification 138
refranation 151
Regiomontanus house system 80
Regulus 128, 158
relationships 178–79
   charts 139, 178
relocation astrology 26
Renaissance astrology 25
retrograde 150
revolution 150
right ascension 110
rising signs see ascendants
Rome, ancient 10, 12, 24
   calendar 118
Royal Stars 158
rulers 145

S
Sabian symbol 92
Sagittarius 48–49, 54, 56, 57, 58
saros cycle 135
satellites 126
Saturn 19, 21, 66, 143, 144, 145, 157, 158
   Saturn return 140
Scorpio 47–48, 55, 56, 57, 58
second house 84
secondary progression 104
   calculation 181–83
seconds 119
see-saw 94
semi-decile 74
semi-sextile 74
semi-square 75
separation 149
Sepharial 105
septile 75
sesquiquadrate 76–77
sesquiquintile 76
seventh house 87
sex 99
sextile 72, 174
Shakespeare, William 16
Shanks, Thomas *The American Atlas* 169
short ascension 117
sidereal astrology 33
sidereal time 121
significators 144
signs see sun-signs
sinister 155
Sirius 81
sixth house 86
Sixtus IV 15
slow in course 150

Smith, Robert Cross 19–20
solar arc 114
   solar arc directions 183
solar system 125, 131, 135
solstice 117
   solstice signs 59
southern hemisphere charts 172
southern signs 57
speculum 163
square 72–73, 174
standard time 120
station 150–51
stellium 152
succedent houses 89
Sumerians 125
Summer Time 119, 169
Sun 6, 7, 60, 62, 135, 136, 143, 145, 150, 151
   aphelion 132
   cazimi 137
   ecliptic 134
   luminary 145
   perihelion 132
   solar return 140–41
sun-signs 7, 8, 59, 36–53, 54–59
   glyphs 166
   sun-sign astrology 30
sunrise charts 96
superior conjunction 134
superior planets 68
swift in motion 117
synastry 139, 141–42
   synastry grid 178–79
synchronicity 162–63
synodic periods 131, 135, 150
synthesis 99
syzygy 135, 150

T
t-square 70
tables of houses 114
Taurus 38–39, 55, 56, 57, 58
tenth house 88
term 157–58
tertiary progressions 104, 183
Thales of Miletus 27
Theosophical Society 20, 30
third house 84–86
time 7, 106, 170
   measurements 118–21
   time differences 120
   time zones 120–21
trans-Neptunian planets 21, 32, 69
trans-Saturnian planets 69
transits 7, 104, 180–81
translation of light 151
transpersonal planets 69
travel 101
tredecile 76
trine 73, 174
triplicity 142–43
tripod 94
Tropic of Cancer 109
Tropic of Capricorn 109
tropical astrology 33
tropical year 121
Tropocentric house system 81

true node 92
twelfth house 88

U
under sunbeams 147
Universe 6, 11, 124
Uranian astrology 32
   glyphs 167
Uranus 19, 66, 173
Ursa Major and Minor 128

V
Valens, Vettius 11
Vedic astrology 32, 33, 153, 165
Venus 22, 63, 143, 144, 145, 157
   Herald of the Dawn 146
vernal equinox 121
vertex 93
vespertines 146
Vesta 126
vigintile 74
Villani, Filippo 13
Virgil 10
Virgo 44–45, 55, 56, 57, 58
voice signs 58
void of course 146–47
Vulcan 30

W
waning Moon 130
water signs 55–56
waxing Moon 129
weather prediction 6, 29, 157
Wemyss 92
west point 92
Witte, Alfred 21
   Rules for Planetary Pictures 31

Y
years 119, 121, 136
Yod 70, 77

Z
Zadkiel 19, 29
Zariel 83
zenith 110
Zenith house system 81
Zodiac 6, 34
   Aquarius 51–52, 55, 56, 57, 58, 59
   Aries 36–38, 54, 56, 57, 58, 59
   Cancer 41–42, 55, 56, 57, 58, 59
   Capricorn 49–51, 55, 56, 57, 58, 59
   divisions 54–59
   earth zodiacs 140
   Gemini 39–41, 55, 56, 57, 58, 59
   Leo 42–43, 54, 56, 57, 58, 59
   Libra 45–47, 55, 56, 57, 58, 59
   Pisces 52–53, 55, 56, 57, 58
   Sagittarius 48–49, 54, 56, 57, 58
   Scorpio 47–48, 55, 56, 57, 58
   sidereal astrology 33
   Taurus 38–39, 55, 56, 57, 58
   Virgo 44–45, 55, 56, 57, 58